A Garland Series

The Modern Chinese Economy

Edited by
Ramon H. Myers
HOOVER INSTITUTION

by the same author

Studies in Chinese Price History

The History of Imperial China: A Research Guide

translated from the Chinese

The People's Comic Book

Landlord and Labour in Late Imperial China: Case Studies from Shandong

Studies in Chinese Price History

Endymion Porter Wilkinson

Garland Publishing, Inc., New York & London
1980

Library of Congress Cataloging in Publication Data

Wilkinson, Endymion.
Studies in Chinese price history.

(The Modern Chinese economy)
Originally presented as the author's thesis,
Princeton University, 1970.
Bibliography: p.
1. Grain—Prices—China—Shensi—History.
2. Shensi, China—Economic conditions.
I. Title. II. Series: Modern Chinese economy.
HD9046.C63S68 1980 338.1'3'31 78-24799
ISBN 0-8240-4257-3

For a complete list of the titles in this series, see the final pages of this volume.

All volumes in this series are printed on acid-free, 250-year-life paper.

Printed in the United States of America

STUDIES IN CHINESE PRICE HISTORY

Endymion Porter Wilkinson

A DISSERTATION

PRESENTED TO THE

FACULTY OF PRINCETON UNIVERSITY

IN CANDIDACY FOR THE DEGREE

OF DOCTOR OF PHILOSOPHY

RECOMMENDED FOR ACCEPTANCE BY THE

DEPARTMENT OF

EAST ASIAN STUDIES

May 1970

TABLE OF CONTENTS

Part 2

Tables

Figures and graphs

Maps

ACKNOWLEDGEMENTS

My first thanks must go to the members of the Department of East Asian Studies, Princeton University, who have provided every kind of encouragement and guidance during the four years in which I have been attached to the University. The Department also supported two Summers of Japanese language studies as well as a year's research in Tokyo. I should particularly like to thank Professor James T. C. Liu for doing so much to make my year in Japan a success.

While gathering the materials upon which the thesis is based I had the privilege of attending Professor Yamane Yukio's seminar on Ming History at the Toyo Bunko. Mr. Kozen Tachibana of that institution, by letting me into its stacks, enabled a much closer use of its library resources than would otherwise have been possible. At the Institute for Oriental Culture, Tokyo University, Professor Saeki Yuichi gave me valuable advice and the chief librarian, Mr. Uetani, often went out of his way to help my researches.

Back in Princeton, in the early stages of data analysis, Mr. Leslie Knox, Jr. of the Textile Research Institute, Princeton University, gave me much expert help as also did Mrs. Sheila Gilbert of the Office of Survey Research. At a crucial stage Mr. David Hoaglin of the Department of Statistics, practically took over much of the computing and introduced me to the type of data analysis that was finally used. During this year of writing in Princeton Mr. T'ung Shih-kang, Curator of the Gest Oriental Library, and the staff of the Gest Library often went out of their way to procure books or microfilms at short notice.

To all of these and to the many others too numerous to be named I should like to express my sincere thanks.

The three main readers of this thesis, Professor T. T. Ch'en, Professor James T. C. Liu and Professor F. W. Mote have given me a great deal of advice and constructive criticism for which I am extremely grateful.

FREQUENTLY USED TERMS AND EQUIVALENTS

Administrative Divisions

provincial capital	Sheng-hui 省會
prefecture	fu 府
department	chou 州
district	hsien 縣

Money

tael (silver unit of account)	yin-liang 銀兩
cash (copper unit of account)	-ch'ien 錢
cash (copper coin)	-ch'ien 錢

Weights and Measures

bushel	shih 石 (approx. 100 litres)
granary bushel	ts'ang-shih 倉石 (107.5 litres)
peck	tou 斗 (approx. 10 litres)
picul	tan 擔 (20 tan = 1 ton)
catty	chin 斤 (2000 chin = 1 ton)
hectare	= 15 mou 畝

CHAPTER I

General Introduction

In this thesis I have attempted to use a body of original documentary sources (some 5000 district grain price reports) to quantify, in the form of exchange and price zones, the relationships between the exchange markets and the grain markets of ninety district towns in a province in north-west China, Shensi. The years covered by the reports were 1900-1910 but since no new forms of transport had come to the province at that time and since the monetary system was essentially as it had been for the previous one hundred years, I selected Shensi rather than Szechwan or Kiangsu (for both of which provinces we also have the same type of reports) in the belief that Shensi at that time might legitimately be regarded as a province at a pre-modern stage of development.

Before beginning the analysis of the exchange rates and the grain prices in the Shensi markets however certain preliminary questions with regard to the grain price reports and exchange reports had to be answered, for, so far as I know, this type of report has never been used in Chinese historical studies before.

The first Chinese historian to draw attention to the importance of grain price reports and exchange reports was Chang Hsüeh-ch'eng in the 18th century. Chang commented that although the summaries of these reports which were sent to the Emperor were probably not too reliable, the original documents upon which they based were much more so. He recommended that compilers of gazetteers record commodity and grain prices in each district every ten years. Unfortunately few if any followed his advice.[1] Of modern Chinese historians only Liu I-cheng drew attention to the grain price reports, in an article on rice prices in Kiangsu. As an appendix to the article he published selections from a series of price reports with the terse comment:

> It was a Ch'ing institution that local officials report on grain prices to provincial governors. The governors memorialized on them to the central government. Usually every month. If we look at the Vermilion Endorsements and Edicts (of the Yung-cheng period) we can see that at that time (1723-1735) provincial officials had to send in reports (on grain prices) punctually, based on the investigations of the local officials.[2]

Since Liu wrote these words several historians have worked on the rice prices contained in the memorials of provincial governors in the Vermilion Endorsements and Edicts (of the Yung-cheng period), notably Abe Takeo and Ch'üan Han-sheng with the collaboration of Wang Yeh-chien.[3] None of these

---

[1]See Chang Hsüeh-ch'eng (1790), chüan 24, p. 29b.

[2]See Liu (1930), p. 8. See also note 49, chapter 4 of this thesis where the reports published by Liu are listed.

[3]See Abe (1957) and note 22, chapter 4 of this thesis for references to Ch'üan and Wang's work. I published a preliminary evaluation of the price quotations in a series of district price reports (as opposed to the summaries of this type of report found in the memorials of provincial governors) shortly after discovering several thousand original district reports in Tokyo. Upon returning to the United States I heard that Professor Ch'üan in collaboration with Dr. Richard Krauss of Harvard University, had prepared an English version of his work on rice prices in the early 18th century. The English version contains many new insights including an

scholars however related the price summaries in the memorials to the original district reports or discussed the purposes for reporting on prices and the methods used to collect them. As a consequence when I found several thousand original district price reports in a Tokyo collection there was no immediate way of knowing what type of prices they were, who had collected them and for what purposes they had been collected. Parts of chapter three and all of chapter four of this thesis are attempts to answer these questions. Why such a lengthy effort was required to evaluate what was after all a routine administrative activity, not only in imperial China, but also in many other pre-industrial societies, is a question whose answer leads us to a brief consideration of the nature of Chinese historical sources.

During the 19th century when historians in western countries were beginning to emphasize the importance of archival sources as opposed to essentially literary sources, Chinese historians were still drawing on a long tradition of handling and quoting from archival sources. For historical reasons however that tradition never developed in this century into a full scale assault on national and local archives; there were many notable attempts to preserve the national

---

evaluation of the nature of the grain price quotations in the memorials printed in the Vermilion Endorsements and Edicts (of the Yung-cheng period). This evaluation is based upon a very close reading of that source and does not therefore cover the type of source which I have used in chapter 4. I am extremely grateful to Dr. Krauss for letting me see the typescript of his and Professor Ch'üan's new work. Many of the points which I made in Wilkinson (1969) are substantiated in the evaluation of the price quotations made by the two authors. (Their work was later published as <u>Mid-Ch'ing Rice Markets and Trade</u>, Cambridge, Mass. 1975).

archives, to edit and publish the materials in them, but these efforts were only able to skim the surface. At the local level the collecting and preservation, not only of the type of materials to be found in local yamen, guild headquarters etc., but also such private documents as deeds of sale, contracts of all sorts, account books etc., never really even began. Local and private materials were almost totally neglected and vast quantities of them must have been lost or destroyed in the upheavals of these years.

Those who approach the study of Chinese history can therefore draw on a highly developed historiographical tradition but they are often not in a position to check or corroborate works produced in that tradition. Nor, frequently, if they decide to move outside the essential areas covered in that tradition, can they draw on the type of source often taken for granted in other countries. Thus China had a long and highly developed commercial history, for example, but few if any of the account books of even the most famous businesses have been brought to light by historians.[4] Turning to a more familiar field for another example, that of administration, we have at least sixteen editions of the administrative regulations of the Board of Revenue (Hu-pu tse-li) in the Ch'ing period, but we do not have the accounts

[4] I went to some trouble to locate Chinese account books hoping to be able to use them as a subsidiary source to the price reports; the few that I was able to find are listed in References Cited 1, Chinese manuscript sources, Account Books.

and receipts of the central government, nor do we have the accounts and receipts of the provincial and district governments which were kept in the archives of the Board. We have the five editions of the Collected Statutes of the Ch'ing Dynasty (which carry the administrative regulations of the entire central government) but we only have a few of the provincial equivalents of this work (the sheng-li) and practically none of the cases and investigatory reports which would allow us to gain some idea as to how these regulations worked in actual practice.

At the provincial and district levels there are, to be sure, the enormous resources of the provincial and local gazetteers. These works however were never intended as a substitute for the local archives nor were they intended as practical guidebooks to local administrative problems. Usually only edited two or three times in a hundred years their primary purpose was to enshrine the notable people, places and literary output of a given locality. They contain much else besides however, and their utilization can provide insights which the non-availability of local documentary sources makes particularly valuable.

In the case of a system such as price reporting, which was based upon a local administrative activity (the gathering and summarizing of district market prices) the gazetteers, as Chang Hsüeh-ch'eng deplored, have nothing to offer. Nor do the great central government compendia of administrative regulations, by their very nature, present the type of material required for the evaluation of this kind of local activity. In evaluating the price reporting system therefore I turned to the type of informal source so brilliantly used by Ch'ü T'ung-tsu in Local Government in China Under the Ch'ing. By good fortune I found about half a dozen handwritten copies of handbooks written by secretarial assistants in charge of financial matters (ch'ien-ku lao-yeh 錢穀老爺 as they were familiarly referred to) active in Shantung and Fukien in the first part of the 19th century.[5] On the basis of these works and various compendia of provincial administrative and legal regulations I was able to attempt a reconstruction of the price reporting system with the object of establishing the nature of the price quotations in the reports. I have also made the suggestion, in the course of this reconstruction, that such a system was a Ch'ing innovation at least insofar as the entire process of reporting and summarizing was regularly carried out at every level of the bureaucracy. The implications of this tentative finding however are not fully explored for my original purpose in reconstructing the price reporting system was not to make a comment upon the historical evolution of a key area of Chinese administrative concern. It was, rather, to provide some grounds for deciding whether to put aside or use that highly unusual type of Chinese historical source which

---

[5]See References Cited 1, Chinese manuscript sources, for a list of the handbooks of this type used in this thesis. See also Wilkinson (1970) for a longer discussion of these works as well as the provincial regulations etc. referred to above.

chance had placed in my hands; a body of basic documentary materials, a series of some 5,000 district price reports.

In the event I reached the conclusion that the price quotations in the district reports were market prices and that they were not customary assessments for tax commutation or means of assessing additional fees as part of that system. The positive part of this conclusion was based upon the reconstruction of the entire price reporting system as it had developed in the Ch'ing period. The negative part was rapidly arrived at simply by checking on the tax systems of one of the provinces (Shensi) from which several thousand of the reports had been submitted.[6]

That so much work had to be spent upon the evaluation of the basic documents used in this thesis and that the evaluation had often to be done using rare or informal (i.e. not printed) sources arose from the fact that the type of work on basic documents which can be taken for granted in other areas of historical writing has simply not been done, as I have suggested above, in many fields of Chinese history.

The evaluation of the documents and their contents occupies portions of Chapter 2 (2.4 Recording and Reporting Cash/Silver Exchange Rates) and all of Chapter 4 (Grain Price Reporting and Grain Price Quotations during the

---

[6]The works I used for this checking were (1) The Complete Book of Taxes and Labour Services of Shensi (1844) (<u>Shan-hsi sheng fu-i ch'üan-shu</u> 陝西省賦役全書) and (2) The Guide to the Reform of the Finances of Shensi (1909)、 (<u>Shan-hsi ch'ing-li ts'ai-cheng shuo-ming shu</u> 陝西清理財政說明書). I am grateful to Professor Saeki Yuichi for suggesting this method of checking.

the Ch'ing). Both reporting on cash/silver exchange rates (C/S rates) and reporting on grain prices are found to have been conducted for the first time on a regular basis in the 18th century. Decisions on the allocation of grain were now being taken on a much higher level than before. Although all the elements of the 18th century system had existed for many centuries the achievement of the 18th century was the regularization on a national scale of the system of reporting and scrutiny implied in the development of the practice of monthly grain price reports. The emergence of this system at this time was presumably connected with the increasing awareness that population was running ahead of resources and that grain prices were rising more rapidly than ever before. The mid-Ch'ing government, no doubt spurred by this realization, was the first to conceive the entire system of public granaries as being controlled and operated on the basis of the monthly district price reports. It is a selection from these reports which forms the basis of the analysis of the Shensi grain market in Chapter 5.

Before turning to the Shensi grain price quotations however a number of monetary problems are considered. In Chapter 2 (Money), I have given the basic monetary terminology necessary for an understanding of prices and price quotations. Short sections on the two sectors of the Chinese monetary system i.e. the cash (copper) sector and the silver sector (2.2 and 2.3) are followed by an examination of long-term and short-term factors affecting changes between the two sectors as reflected in the C/S rates. These rates were quotations of the amount of a given type of cash which exchanged for a given type of tael (silver unit of account). They had not survived in sufficient numbers to trace differences between many different markets within a single region or province until the discovery of the grain price reports from Shensi which I have already referred to. Since these reports also include C/S rates I have been able to present (in Chapter 3, Cash/Silver Exchange Rates in Shensi, 1900-1910) a preliminary study of differences of C/S rates in 90 district towns over a period of ten years. This chapter shows the extremely dislocated nature of the money or exchange markets within a province which was one of the richer of China's poor provinces. After testing integration between exchange markets in a number of different ways, I divide up the province into about fifteen groups of towns having similar levels of C/S rates. That there was no national exchange market(as pointed out in Chapter 2) covering the whole of a country the size of Europe should not surprise us, but that C/S rates even within the boundaries of only one province were not integrated is surprising. The fact that they were not is taken as a reflection of the monetary chaos into which China had fallen from the end of the 19th century on the one hand, and on the other, as a reflection of the slow communications and high transport costs in this part of China.

In order that others may use the data in the reports I have appended all the C/S rates from the Shensi district towns at the end of this chapter as well as the statistical analysis.

Chapter 5 (Shensi Grain Markets, 1900-1910) opens with a brief account of the agricultural sector of the Shensi economy at this time. Since the total product of the province was almost entirely derived from this sector no attempt was made to allow for other sectors. I have attempted to calculate production per capita expressing output in terms of a single unit, namely kilograms of wheat equivalent per person per year (kw/p/y). The basis for calculating these equivalents are the typical province wide prices of the different grains which were derived from the Shensi grain price reports (the data and statistical analysis are contained in Chapter 5, appendix 1 and 2). All steps leading to the calculation of the wheat equivalents are given and various alternative estimates are put forward. These are then compared with similar estimates calculated from data in J. L. Buck's farm surveys from thirty years later. The conclusion is reached that kw/p/y had fallen between the 1900's and 1930. In the light of corroborating evidence on crop disasters and civil unrest from the 1860's on, standards of living in this crucial period of the province's history are held to have been falling.

The major portion of Chapter 5 contains an analysis of the price zones of wheat, rice, millet and field peas as reflected in the prices of these foods in the markets of the

90 district towns in Shensi. These markets with no exception were the major grain markets of the province. Various criteria are put forward to test for situations where grain can be considered to have moved between towns and conclusions as to the size of the market areas for each of the grains are drawn.

Based on the analysis of exchange markets in Chapter 3, as well as on the estimates of kw/p/y and the analysis of grain markets in Chapter 5, there begins to emerge a detailed picture of a near subsistence agricultural economy, split into small price zones, the largest of which was centered upon the capital of the province, but the majority of which were confined to the limits of single districts.

CHAPTER 2

Money

2.1 Introduction

The object of this chapter is to provide the monetary terminology and background necessary for an understanding of price quotations and price changes in China in the three centuries or so preceding 1900. No attempt is made to provide a general description of the entire monetary system.[1] The discussion begins with the copper cash and the silver tael. Next long-term trends and short-term fluctuations of the money market are considered. A concluding section takes up the problem of regional and local differences and serves to introduce the more detailed discussion of local exchange markets contained in Chapter 3.

During the period 1600-1900 copper cash and silver bullion were the most widely accepted monetary means of payment for goods and services. Prices with few exceptions were measured in units of account of one or the other; in terms of one or another of the many cash units of account (ch'ien 錢) or in one of the many different silver units of account (taels or in Chinese, yin-liang 銀兩). To a

[1] The best general descriptions of the Ch'ing monetary system are P'eng Hsin-wei (1958); Kato Shigeshi (1915) and King (1965).

greater extent than at any previous time payment in kind was receeding to a secondary position in the private sector (rent, wages and transactions), as well as in the public sector (government taxes).[2] Although many other forms of money were used in this period, with the exception of bills of exchange and foreign dollars, their use was sporadic and local.

2.2 Cash

At the Metropolitan and provincial levels government operated mints struck copper coins according to annual quotas.[3] The quotas as well as the metallic content of the coins were adjusted or suspended at different times in the different

---

[2]Data on rent and wages is scarce but scattered studies on 19th century conditions (e.g. Jamieson (1888); Gamble (1944); Li Wen-chih (1956); Fu 1-ling (1961); Muramatsu (1966); Perkins (1969); would support this generalization. Furthermore the process of monetization is well attested in the public sector which is taken as an indication of a parallel if not anterior development in the private sector.

[3]Various attempts have been made to estimate the total amount of cash minted annually throughout the Ch'ing dynasty. The task is not a simple one; the only statistics are incomplete copper production statistics (Yen Chung-p'ing, 1957) and mint quotas. The quotas are for the Metropolitan mints only plus a few provincial quotas which in aggregate produced about as much cash as the two metropolitan mints. Nor are the production figures and mint quotas any adequate indication of the amount of cash in circulation for it should be emphasized that it is not the annual production of copper (or cash) which influences the price level but rather the total amount of cash in circulation. Therefore to the annual government figures must be added the estimated amounts which were in circulation from previous reigns and dynasties plus the estimated amount of counterfeit cash and imported foreign cash. Seen in this light the task of estimating the total amount of cash in circulation at any given time is practically impossible.

mints as part of the effort to maintain the value of the cash as measured against silver. One result of these many and varying issues was that cumulatively the cash coins in circulation in any given money market became more and more uneven in quality.[4] The situation was further exacerbated, particularly at times of weak or corrupt government, by the import of foreign cash of poor quality (from Cochin China and Japan), by the illicit striking of short-weight coins at the provincial mints as well as by the efforts of melters, clippers and counterfeiters.

The extent of the use of cash (as opposed to silver) varied widely depending upon the period and the place. In general however cash was used for small transactions, daily wages, army pay and small tax and rent payments. Silver was usually used for long distance commerce, most taxes payable in money and annual salaries.[5] Since silver was much more plentiful in the commercially developed areas of the south it was also used there for small transactions. This question is taken up in greater detail below (see 2.7, Regional and Local Variations).

Cash were counted in single units as <u>wen</u> 文 and in large units as <u>ch'uan</u> or <u>tiao</u> 串 , 吊 . The strings

---

[4]Compare the similar situation with regard to circulation of uneven coins in all European countries in pre-modern times as described in Braudel and Spooner (1967), p. 379.

[5]In 1742 an attempt was made to limit the use of cash to small payments and retail purchases (<u>Ta-Ch'ing hui-tien shih-li</u> (1899), hereafter referred to as <u>shih-li</u>, pp. 8020-21). The attempt was not successful in the private sector nor does it fully describe the use of cash in the public sector.

(<u>ch'uan</u> or <u>tiao</u>) (a form of convenience not unlike the practice in banks today whereby cents or pennies are packed in rolls for ease of handling and counting) varied in size (i.e. number of cash) according to the custom of a given market. Frequently account books do not mention the size of the <u>ch'uan</u> in which a particular payment was made or debt recorded since size of the local string was taken for granted or was a subject for negotiation. When the string is specified we find a statement such as "seven-two <u>ch'ien</u>, six <u>ch'uan</u> and 300 <u>wen</u>" 柒貳錢陸串叁佰文 , which should be taken to record a payment satisfying a debt of six <u>ch'uan</u> each made up of 720 <u>wen</u> plus 216 <u>wen</u> (3/10's of 720) in other words a total of 4536 <u>wen</u>. How many actual cash changed hands in this instance is uncertain for not only did strings differ in size they also differed in the type and quality of the individual cash contained in them.[6] Where the <u>quality</u> of cash in a given string is specified we find a statement such as "three-seven <u>ch'ien</u>, six <u>ch'uan</u> and 300 <u>wen</u>," 叁柒錢陸串叁佰文 which should be taken to record a payment of six strings and 300 cash in which each string or fraction of a string contained three parts debased cash and seven parts standard cash. Where the quality of the cash is numerically signified the first digit is small e.g.

---

[6]See Chang Chia-hsiang (1925), section 2, Chapter 5, pp. 97-98 for a list of different string systems. See also King (1965), p. 62.

"one-nine *ch'ien*; two-eight *ch'ien*; three-seven *ch'ien*" etc. Where the length of the string is numerically indicated the first digit is large e.g. "nine-one *ch'ien*; eight-two *ch'ien*; seven-three *ch'ien*" etc. Besides numeric indicators size of string and quality of cash were specified by many different names whose use depended upon local custom.[7]

It goes without saying that in order to assess a price quotation which is recorded in *ch'ien* it is essential to know in which particular 'string system' the payment was recorded. For example if a daily wage was recorded in one area as 30 *ch'ien*, in another area as 60 *ch'ien* and in a third as 300 *ch'ien* the workers in question would each have received the same wage-equivalent of 30 *ch'ien* a day where the strings in use in the three areas belonged to the 1000 cash per string or *ch'ang-ch'ien* 長錢 system, the 500 cash per string or *chung-ch'ien* 中錢 system and 100 cash per string or *hsiao-ch'ien* 小錢 system respectively. The assumption being that in each case payment was made with the same quality of cash.[8] Fortunately the situation is a good deal less complex in the public sector for the government operated with one cash system throughout the Empire, the *ch'ang-ch'ien* or 1000 cash per string system, moreover it required payments to be made with 1000 standard cash or *chih-ch'ien* 制錢 to the string.

---

[7]See Miyayshita Tadao (1952), note 8, p. 38 for names of local strings used in payment to different creditors. See also Chang Chia-hsiang (1925), section 2, Chapter 5, p. 99.

[8]This example is adapted from Gamble (1944), p. 44.

The weight of the cash[9] and the consequent difficulties and expense of transporting them especially in North China gave rise to the extensive use of privately issued promissory notes, <u>ch'ien-p'iao</u> 錢票, referred to in accounts as "printed <u>ch'ien</u>" 印錢, the terms of redemption being entered upon the note in question. The issuance and effects of these notes are subjects taken up in sections 1.4 and 1.5.

2.3 <u>Silver</u>

Large payments as well as government taxes were mainly payed in silver bullion, the units of account of which were therefore based on units of weight: the <u>tael</u> 銀兩, <u>ch'ien</u> 錢 and <u>fen</u> 分 etc. Just as with cash so also with silver bullion; throughout the empire there were a large number of customarily accepted units differing in weight and fineness of the metal. In the private sector custom or the guilds frequently fixed the use of one or other of these <u>taels</u>,nevertheless each transaction was frequently the occasion for negotiation over the <u>tael</u> to be used.[10] In the public sector the government specified

---

[9]Cash were extremely heavy. The usual weight given for a string of 1000 cash is 7 catties. By this reckoning one man would have been able to carry a maximum of 12 such strings for a day's journey of 40 km. Also by this reckoning 285 strings of 1000 cash each weighed one metric ton. Not surprisingly a memorialist commented that in provinces like Shensi were river transport was lacking a mule cart was required to move more than 10,000 cash (see <u>Chung-kuo chin-tai huo-pi shih tzu-liao</u> (1964), pt. 1, vol. 1, p. 131). See also Chapter 3, note 11 for a graphic example of moving cash.

[10]Miyashita (1952) contains the most exhaustive description of the different customary and official <u>taels</u> in use at the end of the Ch'ing.

certain standard _taels_ for the different types of tax payment.[11]

As with the metals used in the alloy for the cash so with silver, the government exercised a monopoly over production and distribution. This control had by the late 16th century begun to lose any effectiveness it might once have had for by that time the import of foreign silver began to outweigh by far the silver produced in China itself.[12] By the mid 18th century foreign dollars in their original form were playing an important monetary role in south and east China.[13]

Government monetary policy was centered on maintaining the value of its cash currency in terms of silver

---

[11]Yang Tuan-liu (1962), pp. 78-81 conveniently summarizes the five main official _taels_.

[12]Numerous attempts have been made to estimate the amounts of silver reaching China from the New World from the mid-Ming on. That the influx of silver dollars increased enormously during these centuries to the point where they were no longer melted down but circulated in their original form is beyond dispute as is also the gradual decline of the influx from about 1750. There are however no reliable statistics available. When the balance of trade turned against China in the 19th century and silver began to flow out of the country the problem was linked specifically to the opium trade which both at the time and later was held to be the sole cause of the loss of silver and the consequent high cash price of silver. There were however many other causes leading to scarcity of silver than the opium trade, the estimated extent of which was not large enough to have had an empire wide effect. See King (1965), pp. 141-142.

[13]See for example Cheng Kuang-tsu (1855), _tsa-shu wen_, _chüan_ 6, pp. 44-45. Miyashita (1959), p. 19 shows that foreign dollars even came to be used as an official tax-paying money in some of the southern provinces before 1840.

bullion but since it was unable to control the silver supply and hence the price of silver or the minting of cash sufficiently closely to prevent illegal striking etc., the normative exchange ratio set at the beginning of Ch'ing (1000:1) remained a dead letter. In practice therefore the Ch'ing monetary system was not bimetallic in the usual sense at all since the value of each metal was not defined at fixed rates in terms of the other.[14] Each market differed from the next in the condition of its silver and cash sectors. Since there was no fixed ratio between the two sectors or indeed any fixed ratio between either of the two sectors in any given market and those of any other market every single transaction required weighings, assayings and negotiations.[15] These activities were carried on by tradesmen of all types and also by an increasing number of specialized cash shops.

In less commercially developed markets non-specialized stores undertook the exchange functions of the cash shops while in local markets itinerant operators of 'cash tables'

---

[14] See King (1965), p. 40 for further comments.

[15] Thus traders usually took a balance with them or small steelyard when travelling to another district in order to make comparisons with their own customary weights and measures. See Morse (1889), p. 94.

(<u>ch'ien-chuo</u> 錢桌) took their place.[16] Most of the cash shops issued promissory notes or bills while certain of the larger ones built up national networks during the 19th century.[17] The cash shops arranged exchanges of cash and taels in the private sector and they also performed the same service for the government. In the larger centres as explained in the next section, it was the cash shop guilds which set the daily exchange rates. Where these have survived they form a useful tool for tracing trends in a given market.

2.4 Recording and Reporting Cash/Silver Exchange Rates

Market exchange rates were recorded by the cash shops in their account books. They were also recorded although less systematically by all businesses using both cash and silver. The exchange rates were also investigated and reported on by local officials and provincial governors.

---

[16] For the growth of the cash shops see Kato Shigeshi (1947). In Peking there were 389 cash shops in operation between the early 18th century and 1830. By 1830 the number had risen to 511. In Shanghai there were 106 cash shops in 1796, in Canton there were 60 or 70, (See *The Canton Register and Price Current*, May 17, 1828). In Suchow in the early 19th century there were about 50 while in Fuchow there were 30 large ones and over 70 small ones in the suburbs. See P'eng Tse-i, (1961), pp. 45-46 and Parkes (1852). By the very end of the empire even small district towns in out of the way places usually had anything up to ten cash shops. See *Shina shōbetsu zenshi* (1915).

[17] See Yang Lien-sheng (1952), pp. 78-88 for a general introduction to 'proto-banks' and 'old-style banks'.

The most detailed description of how the cash shops or banks kept themselves informed of the rates comes from an outline of the Fuchow exchange market in 1848:

> "The bankers are kept most accurately informed on the subject (of exchange rates) by some twenty men in their general employ, whose sole business is to be in constant attendance in the market, and to acquaint the banks of everything that is going on, when they, guided by the transactions of the day, determine and fix upon, between themselves, the various prices of notes, sycee, and dollars...."[18]

There were 30 large banks in Fuchow at this time as well as about 70 smaller cash shops. In smaller money markets recording and setting the rates would have been a much more simple matter. The author of the above passage also adds that the "reporters" had also "to report the prices of silver every morning at the Magistracy."[19] None of the official regulations on reporting exchange rates required daily reports; Fuchow at this time was probably an exceptional case, the reason being as Parkes suggests, the concern over the increasing value of silver.

The first central government order on investigating and reporting exchange rates is contained in a regulation of 1734: the two metropolitan districts were to appoint cash brokers who were to check exchange rates at the major markets and personally report on them every ten days to the

---

[18] Parkes (1852), p. 182. See also Imahori Seiji (1955), pp. 354-357 on the cash shop guild in Kui-sui district town.

[19] Parkes (1852), p. 182.

Board of Revenue.[20] In 1786 this regulation was extended to all provinces to the extent that they were to make monthly investigations of the market exchange rates and report them to the Board of Revenue every quarter.[21] This regulation was still in operation in 1826 when the governor of Kiangsu in a memorial on cash shops was able to quote from monthly district reports throughout Kiangsu on exchange rates.[22] References to such reports can also be found in other 19th century memorials. Exchange rates were also reported on in connection with the grain price reports.[23] Surviving grain price reports from the very last years of the Empire attest that they were indeed reported.[24]

Quite apart from the reporting of exchange rates the yamen of district governments all recorded exchange rates as a basic accounting practice.[25]

---

[20] Shih-li, p. 8020.

[21] Shih-li, p. 8021.

[22] Memorial reprinted from Central Archives in Chung-kuo chin-tai huo-pi shih tzu-liao, 1964, pt. 1, vol. 1, p. 138.

[23] Sheng-li, Fu-chien (1873?), chüan 6, pp. 118-125 contains memorials dated 1781 and 1795 which state that district reports on grain prices are to include current exchange rates.

[24] The Shensi Reports (see Chapter 3) give monthly exchange rates using exactly the same formula as found in the Fukien regulations referred to in the previous note.

[25] On the different types of yamen accounts (which were basically the same as the different types of account kept in the private sector) see Ts'ai Shen-chih (1941), p. 15. Gamble and his co-workers used the yamen accounts from Ting district, Hopei, to compile an annual index of exchange rates from 1857 to 1930 (Gamble 1954, pp. 246-251). Gamble states that the yamen rates differed from the rates found in store account books by less than 1.5% (for 1928). This would support the suggestion that the officials and the guilds both recorded market rates which they may have derived from the same sources, i.e. guild agents. Annual government accounts usually give the market exchange rate of the 12th month.

In addition to the account books of cash shops and yamen accounts, official reports and memorials (or the vestiges of these sources which have often survived in summarizing compendia rather than in their original form) a third type of source for exchange rates should be mentioned. A very small number of private writers interested themselves in prices and exchange rates and either recorded their own observations or copied from tax quotas etc. These men had often worked as clerks or private secretaries.[26]

Few 20th century Chinese historians have shown an interest in the types of sources on exchange rates and

---

[26] Four of the most outstanding of such men were:

1) Yeh Meng-chu 葉夢珠 (1630?-1700?) from Kiangsu. His _Yüeh shih pien_ 閱世編 (Notes on Practical Affairs) written in the 1690's had to wait until 1935 before it was printed for the first time. It contains extremely detailed descriptions of life in the neighbourhood of Shanghai during the period of his life. His data on prices and exchange rates is drawn on in section 1.5 of this chapter. Nothing is known of Yeh's life.

2) Wang Hui-tsu 汪輝祖 (1730-1807) from Chekiang. His life as a private secretary to numerous local officials has recently been excellently sketched in P.T. Ho, 1963, pp. 292-294. Sasaki Masaya (1954) analyzes the data on prices and exchange rates in Wang (1796 and 1807).

3) Ch'ien Yung 錢泳 (1795-1844) the painter, from Chekiang. Sasaki (1954) has used the data on exchange rates and prices in Ch'ien (1870).

4) Cheng Kuang-tsu 鄭光祖 (1775-1850?) from Chekiang, accompanied his father on several trading trips. He may later have served as a private secretary. The data on exchange rates in Cheng (1855?) is given in map 1 of this chapter. I am indebted to Professor Yamana Yukio for bringing Cheng's work to my attention.

prices mentioned above although as early as 1922 Liang Ch'i-ch'ao had emphasized the importance of such sources.[27] Apart from the Ting district studies and the excellent team work done on a set of account books from a store near Tientsin little has been done in the fifty years since Liang wrote.[28] Studies of exchange fluctuations mainly based on central government compilations and therefore sketchy in their coverage, were pioneered by Japanese scholars.[29]

As a result of the failure to work on basic primary sources at a time when these were available in the '20's and '30's Chinese price history and that part of it with which we are concerned here, monetary history, has to be approached at least up to 1800 through spot quotations found in memorials or preserved in central government compilations.[30] After 1800 a few more detailed sources become available while at the end of the century fluctuations in the Treaty Ports can be followed in such newspapers as <u>Shen-pao</u>.

---

[27]Liang Ch'i-ch'ao (1922), Chapter 4, p. 16.

[28]For the Ting studies see note 25. For the Tientsin study see Yen Chung-p'ing (1955). In this study annual averages of exchange rates from a store in Ta-liu market town (大柳鎮), Ning-chin district (寧津縣,河北) for the years 1798-1850 were compiled in addition to annual averages of selected commodities for the same years.

[29]Notably Otake Fumio (1932).

[30]This was the approach pioneered by Otake and later followed by others. Recently Ch'en Chao-nan has used the same type of source as Otake for a more detailed study of the period 1723-96 (Ch'en, 1966).

Two major but unavoidable drawbacks should be mentioned with regard to basing reconstructions of exchange rates on spot quotations. Firstly it is often impossible to know when a quotation is high or low simply as the result of seasonal, short-term or random factors. Secondly the quotations do not come from one region or market but from a haphazard scattering of markets in different regions. Just how misleading this can be is suggested in Chapter 3 where the disparities within one province at a given time are dealt with in some detail. What follows is therefore a brief and necessarily generalized account of long-term trends in the money markets of China during the three-hundred or so years 1600-1900. It is based on reconstructions of trends in the fluctuations of cash/silver exchange rates during those years.

2.5 Long-Term Trends

A. 1630-1680

Official data on these years is lacking since official reporting had not yet begun. The extent of the breakdown of the monetary system may be gauged from scattered accounts in district gazetteers and private writings.

One of the concomitants of Ming decline was the dislocation of the cash monetary system and the depreciation of the coinage.[31] The extent of the famine and market dislocation is seen in the massive rice price differentials all over China at this time. Several contemporaries described the onset of famine, flood, bad harvests, debased cash and high prices in their localities.[32] The fullest account of monetary and price changes during this interim period is contained in the work of a contemporary writing of conditions in the neighborhood of Shanghai district town, Yeh Meng-chu.[33] Some of Yeh's data is tabulated on the next page.

The debasement of cash (as reflected in the cash/silver exchange rates (C/S rates), see table of Yeh's data on next page) had already begun some twenty years before the fall of the Ming. In 1642 cash had fallen two and a half times and by the next year, to three and a half times the value it had been before 1628 or the value it was to recover by the 1680's and '90's. In 1645, '46 and '47 only

---

[31] Details in occasional writings e.g. Cheng Kuang-tsu (1855?) Tsa-shu wen 6, p. 41; Yeh Meng-chu (1700?) has been relied on for much of the following paragraph. See also Wang Ch'ing-yun (1898), p. 485ff.

[32] See for example, Shen-shih, Ch'i-huang chi-shih and T'ung-hsiang tsai-i chi both describing conditions in Chekiang localities at this time and reprinted in Ch'en Heng-li (1956) pp. 289-291; 324-326. Ch'üan Han-sheng (1957) pp. 354-355 describes national economic dislocation.

[33] See Yeh Meng-chu (1700?) chüan 7, pp. 1-17b and chüan 1, pp. 17b-20b. See also Cheng Kuang-tsu (1855), Tsa-shu wen, chüan 6, pp. 41-48.

Table 1

Cash/silver exchange rates and rice prices in Shanghai district, Suchow prefecture, 1628-1690. (1685 = 100)

Year	C/S index number	Rice (tael) price	Rice (cash) price
1628	122		
1632	130	110	
1637			130
1638	185	205	110
1640	220		330
1641	275		
1642	266	555	1330
1643	365	270	930
1645	925		
1646	1000	270	1100
1647	1100	440	
1648	445		
1650	290	185	
1651	231	430	920
1652		440	
1657		90	
1659		220	
1661		385	
1662	120	230	250
1663		100	
1670		130	
1671	130		
1671/11	120		
1674/4	125		
1674/8	185		
1675	375		
1678	125		
1679	117	195	204
1680		180	
1681	138		
1682/4	123		
1685	100	100	100
1689	108		
1690/2	91		

Source: Yeh Meng-chu (1700?), chüan 7, pp. 1-17b

the old debased cash circulated leading to an enormous devaluation of the cash not to be equalled until the 1920's. Gradually the new government brought the situation under control by recovering the old coins, strictly enforcing laws against melting and by decreeing that up to 30% of commuted taxes be paid in the newly coined cash. Civil disturbances could nullify these trends as is shown by the rapid fall in the C/S rates following the arrival of the news of the revolt of the three southern feudatories which sent the rate climbing from 125 in the 4th month of 1674 to 185 in the 8th month and 375 in the following year. Recovery was rapid, the rate having fallen to 125 by 1678 and 117 by 1679. Apart from these national factors Yeh stresses the importance of the degree of energy which the local officials were prepared to put into the enforcement of laws against melters, clippers etc. Successful implementation could have dramatic short-term effects on the state of the currency and both he and Cheng amongst others gave examples of effective local action.

The effects of cash debasement as opposed to famine on rice prices is seen in the marked differences in the index numbers for <u>tael</u> and cash prices of rice in table 1. The <u>tael</u> price of one <u>tou</u> rose to 5½ times the normal level by 1642 and thereafter declined reaching cyclical but diminishing high points in 1647, 1651 and 1652, 1661 and 1679. These high points were in years of harvest failure and market collapse and it is significant that as order returned the cycle of disaster effects grew longer and less marked. Prices of cash crops such as cotton, tea and tobacco (not shown in table) as well as prices of manufactured goods (paper, cloth and silk) did not fluctuate nearly as much as the grain prices. Turning to the cash prices of rice (and also wheat, soy beans etc; not shown in table) to the disequilibriating effects of harvest failure and breakdown of communications must be added the effects of debasement. Cash prices not only rose twice as much as tael prices but they also remained at these cripplingly high levels much longer. Moreover cash prices were the prices which affected the overwhelming majority of people who relied on the market for their grain. Throughout the Ch'ing cash prices of rice were much less stable than tael prices of rice. The only exceptional period in this respect being the years of comparative monetary stability from about 1710 to 1770. In periods such as the one under review it is easy to appreciate that the basis of ordered government at the district level, the capacity to support the grain requirements of a district town, could be easily and rapidly removed in a mutually enforcing downward spiral of civil unrest, political insecurity, market collapse and monetary instability. So great was the extent of the collapse of the grain market in the mid-17th century that in some areas of Suchow prefecture for example the prices of land fell to an all-time low and buyers could not be found. It was only after the resumption of order in the 1650's and '60's that land prices evened out and estate-building began in earnest.[34] The market collapse and monetary instability of the years 1628-1660 were only to be equalled by the deteriorating situation at the beginning of the 19th century culminating in the years 1832-1860, but by that time the population had risen at least by 400% and the state was fighting a foreign enemy. The recovery in the second half of the nineteenth century (no mean achievement) was as we shall see totally destroyed in the great collapse of 1917-1930. In the 17th century without the complications of western invasion the disruptions of the Manchu conquest can be seen as a marking a hiatus, at least in the south-east, to the expansion already begun in the late Ming. Looking back at the end of the century Yeh Meng-chu was thus able to point out that many items of luxury consumption at the beginning of the century had in fact fallen in price with the development of manufactures and city markets while at the same time falling in quality as they became more widely diffused.

B. <u>1680-1729</u>

Despite the consolidation of the new cash system adopted from the Ming in all essentials, fluctuations reflecting civil unrest as well as temporary alterations in the content of the coins marked this period. Cash was in

---

[34] Yeh, <u>ibid.</u>, <u>ch'üan</u> 1, pp. 17b-20b.

a strong position in relation to silver and prices in cash were low. After the resumption of foreign trade in 1683 silver imports began to increase setting the stage for the next period.[35]

C. 1729-1770

A happy balance was achieved in this period as regards the content of the cash coins which was not changed after 1734. After 1740 the Yunnan copper mines began to operate at full strength thus providing a reliable domestic source to replace Japanese copper.[36] Prices in *taels* began to advance very rapidly which has been explained in terms of the increasing quantity of bullion entering the country.[37] This explanation however is probably too bullionist; contemporaries saw the rise in prices particularly of rice prices in terms of the increasing population and their point of view corresponds with the view of those who have questioned the simple quantity or bullionist theory in another context.[38] Prices in cash may have risen less than prices in *taels* owing to the relative shortage of copper but data is lacking on this point.

---

[35]See Ch'en Chao-nan (1966); Otake (1932); Abe (1959).

[36]See Yen Chung-p'ing (1957).

[37]Ch'üan Han-sheng (1957) follows Hamilton's use of the quantity theory with no regard to the general disrepute with which Hamilton's use of that theory is now held. See next note.

[38]See Hammarström (1957).

D. 1770-1834

The purchasing power of silver continued to fall while cash also began to depreciate as a result of failing copper supplies leading to dilution of the metallic content of the cash coins; a boom in paper cash notes issued by the cash shops and the government inability to control the spread of debased coins.[39] For the first time since the fall of the Ming prices in cash were beginning to rise more rapidly than prices in *taels*.[40] The extent of the decline of cash by the 1790's may be seen in the chart of Cheng Kuang-tsu's trip to the south-west (Map 1). With the gradual build-up of the Opium and cotton trades the stage was set for the next period in which the balance of trade turned against China for the first time in its history and as a result acute silver shortage began to be felt at least in the crucial south China region. A temporary reform of the cash coins was successfully achieved at the beginning of the 19th century, but by the 1830's the situation was beginning to get out of control again.

E. 1834-1856

During the 1830's the *tael* price of cash began to fall very rapidly, no doubt in part as a result of the shortage of silver as bullionists at the time and later have argued, but also as a result of the debasement of the cash.

---

[39]See Sasaki (1954), p. 17.

[40]Sasaki, *ibid.*, p. 19.

Map 1

CHENG KUANG-TSU'S OBSERVATIONS c. 1795

Explanation of numbers in inset:
1. Major centres from Wuchang east all using standard cash
2. Mainly counterfeited medium cash in use in this area
3. Shortage of cash; mainly using high quality cash of previous reigns, 800:1
4. See plan below

Dotted line on inset represents route taken by Cheng; for details see plan below
Double line represents rivers

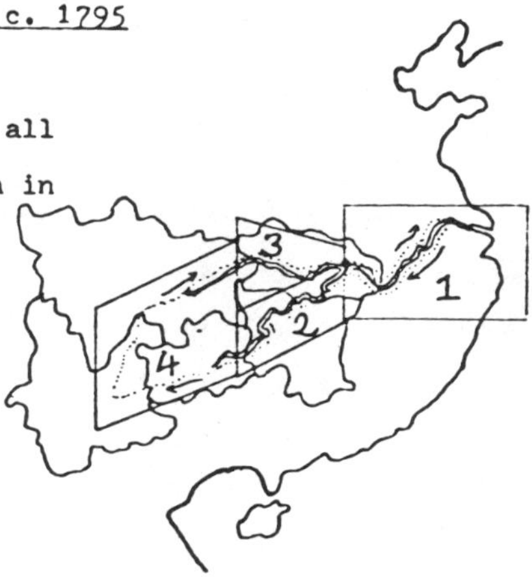

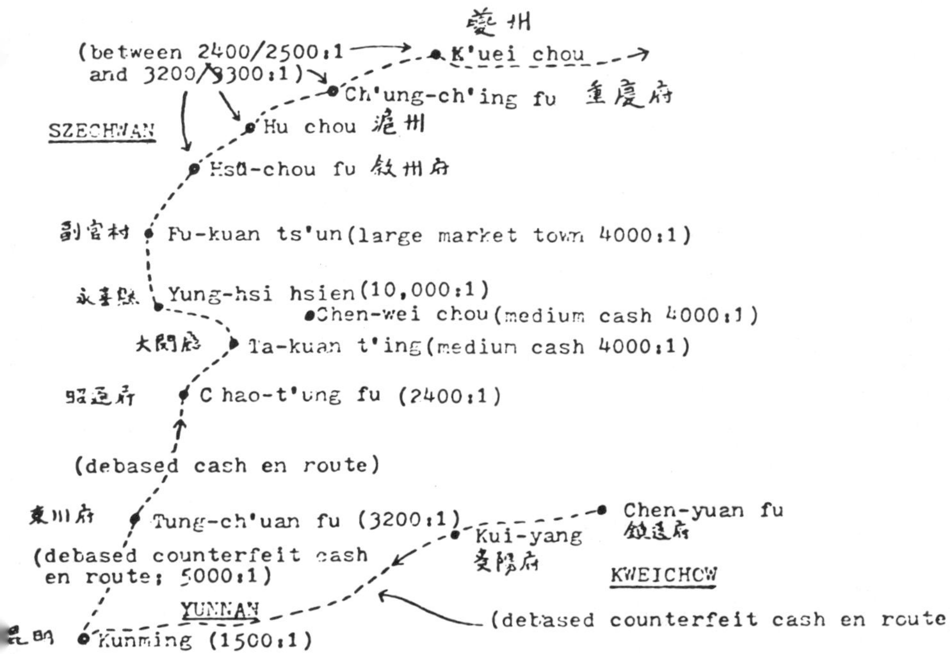

Source: Cheng Kuang-tsu (1855?), tsa-shu wen, chüan 6, pp. 42-43b.

For the first time more detailed sources are available (see graph 1).

F. 1856-1880

Monetary reforms leading to chaos in the metropolitan region followed the massive debasement of the cash coins which can be seen on graph 1. The breakdown of the coinage was hastened by the collapse of the domestic copper supply during the Moslem rebellion in Yunnan (1856-1874) and the cutting off of the capital from its copper supplies by the T'ai-p'ing armies. There were two short-lived periods of recovery at the beginning of the T'ung-chih and Kuang-hsü reigns (see graph 1).[41]

G. 1880-1900

The abandonment of the silver standard in many countries from the 1870's on led to the depreciation of silver in China which coupled with cash reforms and reduction of mint quotas saw the gradual falling of the cash price of silver towards the end of the century.[42] The purchasing power of cash was falling however in this period much more rapidly than the purchasing power of silver.[43]

---

[41] Monetary changes in this period have received more attention than in any other, see King (1965), pp. 144-164 for a recent appraisal.

[42] See Japanese Currency Commission Reports quoted in Fisher (1911), pp. 243-245.

[43] See Buck (1925); Ch'üan and Wang (1963); Chang (1932) for data on commodity prices from Hopei, Szechuan and Kiangsu respectively.

<u>Graph 1</u> <u>C/S rates, 1800-1915. 1821 = 100 (1226:1)</u>. The line on the left-hand side of the graph is based on Yen Chung-p'ing (1955) C/S rates from Hopei (see note 28). The right-hand side is based on Gamble (1954) C/S rates, also from Hopei (see note 28). These isolated series fit well with scattered data in P'eng Tse-i (1961); Gamble (1944) and also with the personal observations of Cheng Kuang-tsu. The mean of the Shensi rates adjusted to the same base year are marked in dotted line.

H. 1900-1930

Depreciation in both sectors continued although cash depreciation was much more rapid. Banking and monetary reforms introduced at the last minute by the Ch'ing government were swept away as the government lost any control over provincial mints. Hyper-infalation set in after 1919 and continued for the next ten years. By 1933 the old monetary system had practically ceased to exist.

2.6 Seasonal Fluctuations

The practice of settling both public and private debts at regular seasonal intervals was one major factor affecting seasonal fluctuations in the exchange rates. Another was the practice of marketing agricultural produce in the weeks immediately following the harvests. A third but less important regular seasonal factor was the increased demand for cash at festival times.[44]

In both the public and private sectors accounts were wound up at the end of the year and in the private sector debts were usually settled before the First of the First month. Increased demand for cash towards the end of the year resulted in a marked rise in the value of cash in relation to silver which has been documented for at least one district.[45] To a lesser extent the same happened at

---

[44] On all these points in the pre-modern period see Ch'en Chao-nan (1966), pp. 60-63. For the 1920's and '30's see Block (1935).

[45] For Ting district town, see Gamble (1954), pp. 250-251.

the other two main debt-settling times, the 5th of the 5th month and the 15th of the 8th month. The demand for cash at the New Year was of course heightened in town and country alike by preparations for New Year spending.

Commuted taxes which were largely payable in silver were collected after the autumn harvest in the 8th month. As a result taxpayers hastened to sell their harvest to obtain the cash to exchange for the silver to pay their taxes. Since at harvest time the purchasing power of cash rose they received less cash for their crops which in turn had to be exchanged at unfavourable rates for silver which was much in demand. Furthermore the cash which remained after the payment of taxes had fallen in value when the time came to use it in the late winter and spring.[46] Although at tax collection time the cash price of silver increased in the countryside the reverse was true in the towns.[47] Needless to say the cash shops were frequently accused of manipulating seasonal rates to their own advantage. In districts with large garrisons issuance of pay (which was in cash) could have depreciating effects on the cash/silver exchange rates.

---

[46]See Block (1935), p. 621.

[47]Silver Prices in China (1935), p. 73: "In areas... where coppers are a common currency for buying and selling, but where silver is required for the payment of debts and taxes...when taxes are levied the price of silver increases in the farm villages but decreases in the cities and towns."
See also P'eng Tse-i (1961) who discusses at length the hardships which this phenomenon entailed for producers in the 19th century.

The above are some of the regular factors affecting seasonal changes in the value of cash. There were also many random factors. Internal wars or famine usually saw the unloading of cash on the market followed by depreciation. On such occasions silver was frequently sought as being more easily transported. To the extent that civil unrest was a sign of the weakness of official control, laws against illicit melting, striking etc. were relaxed and debasement may be presumed to have followed. At times of famine large quantities of cash were sometimes handed out in the towns which also had an inflationary effect on cash prices.

2.7 Regional and Local Variations

Although most of the money markets in China shared general institutions and terminology there was nothing approaching a national money market.[48] The central government assumed control of the metropolitan money market which abosrbed approximately half the annual production of copper and was also probably the best regulated. But it did not suppose that methods suitable in the metropolitan market were necessarily suitable for the provinces. Thus in 1747 the Ch'ien-lung Emperor had circulated a set of regulations found effective in the capital asking the provincial governors

---

[48] See King (1965) pp. 121-133 for some excellent comments on this point.

to report which if any of the regulations might prove effective in their provinces.[49]

Each province was responsible for its own minting policy; provincial mints altered or stopped altogether their output according to their own rhythms. They also took action on such questions as the movement of cash outside their own boundaries usually with scant or no regard to the needs of neighbouring provinces unless officials there were successful in making complaints known to higher levels. The following remarks about regional differences are intended therefore as broad generalizations, as background against which the multifarious local scenes may be placed.

The border areas, Tibet, Sinkiang, Mongolia, Korea etc. had their own special currencies which differentiated them from the rest of the empire. In the northern cities as in the south the provincial capital and the major markets of the province stood out as little islands of cash in seas of great monetary scarcity and hence frequently of monetary debasement. The situation is graphically presented in the chart of the observations made by the young Cheng Kuang-tsu on a journey from Suchow to Kunming and then back via Chungking and the Yangtze (see Map 1). The journey was made in 1796 at a time when complaints of debased cash spreading from the south-western provinces especially Yunnan were becoming common.[50] At about the time of Cheng's

---

[49]See Kao-tsung shih-lu, chüan 232, pp. 6-13; chüan 243, pp. 23-25; chüan 251, pp. 24-26.

[50]See Yang Tuan-liu (1962), p. 56.

journey an effort was made to bring the situation under control in Yunnan by temporarily halting the production of copper and also by calling in short weight cash and minting full-bodied coins.[51] These efforts were largely unsuccessful in the long run as the continued debasement of cash attests.

The degree of articulation between exchange markets as gauged by similar exchange levels of C/S rates is difficult to assess because of lack of data. In the greater Yangtze delta region it was probably considerable owing to the extensive use of the lighter metal silver and also to the availability of cheaper and more rapid means of transport. One early 19th century source reports that exchange rates were rushed from Suchow to Ningpo by carrier pigeon.[52] In the north however even when cash shops could have made a large profit by moving cash only thirty miles to play the exchanges the costs and dangers of transport were prohibitive.[53] The same held true of course for the less accessible areas in the southern provinces.[54]

Generalizations on differences in the use of cash and silver in north and south are common. Most observers agreed that cash was used in the north for much larger

---

[51]See Yen Chung-p'ing (1957), pp. 42-44.

[52]See Martin (1847) quoted in Williams (1897), p. 192. See also MacGowan (1886) pp. 157-158 on the "Wall Street" of Ningpo.

[53]See Lin Tze-hsu (1885) <u>chüan</u> 12, pp. 7-11.

[54]The comment was made of the mountainous areas in S-W Kiangsu by the Emperor Ch'ien-lung, see <u>Kao-tsung shih-lu</u>, <u>chüan</u> 232, p. 14.

transactions than in the south, even for payments of 50 or 100 and more <u>ch'uan</u>.[55] In the south on the other hand where silver was more plentiful silver was often used for very small payments.[56] In 1742 an attempt was made to limit the use of cash to small payments and retail purchases.[57] The attempt was not entirely successful for especially in the 19th century when silver became very scarce we find wholesale grain purchases of up to 20 or 30 bushels made in cash.[58] In local or even regional centres according to a modern authority cash was used for wholesale transactions.[59] It would be an oversimplification to suppose therefore that cash was used for retail purchases and silver for wholesale transactions. In general the less developed a market the more likely it would have been to use cash. By definition long distance trade was not conducted in such markets which were more typical of the north than the relatively silver-abundant south. The situation at the end of the Ch'ing is summed up in a memorial submitted by Chang Chih-tung in 1904.[60] Since he was arguing against the adoption of a gold standard he stressed the role of cash:

> "It is only in the big treaty ports along the coast and up the Yangtze that gold and silver bullion and

---

[55]See K'o Tsu-liang, <u>Ch'ien-fa i</u>, (in Yang, 1962, p. 74).

[56]See Cheng Kuang-tsu (1855), <u>Tsa-shu wen</u>, p. 41.

[57]<u>Shih-li</u>, p. 8020-21.

[58]See References cited 1, Chinese manuscript sources, account books, especially items 2 and 5.

[59]See Miyashita (1956), p. 16.

[60]Chang's memorial is quoted in Chang Chia-hsiang (1925), section 3, Chapter 2, pp. 17-22. The memorial is also freely translated in Wagel (1915), pp. 104-105.

dollars are used. In the interior Chinese goods whether wholesale or retail are reckoned in cash and only in long-distance commerce are the prices converted to silver bullion. Cash still remains the basis.
Generally speaking in Kwangtung, Kwangsi, Yunnan, Kweichou and in the ports and towns of Kiangsu and Chekiang silver is used 70 or 80% of the time. In the river ports and towns along the Yangtze cash and silver are used about half and half together. In the prefectures and districts (i.e. less important commercial centres) of the central and upper Yangtze cash is used 90% of the time. As for the provinces in the Yellow river region they use cash 99% of the time. Cash and silver are used throughout the country but the regions using cash are ten times those using silver. Generally speaking national accounting is done in silver whereas the accounting of the people is largely in cash.

Very large differences, as we should expect from the above, existed between C/S rates within provinces. Early in his reign at a time of comparative monetary stability, the Ch'ien-lung Emperor had complained that the silver price of standard cash could not be unified and that it differed in every prefecture, sub-prefecture and district, and moreover that even within a single district the rates were constantly fluctuating.[61] By the end of the 18th century, admittedly at a time and in an area where the circulation of underweight coins was notorious, provincial, district and non-administrative centres all differed amongst themselves while at the same time standing out sharply from their rural hinterlands as islands of semi-standard cash in seas of debased coinage (see Map 1 showing Cheng Kuang-tsu's

[61]See Kao-tsung shih-lu, chüan 115, p. 32.

trip to the south-west in 1796.) The situation was not much better in Chekiang at this time as the following description of exchange conditions in the neighbourhood of Hsiao-shan makes clear:

> "In the district town of Hsiao-shan as well as in nearby Nan-hsiang and Tung-hsiang, 100 *wen* of the market cash[62] used in trade exchanges for 95 *wen* of standard cash. In the more distant *hsiang* east as far as the prefectural town (about 35 miles away) 100 *wen* of market cash exchanges for 90 *wen* of standard cash."[63]

The situation was to grow worse as official control weakened during the course of the 19th century and the coins in a string of cash grew more and more uneven.[64] Nor should the diversity in local exchange rates surprise us. At no time was the condition of the cash uniform. Not only did the metallic content of the coins differ from casting to casting and from provincial mint to provincial mint but also coins from previous dynasties, not to speak of foreign coins, were constantly in circulation. When it is remembered that even granted a full string of standard cash identical in two different markets, its value in each would depend upon the demand conditions in both markets as well as upon the supply of any of several hundred varieties of silver

---

[62] The phrase 'market cash' (*shih-ch'ien* 市錢), was a general term describing whatever cash happened to be circulating in a given market. It did not necessarily refer to strings of cash made up of six parts standard and four parts debased cash as implied in Miyashita (1952), p. 38, note 8.

[63] Ch'ien Yung (1796) quoted in Ch'en Chao-nan (1966), pp. 32-33.

[64] Of the many descriptions of the diverse contents of a 'handful of cash' see for example Brewitt-Taylor (1899), pp. 357-359.

in both markets.

The degree of integration as well as long-term trends in a large number of district exchange markets in one province is the subject of the next chapter.

CHAPTER 3

Cash/Silver Exchange Rates in Shensi, 1900-1910

3.1 The Data

In 1900 Shensi was virtually untouched by the changes apparent in the richer provinces to the south and east.[1] Its agriculture, industries, trading patterns and communications were much as they had been for the last several centuries. Monetary innovations which had been introduced into many provinces from the 1890's on were slow in arriving in Shensi. Throughout the province the basis of the monetary system remained the cash and the tael although by 1910 silver dollars (yin-yüan 銀圓), and 'coppers' (t'ung-yüan 銅圓) had begun to be minted at the provincial mint and to circulate alongside the old money. The provincial government had also just begun to print paper money but not in sufficient quantity to produce inflation. Exchange services between the cash and silver sectors were largely carried on as they always had been in Shensi by general stores, oil shops, grain stores etc. rather than by specialized money shops. Thus provincewide, of about 1000 stores offering exchange services, only about 200 at

[1] See Chapter 5, part 1 for a general introduction to the economy of Shensi at this time.

the very most were specialized money shops. Both the stores and the money shops operated with capital of only a few thousand _taels_ and many of them with less. Most of the stores continued to issue cash notes as they had since the 18th century.[2]

The pace of change only began to alter in Shensi after the revolution in Sian followed by the introduction of new ideas, a new administration, the railway (in 1915), war, famine and a continual issue of unredeemable paper which caused heavy inflation. These changes however lie beyond the scope of this chapter which is concerned with the old rather than the new.

What follows is an analysis of exchange markets in Shensi in the ten years prior to the revolution of 1911. The analysis is based on monthly reports on cash/silver exchange rates (C/S rates) submitted by the 90 administrative units into which Shensi was divided at this time.

The exchange quotations analyzed in this chapter are drawn from 2,250 routine grain price reports of the type introduced in Chapter 4. The set of reports used in the present chapter (the Shensi Reports) contain quotations for the prices of major grains as well as cash/silver exchange

---

[2]This paragraph is based on material contained in _Chung-kuo chin-tai huo-pi shih tzu-liao_ (1964) in addition to _Shina shōbetsu zenshi_ (1918), vol. 7, part 8, "Currency and monetary institutions", pp. 686-786.

rates (C/S rates). They were submitted by the 90 sub-prefectural departmental and district yamen in Shensi at this time for each of 25 months during the years 1900-1910.[3] Each month each district town yamen sent the report on grain prices and C/S rates to its superior yamen (there were twelve in Shensi at this time) where a brief summary was tacked to the front of the reports from the districts subordinate to that yamen before they were sent on to the Provincial Treasurer at Sian.[4] At the Treasurer's yamen the twelve groups of district reports were then roughly stitched together, each report being stamped with the seal of the Provincial Treasurer. A note was added following the last report stating the type of grain measure to which local measures had been converted as well as the fact that local _taels_ had been converted to _Kuping taels_.

The reports have survived today in the form in which they were bound together at the provincial capital every month. Thus for each month there is one volume containing 102 documents (90 reports plus 12 summaries). Reports from

---

[3] See References Cited 1: Chinese manuscript sources, Shensi Reports, for full titles and present whereabouts of the reports.

[4] The summaries prepared at the superior yamen simply state the highest and lowest C/S rate found amongst the districts in that department or prefecture. In Shensi at this time there were 7 prefectures (_fu_); 5 independent departments (_chih-li chou_) which I refer to throughout as "superior yamen." In addition there were 5 sub-prefectures (_t'ing_); 1 department (_chou_); 79 districts (_hsien_). The five independent department yamen submitted their own reports as well as summaries of their subordinate districts. In all therefore throughout the province 90 yamen sent in reports which were summarized at 12 superior yamen before arriving at the provincial treasurer's yamen in the provincial capital.

Table 1

Months covered in the Shensi Reports, Chinese and Western Calendars

	Chinese Calendar			Western Calendar		
1.	Kuang-hsü 26,	5th month	May 28	to June 26	1900
2.	" " ",	8th month	August 25	to Sept 23	"
3.	Kuang-hsü 28,	4th month	May 8	to June 5	1902
4.	Kuang-hsü 29,	4th month	April 27	to May 26	1903
5.	" " ",	5th month*	June 25	to July 23	"
6.	" " ",	6th month	July 24	to August 22	"
7.	" " ",	7th month	August 23	to Sept 20	"
8.	" " ",	8th month	Sept 21	to Oct 19	"
9.	" " ",	9th month	Oct 20	to Nov 18	"
10.	" " ",	10th month	Nov 19	to Dec 18	"
11.	" " ",	11th month	Dec 19	to Jan 16	1903-04
12.	Kuang-hsü 31,	1st month	Feb 4	to March 5	1905
13.	" " ",	5th month	June 3	to July 2	"
14.	" " ",	8th month	August 30	to Sept 28	"
15.	Kuang-hsü 32,	2nd month	Feb 23	to March 24	1906
16.	" " ",	10th month	Nov 16	to Dec 15	"
17.	Kuang-hsü 34,	5th month	May 30	to June 28	1908
18.	Hsüan-t'ung 1,	3rd month	April 20	to May 18	1909
19.	" " ",	5th month	June 18	to July 16	"
20.	" " ",	6th month	July 17	to August 15	"
21.	" " ",	8th month	Sept 14	to Oct 13	"
22.	" " ",	9th month	Oct 14	to Nov 12	"
23.	" " ",	10th month	Nov 13	to Dec 12	"
24.	" " ",	11th month	Dec 13	to Jan 10	1909-10
25.	" " ",	12th month	Jan 11	to Feb 9	1910

	1900	1902	1903	1904	1905	1906	1908	1909	1910
Jan				XX					XX
Feb					XX				
Mar						XX			
Apr									
May		XX	XX					XX	
Jun	XX				XX		XX		
Jul			XX					XX	
Aug			XX					XX	
Sep	XX		XX		XX			XX	
Oct			XX					XX	
Nov			XX			XX		XX	
Dec			XX					XX	

* Inter-callary month

25 months have survived making a total of 25 volumes containing 2,250 documents in all. Each document is written in a different hand although many already had the report formula crudely wood-block printed, only the changing figures being filled in by hand.

The C/S rate is recorded in front of the grain prices using exactly the same formula for this type of report found in various 18th century regulations:

> "One Kuping tael exchanges for so many ch'uan (or so many thousand) and so many 100's and 10's of standard cash." (庫平紋銀每兩換制錢 ... 千(串) ... 文)[5]

There are three exceptions to the above formula:

1) The 25 reports from Pin chou (邠州 No. 71, see Map 1) use the expression "One Kuping tael of commuted land-tax silver" instead of the regular formula "one Kuping tael." This was presumably a copyists slip for commuted land-tax was payable in Kuping taels.[6]

2) One of the 25 reports from Chung-pu (中部 No. 85, see Map 2) gives the amount of cash for which the local tael exchanged in addition to giving the standard cash/Kuping tael exchange rate. Such information was not required to be entered in reports going to higher levels and was presumably included as the result of a copyists slip.

---

[5]For the 18th century regulations see Chapter 2, note 23. A Fuji-copy of one of the district reports as well as of one of the prefectural summaries may be found in Chapter 4, figs. 1 and 2.

[6]The phrase in these reports is k'u-p'ing liang-yin i-liang 庫平糧銀壹兩 . Liang-yin refers to ti-liang-yin (地糧銀) i.e. commuted land-tax silver, see Hoshi (1966), p. 282.

3) The third exception to the standard formula for recording C/S rates occurs in eight of the 25 reports from San-shui (三 水 No. 72, see Map 1) where the following phrase is found:

> "One *Kuping tael* exchanges for one *ch'uan*, 547 *wen* of standard three-seven cash" (庫平紋銀每兩換制參柒錢壹串伍佰肆拾柒文).

Standard cash by definition described 1000 good cash as we have seen in Chapter 2. On the other hand 'three-seven cash' meant seven parts good cash, three parts debased cash (see 2.2). The copyist probably blundered here for the eight C/S rates using this phrase when compared with the remaining rates from San-shui were clearly recorded for local debased cash and not as required for 1000 standard cash. These eight rates have been readjusted to bring them into line with the remaining rates from San-shui.

The C/S rates as well as the grain price quotations were copied from the original reports which were found in Tokyo and were then punched onto IBM cards preparatory to setting up data files for use on the Princeton computer system.

The data in the Shensi Reports contains many wild values which reflect the wide disparities of natural conditions in the province. Some of the months covered in the Reports were famine months which affected some places more than others leading also to unusually high values. As we shall see in Chapter 5, not all places reported on all crops. There are therefore missing values in the data. For these reasons a maximum resistent data analysis method was required (i.e. a method not influenced by wild or missing values). Thanks to the help and generosity of Mr. David Hoaglin of the Department of Statistics, Princeton University, I have been able to make use of the methods of elementary analysis (specifically designed to overcome the type of problems found in such data as the Shensi Reports) outlined in a forthcoming book of Professor J. W. Tukey.[7]

3.2 Province Wide Trends, 1900-1910

In order to estimate province wide trends during the ten years covered by the reports, each C/S rate was arranged on a two-way table by months (in columns) and by places (in rows). Month effects (column effects) and place effects (row effects) were calculated (see note 7). Next a value typical of the data as a whole was calculated. Thus the residual of a given place in a given month + place effect of that place + month effect of that month + general effect = original C/S rate of that place in that month. For the purposes of this section the month effects of the 25 months

---

[7]J. W. Tukey, unpublished preliminary version (Fall 1969) of Introduction to Exploratory Data Analysis, especially chapters 16 to 21. For an example of the type of two-way table set up for the data in the Shensi reports see ibid., chapter 21, Exhibit 1, Elementary Analysis of a Two-way Table.

were used. The month effects were adjusted so as to fall on the mid-day of each equivalent solar month as a preliminary to plotting them on a 4,015 day (i.e. 11 year) time axis.

The plot of month effects vs. time (see fig. 1) brings out very clearly the extraordinarily high rates of the first two months (1900/5 and 1900/8) particularly of 1900/8. 70% of the towns reported rates of 1400:1 or over in these months which stand out from what can be constructed from scattered quotations of the trend in the previous decade (1890-1900). Nor were these heights reached by the end of the succeeding decade despite the beginnings of severe cash depreciation (in 1909 only 30% of the towns reported rates of 1400:1 or over). 1900 saw therefore the worst depreciation in the cash sector in the entire period 1890-1910.[8] The chief cause of this collapse of the cash sector in 1900 must have been the agricultural crisis of the years 1899, 1900 and 1901. These years saw the most severe famine to have struck the province for several decades (see table 3, Chapter 5 for full details). There was unrest in the province and the standard of local government presumably

[8] So unusually high were the month effects for the first two months (for reasons explained below) that the entire set of data was recalculated leaving out the first two months. The resulting changes were too slight however to justify reproducing the recalculation here. That the changes were so slight shows how resistant the data analysis method is.

Fig. 1 Plot of C/S month effects vs. time (source: Shensi Reports)

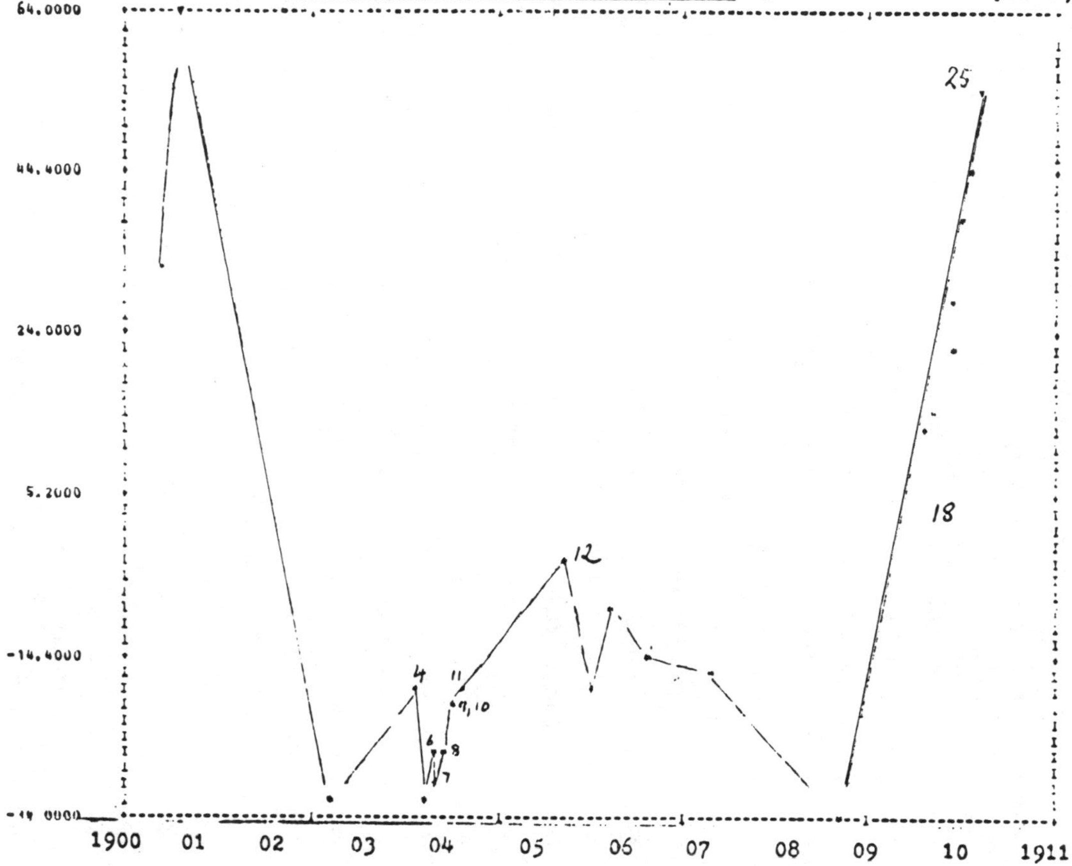

fell leading to the relaxation of the controls on illicit coining, melting etc. Very large numbers of people sought refuge in the towns especially the prefectural cities and took with them their savings (in cash). The situation in the cities must have been that summed up in the saying "there is cash but nothing to buy" (yu ch'ien, wu shih 有錢無市).[9] To the extent that officials took action in the towns they could only have exacerbated the depreciation of cash for they released reserves of cash to be distributed to the refugees. In 1900/10 the court arrived in Sian bringing with it large numbers of troops whose salaries were payed in cash. All these factors must have contributed to the depreciation of cash which in turn hastened the downward spiral as those who could placed their wealth in silver which they hoarded.

In Chapter two we saw examples of civil unrest dramatically reflected in the rapid fall in the purchasing power of cash; the present case is an example of this phenomenon brought about by famine and all the disruptions in its train. The controls on the minting of cash and the attempt to maintain stable rates were weak at the best of times. In assessing the deleterious effects of famine and unrest we should add the collapse of the monetary system

[9]Literally, "there is money but no market or transaction" as there is nothing offered for sale. This saying is frequently found in disaster sections of local gazetteers.

which can only have further contributed to the dislocating of the marketing system and with it the basis of district government upon which a stable cash system was posited.

By 1902/4 the C/S rates had dropped to more normal levels, only to rise slightly by the following year and then drop again that summer. For the remainder of the year the rates rose steadily but only by small increments. In 1905 and 1906 the rates were falling and by 1908/5 had reached their lowest point in 20 years. The decade ends with rapid cash depreciation; the rates for 1909/10 having surpassed the highest rate of 1903. They continued to rise into 1910 although they did not rise to the 1900 level until after the revolution in Sian.

On the basis of present knowledge these trends can only be linked in a very indirect way with movements of silver in the international money market as reflected in the silver/foreign exchange rates of these years in the treaty ports. The fluctuations in Shensi and Shanghai for example show no direct correlation.[10] Broadly speaking however the Shensi trends do compare with the general movement of C/S rates quoted by P'eng Hsin-wei as national averages for these years. They also show some correlation with the rates quoted by Gamble for Ting district, Hopei.[11]

---

[10]For the Shanghai rates see <u>China Year Book</u>, 1914, p. 136.

[11]See chapter 2, graph 1 for the Ting rates and P'eng (1956), p. 588 for the national averages.

Both series show high rates at the beginning of the decade falling towards the middle and then rising again at the end of the decade in the years before 1911. The depreciation of cash in these later years should no doubt be explained in terms of the increased coining of cash and coppers in provincial mints from about 1905 on.

The above account of province wide trends inevitably conceals more complex and sometimes contradictory movements within the three major geographic zones into which Shensi is divided (see map 1). These zones are discussed at some length in Chapter 5. Here we need only note that zone A and zone B were separated by the Ch'in mts. which were usually only crossed at two points (see transport routes, map 2, Chapter 5). Zone C was the poorest of the three zones and had no navigable rivers; only cart tracks connected it with zone A. We would expect C/S rates within the three zones to differ. How they differed and to what extent groups within zones emerged are questions to which, with the aid of maps 2 and 3, we now turn.

3.3 Zones Within the Province

Typical C/S Rates

As explained at the beginning of the previous section the C/S rates were arranged on a two-way table by months (in columns) and by places (in rows). The row effects or place effects are those values typical of each place over all the months; place effect of a given place + general effect =

Map 1

Geographic zones in Shensi

C/S rate typical of that place. The present section is based on an analysis of such typical C/S rates for each place. The object of the analysis is to find how extensive the Shensi exchange market was at this time. The criteria for judging towns to belong to the same exchange market are (1) that they have similar levels of typical C/S rates (the definition of typical is given above, the definition of similar is discussed below) and (2) that they have comparable movements of rates over time. We begin with criterion one.

The province typical C/S rate (general effect) is 1345 while the average of all typical rates in zone A (excluding the provincial capital) is 1217 (see maps 2 and 3 where typical rates are entered for each place). The average of all typical rates in zone B is 1467 while in zone C it is 1422. These averages of whole zones however can tell us very little for as can be seen in maps 2 and 3 there are plateaus of extremely high rates as well as low basins in all of the zones.

In the extreme north of the province towns 48, 49, 51 and 52 have comparatively low C/S rates (average 1218 cash) all within a fairly narrow range (largest differential being 125 cash). Moving southwards however we find that the C/S rates in towns 50, 88, 87, 90, 89, 21, 25, 23 and 18 are unusually high averaging 1608 cash while if we take out 50, 90, and 21 (all in the 1400's) the rest average 1808. To the west towns 24, 26 and 27 have an average of 1384.

Table 2

Typical C/S exchange rates in 90 district towns, Shensi, 1900-1910

1.	1466	46.	1269
2.	1671	47.	1275
3.	1696	48.	1160
4.	1210	49.	1285
5.	1253	50.	1456
6.	1189	51.	1198
7.	1221	52.	1231
8.	1197	53.	1237
9.	1146	54.	1241
10.	1218	55.	1250
11.	1251	56.	1212
12.	1247	57.	1231
13.	1197	58.	1334
14.	1217	59.	1229
15.	1161	60.	1267
16.	1177	61.	1289
17.	1196	62.	1409
18.	1869	63.	1351
19.	1162	64.	1291
20.	1240	65.	1235
21.	1465	66.	1318
22.	1208	67.	1375
23.	1847	68.	1316
24.	1326	69.	1364
25.	1747	70.	1551
26.	1406	71.	1309
27.	1421	72.	1221
28.	1466	73.	1252
29.	1193	74,	1522
30.	1205	75.	1190
31.	1215	76.	1160
32.	1269	77.	1238
33.	1238	78.	1297
34.	1286	79.	1660
35.	1279	80.	1313
36.	1183	81.	1325
37.	1641	82.	1417
38.	1608	83.	1236
39.	1357	84.	1279
40.	1470	85.	1260
41.	1484	86.	1301
42.	1230	87.	1527
43.	1328	88.	1609
44.	1421	89.	2254
45.	1636	90.	1461

Source: Shensi Reports

Key to Map 1

(Unless otherwise specified all towns are district towns. The order is the same as in the reports)

1. Ning-shan t'ing • 寧山廳
2. Hsiao-i t'ing • 孝義廳
3. Hsi-an fu • 西安府
3. Hsien-ning • 咸寧
3. Ch'ang-an • 長安
4. Lin-t'ung • 臨潼
5. Wei-nan • 渭南
6. Kao-ling • 高陵
7. Fu-p'ing • 富平
8. Ching-yang • 涇陽
9. San-yüan • 三原
10. Hui-chou • 耀州
11. T'ung-kuan • 同官
12. Hsien-yang • 咸陽
13. Hsing-p'ing • 興平
14. Li-ch'üan • 醴泉
15. Chou-chih • 盩厔
16. Hu • 鄠
17. Lan-t'ien • 藍田

18-27 see Map 2

28. Lung chou • 隴州
29. Feng-hsiang fu • 鳳翔府
29. Feng-hsiang • 鳳翔
30. Pao-chi • 寶雞
31. Ch'i-shan • 岐山
32. Fu-feng • 扶風
33. Mei • 郿
34. P'ing-yang • 汧陽
35. Lin-yu • 麟遊

36. Liu-pa t'ing • 留壩廳
37. Ting-yüan t'ing • 定遠廳
38. Fo-p'ing • 佛坪
39. Ning-ch'iang chou • 寧羌州
40. Han-chung fu • 漢中府
40. Nan-cheng • 南鄭
41. Ch'eng-ku • 城固
42. Yang • 洋
43. Hsi-hsiang • 西鄉
44. Pao-ch'eng • 褒城
45. Mien • 沔
46. Lüeh-yang • 略陽
47. Feng • 鳳

48-52 see Map 2

53. T'ung-kuan t'ing • 潼關廳
54. Hua chou • 華州
55. T'ung-chou fu • 同州府
55. Ta-li • 大荔
56. Ch'ao-li • 朝邑
57. Ho-yang • 郃陽
58. Han-ch'eng • 韓城
59. Teng-ch'eng • 澄城
60. P'u-ch'eng • 蒲城
61. Hua-yin • 華陰
62. Pai-shui • 白水

63. Han-ying t'ing • 漢陰廳
64. Chuan-p'ing t'ing • 磚坪廳
65. Hsing-an fu • 興安府
65. An-k'ang • 安康
66. P'ing-li • 平利
67. Hsün-yang • 洵陽
68. Shi-ch'üan • 石泉
69. Tzu-yang • 紫陽
70. Pai-ho • 白河

71. Pin chou • 邠州
72. San-shui • 三水
73. Shun-hua • 淳化
74. Ch'ang-wu • 長武

75. Ch'ien chou • 乾州
76. Wu-kung • 武功
77. Yung-shou • 永壽

78. Shang chou • 商州
79. Chen-an • 鎮安
80. Shan-yang • 山陽
81. Lo-nan • 雒南
82. Shang-nan • 商南

83-86 see Map 2

87-90 see Map 2

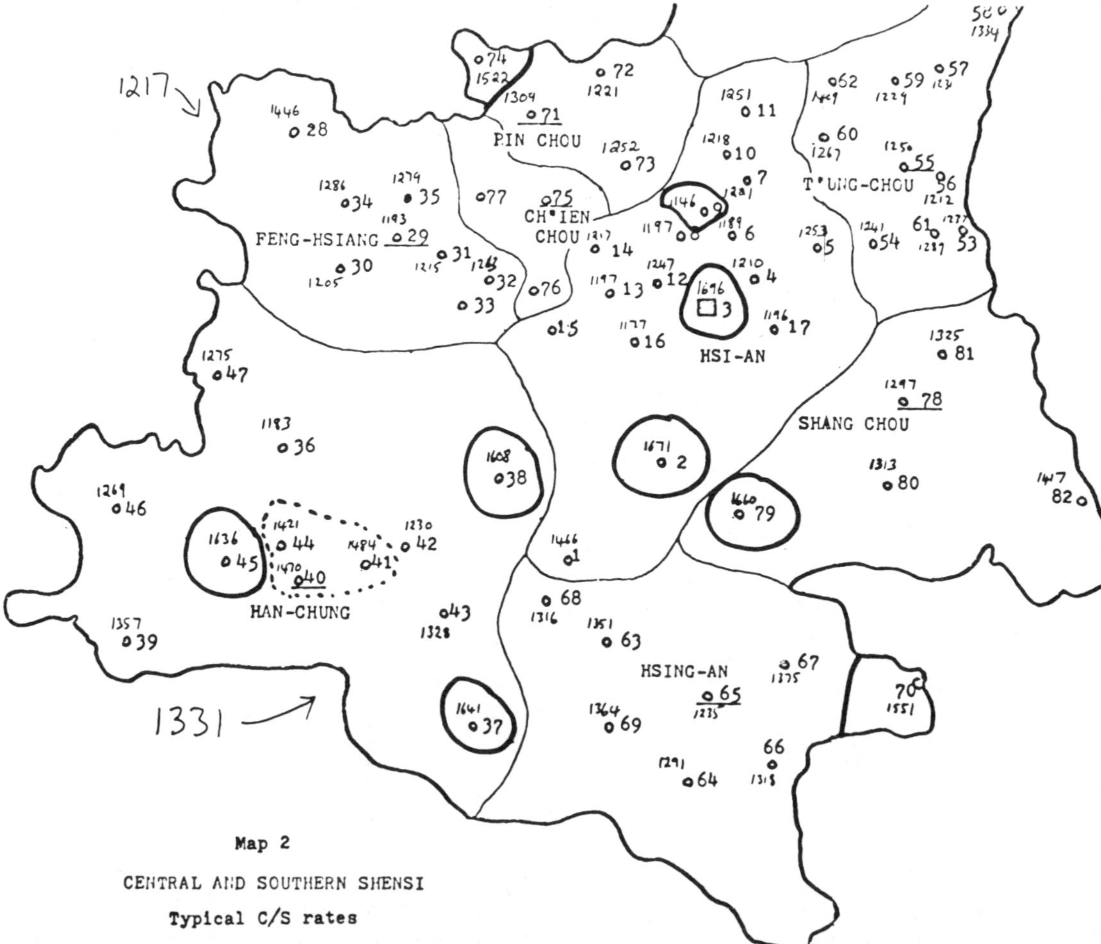

Map 2

CENTRAL AND SOUTHERN SHENSI

Typical C/S rates

Key to Map 3

Unless otherwise specified all towns are district towns. The order is the same as in the reports.

18. Yen-an fu • 延安府
18. Fu-shih • 膚施
19. Kan-ch'üan • 甘泉
20. I-ch'uan • 宜川
21. Yen-ch'uan • 延川
22. Yen-ch'ang • 延長
23. An-sai • 安塞
24. Pao-an • 保安
25. An-ting • 安定
26. Ching-pien • 靖邊
27. Ting-pien • 定邊

48. Yü-lin fu • 榆林府
48. Yü-lin • 榆林
49. Huai-yüan • 懷遠
50. Chia chou • 葭州
51. Shen-mu • 神木
52. Fu-ku • 府谷

83. Lin chou • 鄜州
84. Lo-ch'uan • 洛川
85. Chung-pu • 中部
86. I-chün • 宜君

87. Huan-te chou • 綏德州
88. Mi-chih • 米脂
89. Ch'ing-chien • 清澗
90. Wu-pao • 吳堡

Map 3

NORTHERN SHENSI

Typical C/S rates

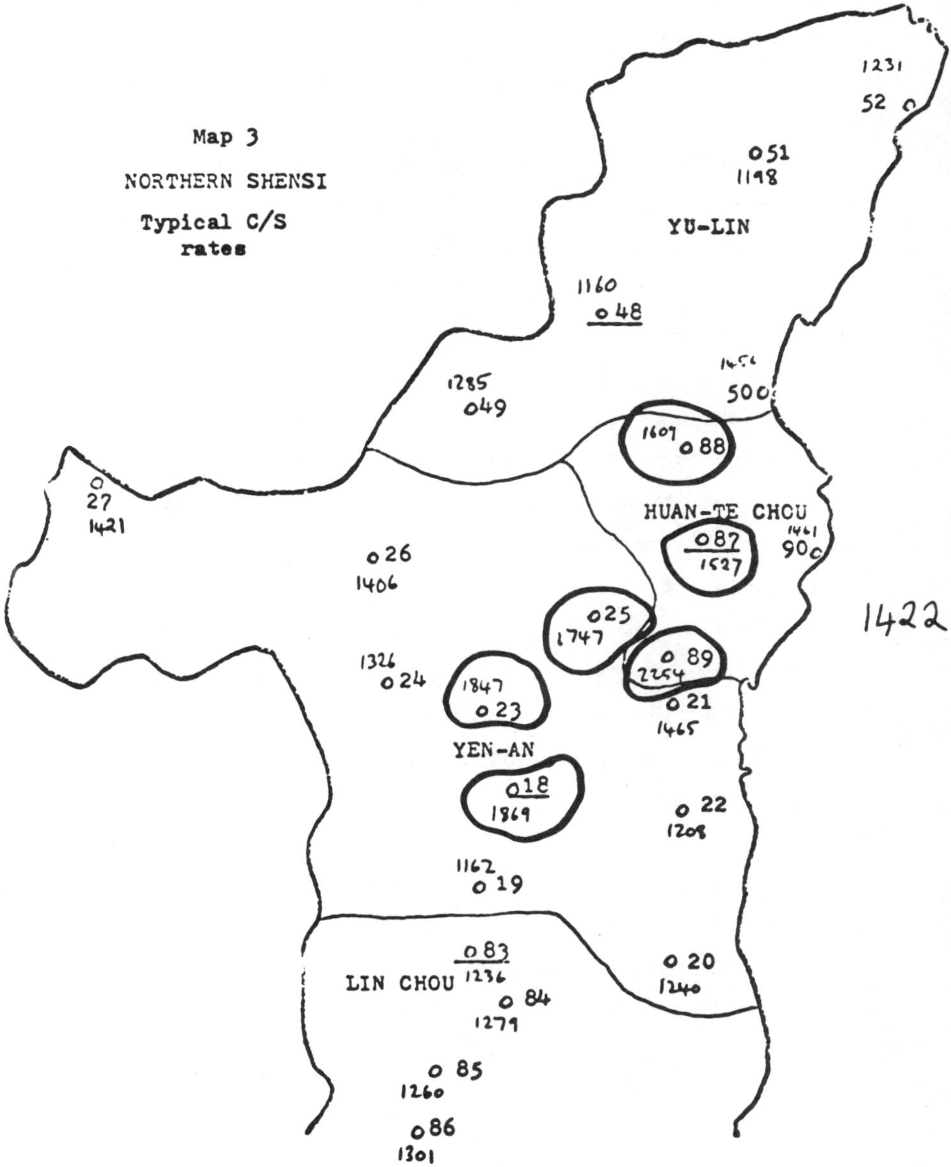

Towards the south again the rates are comparatively low (towns 22, 20, 19, 83, 84, 85 and 86) at 1240. We appear therefore to have two low basins of C/S rates in this zone in addition to two intermediate plateaus and one extremely high plateau.

In the commercially much more developed zone A (centre of the province) the differences are much less marked. In the eastern and western parts of the zone most of the rates are in the 1200's. In the central part of the zone (the greater Sian plain) half of the rates are unusually low in the 1100's while the other half are in the 1200's. The exceptions in this zone are very interesting; towns 74 and 28 at the edge of the zone on the provincial boundary are much higher than the other towns while the provincial capital in the very centre of the zone stands out above all the rest with a typical C/S rate of 1696. These exceptions are discussed below.

In the south of the province (zone B) the situation is almost as complex as in the north (zone C). Towns 79, 2, 1 and 38 (all are in the high range of mountains dividing the two zones) have unusually high rates. Towns 37 and 45 also have very high rates. Most of the rest of the towns are in the 1300's. Town 70 appears to be another exception at the border of the province. To the west towns 40, 41 and 44 stand medium high in the 1400's. Thus in zone B we have several isolated pockets of extremely high C/S rates; a medium high plateau and the rest in the 1200's and 1300's.

These groups of towns with high, medium and low C/S rates as well as the isolated towns with high rates are marked in outline in maps 2 and 3. For the remainder of the discussion we shall discount those towns on the borders of the province (towns 82, 70, 37, 39, 28, 74, and 26) which since they do not fit with any of their neighbours are presumed to belong with exchange markets in neighboruing provinces. It is worth stressing that the groupings outlined on maps 2 and 3 are <u>not</u> coterminous with the boundaries of the administrative units (the prefectures and departments, outlined in black on the maps) into which the province was then divided. Had such a correspondence been found it would have strongly suggested the negative conclusion that the reports reflected regularities in the reporting procedures rather than actual conditions.

Before deciding on the basis of estimated transport costs the differences between levels of C/S rates (in neighbouring towns) greater than which arbitrage can be presumed not to have taken place (and hence defining towns with 'similar' rates) and before offering general and particular reasons for the differences in rates between zones, groups of towns and individual towns, we must test for the degree of integration using criterion two and see whether zones or groups of towns had comparable movements of C/S rates over time.

Clearly in a province as geographically divided as Shensi we should not be surprised to find that although the trend line for the entire province (see fig. 1) moves upward between the first and second months and then falls between the second and third months, a substantial portion of the towns did not follow this trend. Out of 90 towns, 47 showed rising trends between the first two months while 27 showed rising rates and six reported no change. Between the second and third months 51 reported falling rates while 34 reported rising rates and 5 reported no change. We must now examine whether these exceptions to the general trend coincided with the groupings according to place effects as given in the previous paragraphs.

As a convenient way of summarizing monthly movements of C/S rates monthly arithmetic means were calculated for the zones and for the groups (see table 3).

Zone A (table 3, column 2) accords fairly closely with the general trend over the whole province (fig. 1 and table 3, col. 1) with the exception of the eastern part of the zone (table 3, col. 7) which showed no marked rise at the beginning of the decade but only a steady rise throughout. Despite the similarity of general levels therefore the eastern half of the zone does not appear to have been affected by movements in the remainder of the zone. The same applies to the provincial capital which in movements as well as levels stands out from the remainder of the zone.

Turning to zone B (table 3, cols. 9, 12 and 14) we find that the movement of C/S rates does not correlate with zone A movements. Thus the high C/S rates of the beginning of the decade in zone A (typical of the whole province) had

Table 3

Monthly arithmetic means of C/S rates in 17 groups of towns, Shensi, 1900-1910

Months \ Columns	1	2	3	4	5	6	7	8	9	10	11	12	13	14	15	16	17
1.	1450	1502	1543	1460	1923	1693	1294	1518	1348	1232	1396	1346	1245	1411	1420	1488	1455
2.	1487	1482	1498	1424	1989	1600	1297	1425	1432	1267	1593	1330	1218	1454	1480	1652	1600
3.	1393	1288	1207	1297	1450	1415	1226	1581	1413	1317	1464	1328	1248	1374	1432	1691	1643
4.	1358	1259	1219	1276	1218	1106	1277	1633	1399	1307	1427	1320	1237	1378	1330	1715	1641
5.	1342	1224	1164	1237	1228	1142	1234	1643	1378	1263	1431	1323	1229	1361	1320	1733	1668
6.	1348	1238	1170	1276	1252	1155	1232	1633	1363	1253	1399	1316	1226	1369	1292	1771	1697
7.	1340	1237	1172	1271	1261	1155	1225	1659	1348	1230	1391	1317	1223	1350	1217	1754	1685
8.	1334	1232	1173	1194	1273	1186	1242	1680	1344	1230	1379	1315	1220	1338	1217	1758	1684
9.	1337	1241	1177	1241	1239	1190	1251	1700	1352	1246	1381	1315	1222	1338	1232	1738	1683
10.	1336	1242	1188	1229	1246	1190	1251	1685	1358	1251	1393	1309	1217	1347	1250	1721	1671
11.	1331	1252	1207	1233	1272	1183	1262	1664	1353	1240	1393	1309	1217	1351	1250	1669	1581
12.	1326	1276	1226	1283	1269	1229	1256	1763	1349	1236	1406	1315	1210	1355	1227	1615	1418
13.	1319	1248	1185	1255	1260	1186	1242	1711	1378	1251	1471	1326	1219	1362	1250	1620	1416
14.	1333	1258	1198	1278	1287	1186	1239	1737	1431	1269	1606	1337	1272	1359	1242	1631	1416
15.	1343	1243	1175	1263	1258	1193	1239	1706	1480	1336	1654	1447	1388	1402	1230	1606	1414
16.	1319	1229	1172	1231	1232	1201	1256	1674	1422	1281	1573	1426	1352	1431	1272	1544	1367
17.	1315	1202	1142	1162	1200	1174	1231	1648	1449	1293	1622	1446	1388	1416	1285	1590	1380
18.	1345	1243	1197	1185	1237	1177	1276	1737	1474	1320	1607	1489	1454	1430	1270	1572	1411
19.	1353	1256	1221	1183	1270	1177	1284	1716	1453	1300	1574	1485	1448	1449	1270	1587	1413
20.	1355	1260	1225	1195	1270	1177	1282	1700	1449	1283	1589	1487	1450	1452	1275	1592	1413
21.	1365	1275	1235	1202	1273	1220	1301	1726	1455	1296	1592	1491	1457	1438	1290	1605	1416
22.	1371	1285	1248	1211	1266	1229	1320	1742	1445	1290	1572	1496	1464	1449	1307	1605	1416
23.	1377	1290	1257	1213	1283	1229	1320	1737	1444	1290	1567	1407	1466	1501	1312	1619	1416
24.	1386	1307	1275	1269	1274	1242	1326	1752	1439	1283	1562	1523	1485	1487	1295	1620	1410
25.	1390	1311	1288	1241	1286	1249	1340	1758	1449	1286	1587	1523	1485	1507	1332	1603	1403

Source: Shensi Reports

Column	Places	Column	Places	Column	Places	Column	Places
1	all towns	6	75-77	11	40,41/44,45	16	18,21,23,25,48,50 87-90
2	zone A	7	53-62	12	63-70/1,2	17	26,27, 48-52/87-90
3	4-17	8	3	13	63-69		
4	29-35	9	36-47	14	78-82		
5	71-73	10	36,39/42,43/46,47	15	83-86		

no effect on the C/S rates in zone B. Furthermore the upper Han valley (table 3, cols. 9, 10 and 11) had high C/S rates in the middle of the decade in contrast both to zone A and to the lower Han valley whose rates rose gradually over the whole decade with no apparent effect on zone A, with the possible exception of its eastern part (table 3, col. 7).

Finally in zone C we find that the southern part (table 3, col. 15) showed some similarities of movements with zone A whereas the remainder of zone C (table 3, cols. 16 and 17) had C/S rates rising continually from the beginning of the decade. Thus the upper part of zone C took much longer to recover (and indeed most of its towns hardly recovered at all) from the high C/S rates of the early part of the decade in contrast to zone A.

Such broad differences between movements in zones and within zones confirm that we had been led to suspect by the differences in typical levels summarized at the beginning of this section; the province was divided not only into three separate exchange markets but each of these exchange markets was itself divided into small groups.

As a measure of relative dispersion in each of the 17 groups in table 3 (excluding col. 8, a single city) standard deviations (s) were calculated and then divided by the means of each group to give coefficients of variation ($c/v = \frac{100s}{x}$). The coefficients of variation, expressed as percentages, are given in table 4. Certain

Table 4 Coefficients of variation of C/S rates in 16 groups of towns, Shensi, 1900-10

Source: Shensi Reports

Months \ Columns	1	2	3	4	5	6	7	8	9	10	11	12	13	14	15	16
1.	15.2	18.1	20.2	12.4	8.2	13.8	9.6	12.8	6.7	3.1	14.1	9.1	2.3	10.6	8.3	10.1
2.	17.2	20.8	25.8	10.6	14.8	8.6	11.5	14.0	4.7	6.4	14.9	6.8	5.7	17.4	8.3	11.7
3.	16.8	16.4	17.4	11.0	27.3	21.7	5.1	10.0	8.0	6.6	10.9	4.6	1.5	13.1	14.9	14.1
4.	16.2	12.7	14.6	11.2	7.9	1.9	7.1	9.9	4.1	8.3	11.2	4.3	.7	8.9	16.8	19.0
5.	17.4	11.6	8.8	12.7	5.1	5.9	9.2	12.6	5.5	12.6	13.0	4.6	2.4	8.8	16.4	19.2
6.	18.0	11.1	3.5	12.4	2.0	4.0	9.6	12.2	7.2	9.6	13.1	4.9	3.9	10.0	18.1	22.3
7.	17.7	11.4	3.3	13.7	3.7	5.0	9.6	13.8	10.3	10.0	13.8	5.2	5.3	3.6	15.7	19.9
8.	17.6	9.8	3.9	3.2	4.7	3.5	8.5	13.9	10.3	10.8	14.0	5.6	4.8	3.6	15.4	19.8
9.	17.3	9.5	4.7	4.2	2.9	3.6	7.9	13.1	10.0	10.6	14.0	5.7	4.6	3.2	17.3	19.9
10.	17.0	9.2	4.7	4.7	3.8	3.6	8.1	12.7	9.2	10.1	13.4	5.8	2.9	1.9	18.5	20.2
11.	15.7	8.9	4.7	4.7	8.6	3.4	7.8	13.4	9.6	11.1	13.4	5.8	3.2	1.9	16.0	19.4
12.	15.6	9.0	1.7	3.3	5.5	1.4	7.3	11.7	5.6	9.2	13.7	4.8	3.9	3.7	24.8	26.7
13.	16.0	9.4	2.2	3.7	7.8	2.4	6.3	11.6	5.8	7.6	13.7	4.8	2.3	3.8	24.0	27.5
14.	16.3	9.3	3.2	1.6	4.7	2.4	5.4	12.9	6.2	4.4	13.5	5.5	1.5	4.4	24.2	27.5
15.	16.0	9.0	3.1	2.9	2.7	1.9	5.0	11.6	7.4	1.7	9.5	7.7	1.5	3.8	23.3	26.1
16.	15.3	8.1	3.5	4.2	4.7	1.3	4.9	11.2	3.5	4.9	9.3	3.6	1.7	5.2	24.6	26.7
17.	17.1	9.4	4.8	5.3	3.5	3.4	5.6	12.5	5.1	6.3	8.3	5.6	1.3	4.0	24.8	29.8
18.	15.6	9.2	3.9	4.5	5.6	3.4	3.3	11.4	3.8	2.7	6.3	5.5	2.2	2.9	24.3	25.1
19.	15.2	8.7	3.6	3.5	4.8	3.4	3.1	11.8	4.4	4.0	6.6	5.6	2.1	2.8	24.2	25.1
20.	15.2	8.7	3.8	5.6	4.8	3.4	2.6	12.7	3.9	4.5	6.6	5.6	1.8	2.6	23.8	25.1
21.	15.0	8.8	3.2	4.3	5.0	6.2	2.0	12.1	4.5	4.6	6.4	5.6	.8	4.7	23.9	25.0
22.	14.8	8.7	4.1	4.0	4.5	5.2	3.3	11.9	4.4	3.4	6.5	6.1	1.6	3.8	23.9	25.0
23.	14.7	8.4	4.2	4.2	5.9	5.3	2.4	11.8	3.9	3.2	6.5	6.0	5.2	3.5	23.8	25.0
24.	14.6	7.5	3.2	3.5	6.6	3.6	2.3	12.0	4.2	3.2	5.6	4.0	2.0	4.9	24.7	25.1
25.	14.6	7.6	2.3	4.0	7.0	3.6	2.4	12.3	3.8	4.3	5.6	4.0	3.1	3.5	25.6	25.5

Column	Places	Column	Places	Column	Places
1	all towns	6	75-77	11	63-70/1,2
2	zone A	7	53-62	12	63-69
3	4-17	8	36-47	13	78-82
4	29-35	9	36,39/42,43/46,47	14	83-86
5	71-73	10	40,41/44,45	15	18,21,23,25,48,50
				16	26,27/48-52/87-90

striking contrasts emerge; columns 15 and 16 for example (northern part of zone C) have the highest coefficients of variation (c/v) in the entire province and the dispersion becomes larger as time goes on. This should be compared with most of the groups in zone A where c/v decline over the decade. Interestingly Lin-chou (col. 14) has c/v similar to zone A rather than zone C in which for geographic reasons it had been placed. Zone B has very different c/v from zone A although both the upper and lower Han valley had declining c/v over the decade (cols. 8-12). Shang-chou (col. 13) with the exclusion of towns 82 and 79 had the lowest c/v of any group but since there were only three towns included in this group we should expect lower c/v. Finally in zone A the large differences at the beginning of the decade between the western part of the zone (col. 4) and the eastern part (col. 7) should be noted. Both table 3 and table 4 are concerned with groups of towns and each in its own way masks the nature of the differences between individual towns. Such differences we shall now consider with the aid of criterion one, that two towns are judged to be in the same exchange market if they have similar typical C/S rates, where similar is defined as having differentials less than which arbitrage can be presumed not to have taken place.

If we take zone A which both in the typical levels of C/S rates in its towns (see map 2) as well as in the consistency of movement of rates over time (see tables 3 and 4) appears the most integrated of the three zones and if we select those towns lying on a main road across the zone we can then show the differences in C/S rates between these towns and discuss the problem of similar C/S rates between towns in more concrete terms.

TABLE 5

Place	Typical C/S Rate	Differences
53	1237	
61	1289	+52
54	1241	-48
5	1253	+12
4	1210	-43
3	1696	+476
12	1247	-449
13	1197	-50
76	1160	-37
32	1269	+109
31	1215	-54
29	1193	-22
30	1205	+12

Source: table 2. Difference in C/S rates between 53 and 61 for example is 52 cash. The addition sign indicates that town 61's typical C/S rate is 52 cash higher than town 53's typical rate.

The average difference in C/S rates between towns on this route, excluding the exceptional case of the provincial capital (3), was 35 cash while the average difference between places was just over 30 km. Since one man could carry 70 to 80 catties over 30 km. in one day at a cost of about 350 cash (see Chapter 5, table 10 for estimated transport costs in the province at this time) and

since 1000 cash weighed approx. 7 catties (see Chapter 2, note 9) he could carry about 10-12 strings of 1000 cash each, but on this route he would have made a loss:
$\frac{10,000}{1250} \times 35 = 280$ cash which less transport costs = -70 cash. A cart could carry four times as much as a single porter at only twice the cost. Thus a cartload of cash shifted between two towns on this route would have gained a very small profit of 420 cash $\frac{40,000}{1250} \times 35 = 1,120$ which less transport costs of 700 cash = 420 cash). These calculations serve to show the difficulties of transporting such a heavy money. The following quotation from a contemporary witness, the agent of the New York Christian Herald's Shensi famine relief fund, Francis Nichols, underlines these difficulties:[12]

> The transportation of the money from Sian to the place of distribution was one of the most difficult problems of the work. Cash strings were the only available medium by which the funds could be disbursed in small amounts. A string of cash whose value is about seventy cents weighs more than four pounds, so that the equivalent of comparatively few American dollars constituted a load for a cart drawn by two mules. To distribute $800 at Lintoun, (Lin-t'ung, town 4, 15 km. from Sian) fifty-two carts were necessary to carry the cash.

In other words to transport 1,145 strings of cash required 52 two-mule carts, each cart carrying 22 strings. Nichols was apparently exaggerating for by his own figures

---

[12] Nichols (1902), p. 238, writing of conditions in May, 1901.

each two-mule cart carried only very slightly more than a porter whereas carts carried between four and ten times as much as a human carrier depending upon the number of animals in the harness.

We gain perhaps a more clear view of the relative value of cash per weight if we compare it to the same weight of wheat both expressed in terms of silver. The general typical price of wheat in Shensi at this time was 2.28 taels per granary bushel or 30.3 taels per metric ton (see Chapter 5, table 4 and section on weights and measures). The general typical C/S rate for the entire province was 1345 cash to one tael or 185 taels per metric ton of cash (reckoning 1000 cash as weighing 7 catties). Per weight then cash was worth approximately six times more than wheat and this being the case we should expect that C/S rates would have been more uniform than wheat prices. Indeed using an admittedly crude indicator, such as province wide coefficients of variation, we find that C/S rates varied from central values only about half or one-third as much as did wheat prices.

3.4 Conclusions

While it would be possible to continue to calculate with some precision differences between C/S rates in all pairs of towns and then, allowing for distances between all pairs of towns, divide them into groups on the basis of sharing rates whose differences were insufficiently high to have made the absence of arbitrage inexplicable and then, with the groups formed on this assumption, test the groupings already suggested by rule of thumb on the basis of typical levels and movements of rates over time, it is nevertheless felt that enough has already been said to suggest the main outlines of the differences of C/S rates between towns and the above example, concerned with rates in towns on the main road leading across the plain of Sian, must suffice. We turn now therefore to the reasons for these differences.

As we saw in Chapter 2 cash and silver were commodities like anything else; there were specialists trading and speculating in both and the value of both depended upon the supply as well as upon the relative demand for each. In a province such as Shensi where, as we shall see (in Chapter 5) contacts between districts, as reflected in price zones for selected grains, were extremely limited and where geographic barriers and poor transport facilities put a break on trade between districts, we would not expect a well integrated province wide exchange market, rapidly responsive in all parts to changes in one part, but rather many groups of exchange markets; at one extreme forming loose zones and at the other, breaking down into single isolated towns. To this extent therefore the foregoing has confirmed our expectations.

In modern foreign exchange markets the slightest difference between exchange rates in two places leads to an immediate process of arbitrage in these places until the rates become consistent with each other. In Shensi as late as 1900-1910 no such process took place; differences in absolute levels in one zone or group had no effect on other zones or groups; movements over time in one zone or group had no effect on neighbouring zones or groups. The chief reason for the failure of arbitrage to take place lies in the poor communications and expensive transport (see Chapter 5, tables 9 and 10 for time taken between select places and transport costs per ton km. in Shensi at this time). This point was made strongly by Lin Tse-hsu while serving as judicial commissioner in Shensi in the late 1820's. His point, which applies with equal force to the later period, was that merchants found it unprofitable to enter into a process of arbitrage owing to the high transport costs in the province. And if merchants found it unprofitable, he continued, then it would be quite impossible for officials to undertake to unify C/S rates throughout the province.[13]

From scattered remarks in memorials we gained the impression that not only in the 19th century but also in the 18th century differences in rates were very large, even within a single province (see section 7 of Chapter 2). The differences in the early part of the 18th century within one province however are never quoted as being larger than 30, 40 or 50 cash.[14] By the end of the century we saw in one

---

[13]See Lin Tse-hsü (1885), chüan 12, pp. 7-11.

[14]See Saeki (1959) for a selection from memorials on C/S differences drawn from Yung-cheng chu-p'i yü-chih (1738).

example (that of Cheng Kuang-tsu's observations in the south-west, see map 1, Chapter 2) that these differences had grown much larger as the result of the weakening and adulteration of the cash and also as a result of the increasing shortage of silver, the consequence of which was to double the cash price of silver and hence double the differences between rates. The situation had deteriorated even further by the end of the 19th century (although in the short run there had been a recovery from the almost total collapse of the monetary system in the middle years of the century). To the extent that the progressive weakening of the cash sector was a reflection of the weakening of the controls over those who attempted to break monetary regulations, the wide differences in rates may be seen as a failure of government. As a response to the breakdown of the old system new forms of currency and new monetary institutions were already beginning to emerge at the end of the 19th century however, and the old system was already partially abandoned in many provinces (although far less so in Shensi than in the other provinces). The collapse of the old system therefore was due rather to specifically monetary changes as well as to changing economic conditions than to the weakness or corruption of officials.

Levels of C/S rates depended upon the relative demand for each money, which, given the seasonal system of payments produced seasonal shifts in the rates. Unfortunately the Shensi data does not cover a long enough series of continuous months to allow the examination of seasonal fluctuations. Long-term trends also do not show up well in the Reports which only cover ten years. As a result of these deficiencies of the data most of the analysis has been focused on local variations rather than on changes over time.

Explanations for typical levels of rates in a given place (having accounted for the absence of arbitrage between places) would require much greater knowledge than we possess of local factors. There is a possibility that in towns with large garrisons C/S rates were liable to be high owing to payment of troops in cash. There is also the strong likelihood that administrative centres, especially provincial capitals, would have high C/S rates (this was a phenomenon observed by many provincial governors in the 18th and 19th centuries). The reasons for high rates in these cities being that cash was minted in them and was therefore plentiful. Moreover, silver was most in demand in such cities both for tax payments and remittance and also for long distance trade. In Sian as we have seen the typical rates were extraordinarily high in comparison with the rates of towns only 20 or 30 km. distant whose rates were a quarter as low again as those in Sian. Such wide disparities were not found between the prefectural cities and their surrounding towns although some were in the midst of a group of towns having high C/S rates. The case of Sian is hard to account for without presuming some form of artificially maintained rate (either by officials or by the exchange shop guilds) although there is no evidence that such maintainance was practiced that I have been able to find. Other towns in the province with high C/S rates (e.g. towns 37, 38, 2, 79) were amongst the most isolated in the province and can therefore be presumed to have been short on silver and long on debased cash. Towns with the lowest C/S rates were often commercial centres e.g. San-yüan (9) no doubt reflecting plentiful silver and a high demand for cash to pay for the production of cotton which was in this case the commercial staple of the town.

Wide disparities of C/S rates between places, which as we have seen in this chapter was a feature of the old monetary system, were to pass away only with the complete breakdown of the entire system and the growth of new economic forces and monetary institutions after an interim period of great monetary chaos which lasted for nearly fifty years from the date of the last of the Shensi Reports.

In the following chapter we shall be leaving the subject of money and exchange rates and turning to the subject of grain prices in an attempt to evaluate the quotations which along with the C/S rates were entered in the Shensi Reports. In Chapter 5 we return to Shensi to analyze the grain markets of the province, an analysis based on the price quotations in the reports.

APPENDIX I

Original data: C/S Rates from 90 Towns, Shensi, 1900-1910

ORIGINAL DATA: CASH/SILVER EXCHANGE RATES, 1900 TO 1910, SHENSI

PLACE \ MONTH	1	2	3	4	5	6	7	8	9	10	11	12	13
1	1700.	1700.	1400.	1400.	1400.	1350.	1350.	1350.	1350.	1350.	1350.	1470.	1520.
2	1490.	1520.	1592.	1592.	1682.	1682.	1712.	1712.	1712.	1666.	1666.	1658.	1658.
3	1518.	1425.	1581.	1633.	1643.	1633.	1659.	1680.	1700.	1685.	1664.	1763.	1711.
4	1133.	1132.	1133.	1205.	1092.	1174.	1195.	1195.	1215.	1215.	1215.	1205.	1185.
5	1480.	1400.	1160.	1300.	1160.	1240.	1220.	1240.	1270.	1290.	1300.	1230.	1180.
6	1457.	1520.	1541.	1171.	1131.	1131.	1161.	1161.	1161.	1161.	1140.	1222.	1191.
7	1371.	1411.	1174.	1174.	1126.	1177.	1187.	1187.	1217.	1237.	1217.	1246.	1184.
8	1176.	963.	1115.	1130.	1155.	1165.	1165.	1195.	1165.	1225.	1322.	1237.	1207.
9	1085.	1000.	1000.	1140.	1060.	1120.	1120.	1120.	1150.	1160.	1170.	1210.	1140.
10	1902.	1800.	1131.	1140.	1162.	1203.	1230.	1210.	1224.	1185.	1228.	1234.	1218.
11	1800.	2100.	1200.	1170.	1150.	1170.	1200.	1210.	1200.	1230.	1200.	1220.	1220.
12	2037.	1840.	1140.	1114.	1165.	1196.	1196.	1196.	1226.	1227.	1226.	1257.	1226.
13	1935.	1600.	1060.	1050.	1180.	1175.	1165.	1105.	1070.	1080.	1220.	1250.	1180.
14	1480.	1470.	1683.	1714.	1153.	1224.	1183.	1224.	1204.	1173.	1214.	1244.	1193.
15	1849.	2240.	1027.	1144.	1092.	1113.	1113.	1113.	1113.	1154.	1154.	1236.	1163.
16	1401.	1248.	1040.	1124.	1175.	1196.	1175.	1175.	1175.	1196.	1196.	1206.	1155.
17	1500.	1250.	1500.	1500.	1500.	1100.	1100.	1100.	1100.	1100.	1100.	1180.	1155.
18	1530.	1812.	1920.	1770.	1770.	1770.	1770.	1770.	1770.	1770.	1820.	1870.	1870.
19	1540.	1750.	1680.	1110.	1160.	1180.	1150.	1130.	1120.	1130.	1120.	1135.	1140.
20	1370.	1630.	1400.	1340.	1240.	1200.	1200.	1200.	1200.	1200.	1200.	1220.	1220.
21	1550.	1700.	1500.	1600.	1600.	1630.	1700.	1700.	1600.	1600.	1600.	1700.	1600.
22	1700.	1750.	1930.	1350.	1350.	1370.	1400.	1200.	1150.	1120.	1120.	1100.	1100.
23	1655.	1785.	1885.	1885.	1885.	1855.	1855.	1855.	1855.	1855.	1855.	1855.	1855.
24	1400.	1400.	1400.	1400.	1400.	1400.	1400.	1400.	1400.	1400.	1400.	1400.	1400.
25	1500.	1550.	1530.	1600.	1700.	1700.	1600.	1650.	1650.	1650.	1680.	1750.	1750.

14	15	16	17	18	19	20	21	22	23	24	25	
1540.	1510.	1550.	1520.	1500.	1500.	1500.	1500.	1500.	1500.	1600.	1600.	1
1658.	1700.	1700.	1675.	1658.	1667.	1667.	1662.	1662.	1662.	1686.	1686.	2
1737.	1706.	1674.	1648.	1737.	1716.	1700.	1726.	1742.	1737.	1752.	1758.	3
1195.	1174.	1154.	1133.	1215.	1236.	1236.	1257.	1257.	1257.	1267.	1298.	4
1210.	1208.	1209.	1178.	1259.	1270.	1280.	1280.	1280.	1311.	1280.	1311.	5
1201.	1161.	1130.	1140.	1157.	1209.	1222.	1232.	1222.	1232.	1232.	1232.	6
1215.	1174.	1174.	1134.	1215.	1236.	1246.	1267.	1277.	1277.	1277.	1277.	7
1167.	1157.	1162.	1127.	1217.	1217.	1237.	1237.	1237.	1237.	1247.	1257.	8
1130.	1100.	1080.	1100.	1120.	1120.	1120.	1180.	1200.	1280.	1240.	1300.	9
1203.	1182.	1182.	1115.	1185.	1250.	1250.	1250.	1265.	1240.	1264.	1260.	10
1220.	1244.	1240.	1300.	1280.	1280.	1300.	1300.	1300.	1350.	1350.	1300.	11
1287.	1237.	1226.	1196.	1237.	1250.	1257.	1268.	1354.	1328.	1328.	1348.	12
1195.	1160.	1163.	1140.	1220.	1222.	1212.	1214.	1270.	1250.	1325.	1322.	13
1244.	1183.	1203.	1122.	1132.	1224.	1204.	1223.	1244.	1193.	1193.	1295.	14
1163.	1163.	1153.	1112.	1179.	1158.	1179.	1179.	1158.	1179.	1281.	1271.	15
1175.	1144.	1144.	1061.	1144.	1174.	1165.	1165.	1165.	1176.	1269.	1269.	16
1170.	1170.	1200.	1140.	1200.	1250.	1250.	1250.	1250.	1300.	1300.	1300.	17
1920.	1820.	1770.	1870.	1920.	1970.	1970.	1970.	1970.	1970.	1970.	1970.	18
1140.	1100.	1120.	1070.	1090.	1200.	1200.	1200.	1220.	1220.	1220.	1210.	19
1200.	1180.	1220.	1220.	1220.	1240.	1250.	1280.	1280.	1280.	1280.	1340.	20
1600.	1500.	1300.	1200.	1170.	1200.	1250.	1250.	1250.	1250.	1220.	1120.	21
1150.	1080.	1050.	1070.	1190.	1250.	1260.	1300.	1290.	1290.	1290.	1290.	22
1855.	1855.	1705.	1755.	1755.	1755.	1755.	1855.	1855.	1855.	1955.	1955.	23
1400.	1400.	1200.	1200.	1200.	1200.	1200.	1200.	1200.	1200.	1200.	1200.	24
1800.	1800.	1850.	1800.	1750.	1800.	1800.	1800.	1800.	1900.	1900.	1850.	25

	1	2	3	4	5	6	7	8	9	10	11	12	13
26	1680.	1820.	1630.	1650.	1650.	1650.	1650.	1650.	1650.	1650.	1650.	1350.	1350.
27	1550.	1650.	1700.	1700.	1890.	1905.	1905.	1905.	1890.	1890.	1890.	1300.	1300.
28	1535.	1524.	1535.	1420.	1420.	1430.	1430.	1430.	1440.	1440.	1410.	1560.	1560.
29	1346.	1240.	1183.	1142.	1158.	1248.	1280.	1152.	1208.	1183.	1191.	1355.	1300.
30	1615.	1490.	1389.	1236.	1143.	1200.	1159.	1159.	1283.	1190.	1201.	1242.	1300.
31	1680.	1400.	1150.	1200.	1170.	1200.	1200.	1200.	1230.	1230.	1230.	1230.	1246.
32	1657.	1658.	1554.	1580.	1591.	1633.	1658.	1200.	1202.	1202.	1202.	1264.	1176.
33	1252.	1236.	1186.	1219.	1203.	1236.	1186.	1195.	1252.	1285.	1335.	1293.	1219.
34	1349.	1515.	1343.	1313.	1212.	1232.	1232.	1272.	1333.	1333.	1292.	1313.	1293.
35	1326.	1430.	1275.	1244.	1183.	1183.	1183.	1183.	1183.	1183.	1183.	1285.	1256.
36	1252.	1252.	1525.	1330.	1210.	1130.	1030.	1030.	1050.	1080.	1080.	1160.	1150.
37	1730.	1790.	1620.	1620.	1620.	1620.	1620.	1620.	1620.	1620.	1624.	1640.	1640.
38	1410.	1430.	1570.	1620.	1620.	1620.	1620.	1620.	1600.	1600.	1600.	1510.	1510.
39	1340.	1200.	1220.	1360.	1360.	1360.	1360.	1360.	1360.	1360.	1360.	1360.	1360.
40	1445.	1579.	1434.	1414.	1342.	1342.	1342.	1342.	1342.	1370.	1370.	1362.	1440.
41	1370.	1600.	1455.	1345.	1375.	1345.	1315.	1285.	1295.	1315.	1295.	1335.	1475.
42	1280.	1370.	1260.	1210.	1170.	1170.	1130.	1130.	1150.	1150.	1110.	1180.	1250.
43	1180.	1240.	1292.	1294.	1290.	1330.	1330.	1330.	1340.	1340.	1310.	1229.	1299.
44	1350.	1470.	1370.	1350.	1310.	1310.	1310.	1290.	1290.	1290.	1290.	1330.	1350.
45	1420.	1720.	1600.	1600.	1700.	1600.	1600.	1600.	1600.	1600.	1620.	1600.	1620.
46	1100.	1300.	1300.	1300.	1240.	1240.	1240.	1240.	1240.	1240.	1240.	1240.	1200.
47	1240.	1240.	1310.	1350.	1310.	1290.	1290.	1290.	1340.	1340.	1340.	1250.	1250.
48	1300.	1515.	1320.	1200.	1200.	1200.	1200.	1200.	1100.	1050.	1050.	1100.	1140.
49	1340.	1440.	1460.	1460.	1460.	1460.	1480.	1480.	1480.	1480.	1180.	1250.	1250.
50	1520.	1750.	2000.	2226.	2226.	2226.	2226.	2226.	2226.	2226.	1620.	1045.	1045.

14	15	16	17	18	19	20	21	22	23	24	25	
1350.	1350.	1280.	1230.	1250.	1250.	1250.	1250.	1250.	1250.	1250.	1200.	26
1300.	1300.	1200.	1100.	1200.	1200.	1200.	1200.	1200.	1200.	1200.	1200.	27
1570.	1500.	1173.	1420.	1480.	1480.	1470.	1480.	1490.	1480.	1480.	1480.	28
1252.	1200.	1220.	1126.	1124.	1151.	1112.	1142.	1163.	1193.	1265.	1142.	29
1295.	1295.	1220.	1110.	1143.	1151.	1142.	1192.	1198.	1176.	1192.	1209.	30
1265.	1265.	1130.	1120.	1170.	1170.	1180.	1200.	1200.	1220.	1340.	1250.	31
1285.	1305.	1277.	1124.	1150.	1171.	1165.	1176.	1181.	1140.	1254.	1265.	32
1304.	1289.	1273.	1240.	1236.	1167.	1195.	1195.	1178.	1211.	1277.	1277.	33
1292.	1232.	1273.	1262.	1272.	1272.	1272.	1312.	1292.	1292.	1292.	1262.	34
1256.	1256.	1224.	1153.	1200.	1200.	1300.	1200.	1265.	1265.	1265.	1285.	35
1160.	1230.	1240.	1210.	1270.	1250.	1210.	1210.	1210.	1210.	1210.	1230.	36
1640.	1640.	1620.	1650.	1650.	1650.	1650.	1650.	1650.	1650.	1650.	1650.	37
1490.	1490.	1470.	1490.	1690.	1690.	1690.	1670.	1670.	1670.	1670.	1670.	38
1360.	1360.	1360.	1360.	1360.	1360.	1360.	1370.	1360.	1360.	1360.	1360.	39
1630.	1672.	1548.	1600.	1600.	1548.	1548.	1548.	1548.	1548.	1548.	1548.	40
1585.	1665.	1525.	1730.	1590.	1580.	1640.	1660.	1600.	1580.	1560.	1650.	41
1310.	1430.	1250.	1270.	1350.	1250.	1270.	1290.	1260.	1290.	1250.	1250.	42
1339.	1470.	1290.	1380.	1380.	1380.	1300.	1350.	1350.	1320.	1320.	1320.	43
1520.	1610.	1530.	1490.	1570.	1510.	1510.	1510.	1510.	1510.	1510.	1510.	44
1690.	1670.	1690.	1670.	1670.	1660.	1660.	1650.	1630.	1630.	1630.	1640.	45
1200.	1280.	1300.	1300.	1300.	1300.	1300.	1300.	1300.	1300.	1300.	1300.	46
1250.	1250.	1250.	1240.	1260.	1260.	1260.	1260.	1260.	1260.	1260.	1260.	47
1150.	1110.	1100.	1200.	1160.	1160.	1160.	1160.	1160.	1200.	1200.	1200.	48
1250.	1200.	1150.	1100.	1220.	1220.	1220.	1220.	1200.	1200.	1200.	1200.	49
1045.	1210.	1210.	1210.	1210.	1210.	1210.	1210.	1210.	1210.	1210.	1210.	50

	1	2	3	4	5	6	7	8	9	10	11	12	13
51	1400.	1700.	1600.	1300.	1300.	1200.	1200.	1200.	1200.	1200.	1200.	1200.	1140.
52	1230.	1238.	1289.	1208.	1208.	1208.	1208.	1208.	1208.	1208.	1208.	1208.	1137.
53	1313.	1154.	1221.	1212.	1172.	1182.	1172.	1172.	1192.	1192.	1212.	1222.	1212.
54	1198.	1181.	1215.	1256.	1165.	1165.	1146.	1182.	1198.	1162.	1240.	1256.	1198.
55	1495.	1536.	1178.	1331.	1116.	1119.	1132.	1178.	1218.	1208.	1218.	1280.	1244.
56	1210.	1190.	1140.	1160.	1160.	1140.	1140.	1140.	1160.	1160.	1160.	1180.	1190.
57	1137.	1219.	1179.	1200.	1160.	1160.	1160.	1208.	1208.	1208.	1187.	1178.	1168.
58	1400.	1350.	1270.	1340.	1370.	1390.	1380.	1340.	1340.	1350.	1370.	1180.	1240.
59	1200.	1250.	1200.	1230.	1240.	1240.	1220.	1240.	1220.	1220.	1220.	1230.	1200.
60	1229.	1142.	1262.	1270.	1257.	1270.	1244.	1272.	1269.	1269.	1269.	1264.	1247.
61	1480.	1480.	1230.	1290.	1220.	1170.	1170.	1200.	1210.	1250.	1250.	1280.	1280.
62	1281.	1476.	1365.	1481.	1486.	1486.	1486.	1496.	1496.	1496.	1496.	1492.	1444.
63	1200.	1200.	1250.	1320.	1320.	1320.	1320.	1320.	1320.	1320.	1320.	1160.	1200.
64	1100.	1100.	1200.	1220.	1220.	1220.	1220.	1220.	1220.	1190.	1190.	1180.	1180.
65	1280.	1280.	1180.	1154.	1154.	1154.	1154.	1154.	1154.	1154.	1154.	1154.	1154.
66	1250.	1150.	1250.	1200.	1200.	1200.	1200.	1200.	1200.	1200.	1200.	1200.	1200.
67	1340.	1344.	1352.	1260.	1260.	1260.	1260.	1260.	1260.	1260.	1260.	1310.	1310.
68	1130.	1186.	1220.	1240.	1180.	1160.	1140.	1120.	1120.	1120.	1120.	1200.	1200.
69	1420.	1270.	1290.	1270.	1270.	1270.	1270.	1270.	1280.	1280.	1280.	1270.	1290.
70	1550.	1550.	1550.	1550.	1550.	1550.	1550.	1550.	1550.	1550.	1550.	1550.	1550.
71	2000.	2250.	1900.	1280.	1280.	1280.	1280.	1280.	1280.	1300.	1400.	1350.	1330.
72	1741.	1690.	1151.	1267.	1247.	1247.	1210.	1210.	1210.	1210.	1210.	1229.	1305.
73	2028.	2028.	1300.	1107.	1157.	1229.	1300.	1331.	1229.	1229.	1208.	1229.	1147.
74	1420.	1650.	1600.	1560.	1510.	1610.	1600.	1570.	1520.	1500.	1500.	1500.	1500.
75	1520.	1442.	1586.	1088.	1068.	1107.	1107.	1199.	1210.	1210.	1189.	1219.	1169.

14	15	16	17	18	19	20	21	22	23	24	25	
1140.	1140.	1150.	1100.	1206.	1206.	1206.	1206.	1206.	1206.	1206.	1206.	51
1137.	1178.	1178.	1190.	1271.	1271.	1271.	1271.	1291.	1291.	1291.	1291.	52
1202.	1212.	1212.	1212.	1293.	1283.	1283.	1283.	1283.	1293.	1323.	1343.	53
1240.	1223.	1223.	1206.	1297.	1281.	1281.	1289.	1289.	1289.	1297.	1372.	54
1265.	1249.	1321.	1167.	1223.	1280.	1280.	1280.	1280.	1331.	1331.	1331.	55
1190.	1180.	1210.	1210.	1250.	1250.	1250.	1290.	1290.	1290.	1330.	1330.	56
1168.	1178.	1218.	1198.	1285.	1305.	1305.	1305.	1305.	1305.	1305.	1305.	57
1240.	1320.	1320.	1330.	1340.	1340.	1280.	1280.	1360.	1360.	1380.	1380.	58
1170.	1160.	1200.	1160.	1220.	1220.	1220.	1280.	1280.	1280.	1280.	1280.	59
1229.	1232.	1191.	1180.	1243.	1235.	1264.	1320.	1370.	1343.	1309.	1322.	60
1290.	1300.	1330.	1300.	1280.	1310.	1320.	1320.	1350.	1350.	1350.	1380.	61
1396.	1343.	1339.	1352.	1337.	1337.	1337.	1363.	1399.	1361.	1361.	1361.	62
1240.	1400.	1300.	1350.	1450.	1420.	1420.	1420.	1420.	1420.	1420.	1420.	63
1180.	1170.	1300.	1320.	1430.	1430.	1430.	1450.	1450.	1450.	1480.	1480.	64
1154.	1400.	1320.	1300.	1300.	1300.	1300.	1300.	1300.	1300.	1400.	1400.	65
1200.	1350.	1350.	1500.	1530.	1500.	1500.	1500.	1500.	1500.	1500.	1500.	66
1330.	1436.	1425.	1480.	1492.	1492.	1496.	1492.	1472.	1492.	1511.	1511.	67
1200.	1480.	1400.	1420.	1540.	1560.	1560.	1560.	1580.	1580.	1580.	1580.	68
1320.	1480.	1370.	1350.	1440.	1440.	1450.	1480.	1530.	1520.	1510.	1510.	69
1550.	1550.	1550.	1550.	1550.	1550.	1550.	1550.	1550.	1550.	1550.	1550.	70
1330.	1280.	1300.	1250.	1300.	1300.	1300.	1300.	1300.	1350.	1350.	1350.	71
1315.	1277.	1199.	1174.	1162.	1200.	1200.	1200.	1200.	1200.	1182.	1182.	72
1218.	1218.	1198.	1177.	1249.	1311.	1311.	1321.	1300.	1300.	1290.	1326.	73
1500.	1500.	1450.	1450.	1470.	1500.	1550.	1600.	1550.	1550.	1500.	1500.	74
1169.	1179.	1194.	1142.	1172.	1172.	1172.	1232.	1237.	1237.	1237.	1257.	75

	1	2	3	4	5	6	7	8	9	10	11	12	13
76	1960.	1660.	1060.	1100.	1160.	1160.	1140.	1140.	1140.	1140.	1140.	1250.	1170.
77	1600.	1700.	1600.	1130.	1200.	1200.	1220.	1220.	1220.	1220.	1220.	1220.	1220.
78	1416.	1431.	1341.	1292.	1246.	1225.	1184.	1184.	1184.	1225.	1225.	1220.	1266.
79	1500.	1490.	1630.	1700.	1640.	1680.	1650.	1620.	1640.	1620.	1620.	1700.	1650.
80	1360.	1440.	1320.	1280.	1300.	1320.	1300.	1270.	1250.	1270.	1290.	1280.	1320.
81	1360.	1550.	1300.	1300.	1300.	1300.	1300.	1300.	1300.	1300.	1300.	1320.	1320.
82	1420.	1360.	1280.	1320.	1320.	1320.	1320.	1320.	1320.	1320.	1320.	1255.	1255.
83	1300.	1260.	1300.	1300.	1300.	1210.	1210.	1210.	1200.	1220.	1220.	1200.	1200.
84	1280.	1280.	1300.	1300.	1300.	1280.	1280.	1280.	1280.	1280.	1280.	1280.	1280.
85	1560.	1580.	1430.	1500.	1480.	1480.	1179.	1179.	1250.	1250.	1250.	1180.	1220.
86	1540.	1800.	1700.	1220.	1200.	1200.	1200.	1200.	1200.	1250.	1250.	1250.	1300.
87	1340.	1400.	1440.	1480.	1500.	1540.	1620.	1620.	1600.	1500.	1500.	1620.	1680.
88	1340.	1550.	1600.	1610.	1620.	1630.	1660.	1670.	1675.	1685.	1685.	1660.	1660.
89	1650.	1760.	2030.	2030.	2030.	2300.	2030.	2030.	2050.	2050.	2050.	2350.	2350.
90	1500.	1700.	1690.	1750.	1800.	1860.	1880.	1860.	1860.	1830.	1830.	1200.	1250.

14	15	16	17	18	19	20	21	22	23	24	25	
1170.	1180.	1190.	1160.	1140.	1140.	1140.	1140.	1160.	1160.	1200.	1200.	76
1220.	1220.	1220.	1220.	1220.	1220.	1220.	1290.	1290.	1290.	1290.	1290.	77
1280.	1308.	1339.	1318.	1339.	1370.	1370.	1308.	1308.	1474.	1370.	1391.	78
1620.	1680.	1670.	1620.	1670.	1680.	1670.	1660.	1700.	1700.	1700.	1720.	79
1300.	1310.	1300.	1310.	1280.	1330.	1350.	1330.	1320.	1330.	1355.	1370.	80
1320.	1274.	1298.	1284.	1313.	1315.	1320.	1326.	1350.	1432.	1410.	1456.	81
1275.	1440.	1550.	1550.	1550.	1550.	1550.	1570.	1570.	1570.	1600.	1600.	82
1200.	1200.	1200.	1240.	1230.	1240.	1240.	1240.	1280.	1300.	1230.	1300.	83
1280.	1220.	1270.	1270.	1270.	1270.	1270.	1270.	1270.	1270.	1270.	1330.	84
1190.	1200.	1260.	1270.	1260.	1250.	1270.	1270.	1300.	1300.	1300.	1300.	85
1300.	1300.	1360.	1360.	1320.	1320.	1320.	1380.	1380.	1380.	1380.	1400.	86
1680.	1540.	1300.	1510.	1520.	1520.	1520.	1520.	1520.	1520.	1520.	1520.	87
1660.	1660.	1560.	1560.	1560.	1560.	1560.	1560.	1560.	1560.	1540.	1540.	88
2350.	2350.	2350.	2450.	2350.	2350.	2350.	2350.	2350.	2350.	2350.	2350.	89
1250.	1220.	1300.	1350.	1330.	1350.	1350.	1380.	1380.	1380.	1340.	1320.	90

APPENDIX 2

Elementary Analysis of C/S Rates from 90 Towns, Shensi, 1900-1910

ELEMENTARY ANALYSIS OF CASH/SILVER EXCHANGE RATES, 1900 TO 1910, SHENSI

PLACE \ MONTH	1	2	3	4	5	6	7	8	9	10	11	12	13
1	201.707	170.252	-33.158	-48.158	-33.273	-89.738	-86.323	-90.063	-94.828	-96.713	-98.123	7.392	71.642
2	-211.043	-212.498	-43.908	-58.908	45.977	39.512	72.927	69.187	64.422	16.537	15.127	-7.358	6.892
3	-211.037	-335.492	-82.902	-45.902	-21.017	-37.482	-8.067	9.193	24.428	7.543	-14.867	69.648	31.898
4	-108.940	-141.395	-43.805	13.195	-84.920	-9.385	15.030	11.290	26.525	24.640	23.230	-1.255	-7.005
5	195.450	83.995	-59.415	65.585	-59.530	14.005	-2.580	13.680	38.915	57.030	65.620	-18.865	-54.615
6	236.452	267.997	385.587	0.587	-24.528	-30.993	2.422	-1.318	-6.083	-7.968	-30.378	37.137	20.387
7	118.360	126.905	-13.505	-28.505	-61.620	-17.085	-3.670	-7.410	17.825	35.940	14.530	29.045	-18.705
8	-53.137	-297.592	-49.002	-49.002	-9.117	-5.582	-2.167	24.093	-10.672	47.443	143.033	43.548	27.798
9	-92.765	-209.220	-112.630	12.370	-52.745	0.790	4.205	0.465	25.700	33.815	42.405	67.920	12.170
10	652.652	519.197	-53.213	-59.213	-22.328	12.207	42.622	18.882	28.117	-12.768	28.822	20.337	18.587
11	517.448	785.993	-17.417	-62.417	-67.532	-53.997	-20.582	-14.322	-29.087	-0.972	-32.382	-26.867	-12.617
12	758.482	530.027	-73.383	-114.383	-48.498	-23.963	-20.548	-24.288	0.947	0.062	-2.348	14.167	-2.583
13	706.519	340.064	-103.346	-128.346	16.539	5.074	-1.511	-65.251	-105.016	-96.901	41.689	57.204	1.454
14	231.764	190.309	499.899	515.899	-30.216	34.319	-3.266	33.994	9.229	-23.656	15.934	31.449	-5.301
15	655.894	1015.439	-100.971	1.029	-36.086	-21.551	-18.136	-21.876	-26.641	12.474	-11.064	78.579	19.829
16	192.407	7.952	-103.458	-34.458	31.427	45.962	28.377	24.637	19.872	38.987	37.577	33.092	-3.658
17	272.446	-9.009	337.581	322.581	337.466	-68.999	-65.584	-69.324	-74.089	-75.974	-77.384	-11.869	-22.619
18	-371.605	-121.060	83.530	-81.470	-66.585	-73.050	-69.635	-73.375	-78.140	-80.025	-31.435	4.080	18.330
19	346.192	524.737	551.327	-33.673	31.212	44.747	18.162	-5.578	-20.343	-12.228	-23.638	-23.123	-3.873
20	98.242	326.787	193.377	118.377	33.262	-13.203	-9.788	-13.528	-18.293	-20.178	-21.588	-16.073	-1.823
21	52.738	171.283	67.873	152.873	167.758	191.293	264.708	260.968	156.203	154.318	152.908	238.423	152.673
22	460.306	478.851	755.441	160.441	175.326	188.861	222.276	18.536	-36.229	-68.114	-69.524	-104.009	-89.759
23	-224.559	-126.014	70.576	55.576	70.461	33.996	37.411	33.671	28.906	27.021	25.611	11.126	25.376
24	42.406	10.951	107.541	92.541	107.426	100.961	104.376	100.636	95.871	93.986	92.576	78.091	92.341
25	-280.094	-261.549	-184.959	-129.959	-15.074	-21.539	-118.124	-71.864	-76.629	-78.514	-49.924	5.591	19.841

14	15	16	17	18	19	20	21	22	23	24	25	ROW EFFECT	
82.257	58.177	99.732	87.932	31.162	20.967	18.817	10.987	4.997	-3.793	90.052	79.147	121.085	1
-2.493	45.427	46.982	40.182	-13.588	-14.783	-16.933	-29.763	-35.753	-44.543	-26.698	-37.603	323.835	2
48.513	23.433	-7.012	-14.812	37.418	6.223	-11.927	6.243	16.253	2.463	11.308	6.403	351.829	3
-6.390	-21.470	-39.915	-42.715	2.515	13.320	11.170	24.340	18.350	9.560	13.405	33.500	-135.268	4
-34.000	-30.080	-27.525	-40.325	3.905	4.710	12.560	4.730	-1.260	20.950	-16.205	3.890	-92.658	5
21.002	-13.078	-42.523	-14.323	-34.093	7.712	18.562	20.732	4.742	5.952	-0.203	-11.108	-156.660	6
2.910	-32.170	-30.615	-52.415	-8.185	2.620	10.470	23.640	27.650	18.860	12.705	1.800	-124.568	7
-21.587	-25.667	-19.112	-35.912	17.318	7.123	24.973	17.143	11.153	2.363	6.208	5.303	-148.071	8
-7.215	-31.295	-49.740	-11.540	-28.310	-38.505	-40.655	11.515	25.525	96.735	50.580	99.675	-199.443	9
-5.798	-20.878	-19.323	-68.123	-34.893	19.912	17.762	9.932	18.942	-14.848	2.997	-11.908	-127.860	10
-22.002	7.918	5.473	83.673	26.903	16.708	34.558	26.728	20.738	61.948	55.793	-5.112	-94.656	11
49.032	4.952	-4.493	-16.293	-12.063	-9.258	-4.408	-1.238	78.772	43.982	37.827	46.922	-98.690	12
7.069	-22.011	-17.456	-22.256	20.974	12.779	0.629	-5.201	44.809	16.019	84.864	70.959	-148.726	13
36.314	-18.766	2.789	-60.011	-86.781	-4.976	-27.126	-15.956	-0.946	-60.736	-66.891	24.204	-128.972	14
10.444	16.364	7.919	-14.881	15.349	-15.846	3.004	-4.826	-31.816	-19.606	76.239	55.334	-184.101	15
6.957	-18.123	-16.568	-81.368	-35.138	-15.333	-26.483	-34.313	-40.303	-38.093	48.752	37.847	-168.615	16
-17.004	-11.084	20.471	-21.329	1.901	41.706	39.556	31.726	25.736	66.946	60.791	49.886	-149.654	17
58.945	-35.135	-83.580	34.620	47.850	87.655	85.505	77.675	71.685	62.895	56.740	45.835	524.397	18
-13.258	-47.338	-25.783	-57.583	-74.353	25.452	23.302	15.472	29.482	20.692	14.537	-6.368	-183.400	19
-31.208	-45.288	-3.733	14.467	-22.303	-12.498	-4.648	17.522	11.532	2.742	-3.413	45.682	-105.450	20
143.288	49.208	-149.237	-231.037	-297.807	-278.002	-230.152	-237.982	-243.972	-252.762	-288.917	-399.822	120.054	21
-49.144	-113.224	-141.669	-103.469	-20.239	29.566	37.416	69.586	53.596	44.806	38.651	27.746	-137.514	22
15.991	21.911	-126.534	-58.334	-95.104	-105.299	-107.449	-15.279	-21.269	-30.059	63.786	52.881	502.351	23
82.956	88.876	-109.569	-91.369	-128.139	-138.334	-140.484	-148.314	-154.304	-163.094	-169.249	-180.154	-19.614	24
60.456	66.376	117.931	86.131	-0.639	39.166	37.016	29.186	23.196	114.406	108.251	47.346	402.886	25

	1	2	3	4	5	6	7	8	9	10	11	12	13
26	241.541	350.086	256.676	261.676	276.561	270.096	273.511	269.771	265.006	263.121	261.711	-52.774	-38.524
27	96.073	164.618	311.208	296.208	501.093	509.628	513.043	509.303	489.538	487.653	486.243	-118.242	-103.992
28	36.177	-6.278	101.312	-28.688	-13.803	-10.268	-6.853	-10.593	-5.358	-7.243	-38.653	96.862	111.112
29	121.013	-16.442	23.148	-32.852	-1.967	81.568	116.983	-14.757	36.478	9.593	16.183	165.698	124.948
30	378.112	221.657	217.247	49.247	-28.868	21.667	-15.918	-19.658	99.577	4.692	14.282	40.797	113.047
31	433.519	122.064	-31.346	3.654	-11.461	12.074	15.469	11.749	36.984	35.099	33.689	19.204	49.454
32	355.970	325.515	318.105	329.105	354.990	390.525	418.940	-42.800	-45.565	-47.450	-48.860	-1.345	-75.095
33	-17.481	-64.936	-18.346	-0.346	-1.461	25.074	-21.511	-16.251	35.984	67.099	115.689	59.204	-0.546
34	30.860	165.405	89.995	44.995	-41.120	-27.585	-24.170	12.090	68.325	66.440	24.030	30.545	24.795
35	64.974	137.519	79.109	33.109	-13.006	-19.471	-16.056	-19.796	-24.561	-26.446	-27.856	59.659	44.909
36	37.677	6.222	375.812	165.812	60.697	-25.768	-122.353	-126.093	-110.858	-82.743	-84.153	-18.638	-14.388
37	116.630	85.175	11.765	-3.235	11.650	5.185	8.600	4.860	0.095	-1.790	0.800	2.315	16.565
38	-231.008	-242.463	-5.873	29.127	44.012	37.547	40.962	37.222	12.457	10.572	9.162	-95.323	-81.073
39	-49.773	-221.228	-104.638	20.362	35.247	28.782	32.197	28.457	23.692	21.807	20.397	5.912	20.162
40	-57.722	44.823	-3.587	-38.587	-95.702	-102.167	-98.752	-102.492	-107.257	-81.142	-82.552	-105.037	-12.787
41	-147.173	51.372	2.962	-122.038	-77.153	-113.618	-140.203	-173.943	-168.708	-150.593	-172.003	-146.488	7.762
42	18.024	76.569	63.159	-1.841	-26.956	-33.421	-70.006	-73.746	-58.511	-60.396	-101.806	-46.291	37.959
43	-179.405	-150.860	-2.270	-15.270	-4.385	29.150	32.565	28.825	34.060	32.175	0.765	-94.720	-10.470
44	-104.029	-15.484	-18.894	-53.894	-79.009	-85.474	-82.059	-105.799	-110.564	-112.449	-113.859	-88.344	-54.094
45	-248.438	20.107	-3.303	-18.303	96.582	-9.883	-6.468	-10.208	-14.973	-16.858	1.732	-32.753	1.497
46	-200.856	-32.311	64.279	49.279	4.164	-2.301	1.114	-2.626	-7.391	-9.276	-10.686	-25.171	-50.921
47	-67.200	-98.655	67.935	92.935	67.820	41.355	44.770	41.030	86.265	84.380	82.970	-21.515	-7.265
48	108.548	292.093	193.683	58.683	73.568	67.103	70.518	66.778	-37.987	-89.872	-91.282	-55.767	-1.517
49	23.682	92.227	208.817	193.817	208.702	202.237	225.652	221.912	217.147	215.262	-86.148	-30.633	-16.383
50	30.814	229.359	575.949	786.949	801.834	795.369	798.784	795.044	790.279	788.394	180.984	-408.501	-394.251

14	15	16	17	18	19	20	21	22	23	24	25	ROW EFFECT	
-47.909	-41.989	-110.434	-142.234	-159.004	-169.199	-171.349	-179.179	-185.169	-193.959	-200.114	-261.019	61.251	26
-113.377	-107.457	-205.902	-287.702	-224.472	-234.667	-236.817	-244.647	-250.637	-259.427	-265.582	-276.487	76.719	27
111.727	47.647	-277.798	-12.598	10.632	0.437	-11.713	-9.543	-5.533	-24.323	-30.478	-41.383	121.615	28
67.563	21.483	43.038	-32.762	-71.532	-54.727	-95.877	-73.707	-58.697	-37.487	28.358	-105.547	-152.221	29
98.662	104.582	31.137	-60.663	-64.433	-66.628	-77.778	-35.608	-35.598	-66.388	-56.543	-50.448	-140.319	30
59.069	64.989	-68.456	-60.256	-47.026	-57.221	-49.371	-37.201	-43.191	-31.981	81.864	-19.041	-130.726	31
24.520	50.440	23.995	-110.805	-121.575	-110.770	-118.920	-115.750	-116.740	-166.530	-58.685	-58.590	-76.178	32
75.069	65.989	51.544	36.744	-4.026	-83.221	-57.371	-65.201	-88.191	-63.981	-4.136	-15.041	-107.726	33
14.410	-39.670	2.885	10.085	-16.685	-26.880	-29.030	3.140	-22.850	-31.640	-37.795	-78.700	-59.068	34
35.524	41.444	10.999	-41.801	-31.571	-41.766	56.084	-51.746	7.264	-1.526	-7.681	1.414	-116.182	35
-13.773	62.147	73.702	61.902	85.132	54.937	12.787	4.957	-1.033	-9.823	-15.978	-6.883	-162.885	36
7.180	13.100	-5.345	42.855	6.035	-4.110	-6.260	-14.090	-20.080	-28.870	-35.025	-45.930	296.162	37
-110.458	-104.538	-122.983	-84.783	78.447	68.252	66.102	38.272	32.282	23.492	17.337	6.432	263.800	38
10.777	16.697	18.252	36.452	-0.318	-10.513	-12.663	-10.493	-26.483	-35.273	-41.428	-52.333	12.565	39
167.828	215.748	93.303	163.503	126.733	64.538	62.388	54.558	48.568	39.778	33.623	22.718	125.514	40
108.377	194.297	55.852	279.052	102.232	82.087	139.937	152.107	86.117	57.327	31.172	110.267	139.965	41
88.574	214.494	36.049	74.249	117.479	7.284	25.134	37.304	1.314	22.524	-23.631	-34.536	-115.232	42
20.145	157.065	-21.380	86.820	50.050	39.855	-42.295	-0.125	-6.115	-44.905	-51.060	-61.965	-17.803	43
106.521	202.441	123.996	102.196	145.426	75.231	73.081	65.251	59.261	50.471	44.316	33.411	76.821	44
62.112	48.032	69.587	67.787	31.017	10.822	8.672	-9.158	-35.148	-43.938	-50.093	-50.998	291.231	45
-60.306	25.614	47.169	65.369	28.599	18.404	16.254	8.424	2.434	-6.356	-12.511	-23.416	-76.351	46
-16.650	-10.730	-9.175	-0.975	-17.745	-27.940	-30.090	-37.920	-43.910	-52.700	-58.855	-69.760	-70.008	47
-0.902	-34.982	-43.427	74.773	-1.997	-12.192	-14.342	-22.172	-28.162	3.048	-3.107	-14.012	-185.756	48
-25.768	-69.848	-118.293	-150.093	-66.863	-77.058	-79.208	-87.038	-113.028	-121.818	-127.973	-138.878	-60.890	49
-403.636	-232.716	-231.161	-212.961	-249.731	-259.926	-262.076	-269.906	-275.896	-284.686	-290.841	-301.746	111.978	50

	1	2	3	4	5	6	7	8	9	10	11	12	13
51	170.687	439.232	435.822	120.822	135.707	29.242	32.657	28.917	24.152	22.267	20.857	6.372	-39.378
52	-32.211	-55.666	91.924	-4.076	10.809	4.344	7.759	4.019	-0.746	-2.631	-4.041	-18.526	-75.276
53	44.130	-146.325	17.265	-6.735	-31.850	-28.315	-34.900	-38.640	-23.405	-25.290	-6.700	-11.185	-6.935
54	-74.295	-122.750	7.840	33.840	-42.275	-48.740	-64.325	-32.065	-20.830	-58.715	17.875	19.390	-24.360
55	213.682	223.227	-38.183	99.817	-100.298	-103.763	-87.348	-45.088	-9.853	-21.738	-13.148	34.367	12.617
56	-34.066	-85.521	-38.931	-33.931	-19.046	-45.511	-42.096	-45.836	-30.601	-32.486	-33.896	-28.381	-4.131
57	-125.793	-75.248	-18.658	-12.658	-37.773	-44.238	-40.823	3.437	-1.328	-3.213	-25.623	-49.108	-44.858
58	34.059	-47.396	-30.806	24.194	69.079	82.614	76.029	32.289	27.524	35.639	54.229	-150.256	-76.006
59	-60.941	-42.396	4.194	19.194	44.079	37.614	21.029	37.289	12.524	10.639	9.229	4.744	-11.006
60	-69.713	-188.168	28.422	21.422	23.307	29.842	7.257	31.517	23.752	21.867	20.457	0.972	-1.778
61	159.327	127.872	-25.538	19.462	-35.653	-92.118	-88.703	-62.443	-57.208	-19.093	-20.503	-4.988	9.262
62	-160.588	2.957	-11.453	89.547	109.432	102.967	106.382	112.642	107.877	105.992	104.582	86.097	52.347
63	-183.415	-214.870	-68.280	-13.280	1.605	-4.860	-1.445	-5.185	-9.950	-11.835	-13.245	-187.730	-133.480
64	-222.484	-253.939	-57.349	-52.349	-37.464	-43.929	-40.514	-44.254	-49.019	-80.904	-82.314	-106.799	-92.549
65	12.796	-18.659	-22.069	-63.069	-48.184	-54.649	-51.234	-54.974	-59.739	-61.624	-63.034	-77.519	-63.269
66	-100.051	-231.506	-34.916	-99.916	-85.031	-91.496	-88.081	-91.821	-96.586	-98.471	-99.881	-114.366	-100.116
67	-68.075	-95.530	9.060	-97.940	-83.055	-89.520	-86.105	-89.845	-94.610	-96.495	-97.905	-62.390	-48.140
68	-217.520	-192.975	-62.385	-57.385	-102.500	-128.965	-145.550	-169.290	-174.055	-175.940	-177.350	-111.835	-97.585
69	23.244	-158.211	-41.621	-76.621	-61.736	-68.201	-64.786	-68.526	-63.291	-65.176	-66.586	-91.071	-56.821
70	-33.869	-65.324	31.266	16.266	31.151	24.686	28.101	24.361	19.596	17.711	16.301	1.816	16.066
71	658.935	877.480	624.070	-10.930	3.955	-2.510	0.905	-2.835	-7.600	10.515	109.105	44.620	38.870
72	488.623	406.168	-36.242	64.758	59.643	53.178	19.593	15.853	11.088	9.203	7.793	12.308	102.558
73	744.080	712.625	81.215	-126.785	-61.900	3.635	78.050	105.310	-1.455	-3.340	-25.750	-19.235	-86.985
74	-134.841	63.704	110.294	55.294	20.179	113.714	107.129	73.389	18.624	-3.261	-4.671	-19.156	-4.906
75	298.731	189.276	429.866	-83.134	-88.249	-55.714	-52.299	35.961	42.196	40.311	17.901	33.416	-2.334

14	15	16	17	18	19	20	21	22	23	24	25	ROW EFFECT	
-48.763	-42.843	-31.288	-63.088	6.142	-4.053	-6.203	-14.033	-20.023	-28.813	-34.968	-45.873	-147.894	51
-84.661	-37.741	-36.186	-5.986	38.244	28.049	25.899	18.069	32.079	23.289	17.134	6.229	-114.997	52
-26.320	-10.400	-8.845	9.355	53.585	33.390	31.240	23.410	17.420	18.630	42.475	51.570	-108.337	53
8.255	-2.825	-1.270	-0.070	54.160	27.965	25.815	25.985	19.995	11.205	13.050	77.145	-104.912	54
24.232	14.152	87.707	-48.093	-28.863	17.942	15.792	7.962	1.972	44.182	38.027	27.122	-95.890	55
-13.516	-17.596	13.959	32.159	35.389	25.194	23.044	55.214	49.224	40.434	74.279	63.374	-133.142	56
-54.243	-38.323	3.232	1.432	51.662	61.467	59.317	51.487	45.497	36.707	30.552	19.647	-114.415	57
-85.391	0.529	2.084	30.284	3.514	-6.681	-68.831	-76.661	-2.651	-11.441	2.404	-8.501	-11.267	58
-50.391	-54.471	-12.916	-34.716	-11.486	-21.681	-23.831	28.339	22.349	13.559	7.404	-3.501	-116.267	59
-29.163	-20.243	-59.688	-52.488	-26.258	-44.453	-17.603	30.567	74.577	38.787	-1.368	0.727	-78.494	60
9.877	25.797	57.352	45.552	-11.218	8.587	16.437	8.607	32.617	23.827	17.672	36.767	-56.535	61
-5.038	-52.118	-54.563	-23.363	-75.133	-85.328	-87.478	-69.308	-39.298	-86.088	-92.243	-103.148	64.381	62
-102.865	63.055	-35.390	32.810	96.040	55.845	53.695	45.865	39.875	31.085	24.930	14.025	6.207	63
-101.934	-106.014	25.541	63.741	136.971	126.776	124.626	136.796	130.806	122.016	145.861	134.956	-54.724	64
-72.654	179.266	100.821	99.021	62.251	52.056	49.906	42.076	36.086	27.296	121.141	110.236	-110.004	65
-109.501	46.419	47.974	216.174	209.404	169.209	167.059	159.229	153.239	144.449	138.294	127.389	-27.157	66
-37.525	74.395	64.950	138.150	113.380	103.185	105.035	93.205	67.215	78.425	91.270	80.365	30.867	67
-106.970	178.950	100.505	138.705	221.935	231.740	229.590	221.760	235.770	226.980	220.825	209.920	-29.688	68
-36.206	129.714	21.269	19.469	72.699	62.504	70.354	92.524	136.534	117.744	101.589	90.684	19.549	69
6.681	12.601	14.156	32.356	-4.414	-14.609	-16.759	-24.589	-30.579	-39.369	-45.524	-56.429	206.661	70
29.485	-14.595	6.960	-24.840	-11.610	-21.805	-23.955	-31.785	-37.775	3.435	-2.720	-13.625	-36.143	71
103.173	71.093	-5.352	-12.152	-60.922	-33.117	-35.267	-43.097	-49.087	-57.877	-82.032	-92.937	-124.831	72
-25.370	-19.450	-37.895	-40.695	-5.465	46.340	44.190	46.360	19.370	10.580	-5.575	19.520	-93.287	73
-14.291	-8.371	-56.816	-38.616	-55.386	-35.581	12.269	54.439	-1.551	-10.341	-66.496	-77.401	177.633	74
-11.719	4.201	20.756	-13.044	-19.814	-30.009	-32.159	20.011	19.021	10.231	4.076	13.171	-155.939	75

	1	2	3	4	5	6	7	8	9	10	11	12	13
76	768.325	436.870	-66.540	-41.540	33.345	26.880	10.295	6.555	1.790	-0.095	-1.505	94.010	28.260
77	330.738	399.283	395.873	-89.127	-4.242	-10.707	12.708	8.968	4.203	2.318	0.908	-13.577	0.673
78	86.831	70.376	76.966	12.966	-18.149	-45.614	-83.199	-86.939	-91.704	-52.589	-53.999	-73.484	-13.234
79	-193.073	-234.528	2.062	57.062	11.947	45.482	18.897	-14.843	0.392	-21.493	-22.903	42.612	6.862
80	15.774	64.319	40.909	-14.091	20.794	34.329	17.744	-15.996	-40.761	-22.646	-4.056	-28.541	25.709
81	3.780	162.325	8.915	-6.085	8.800	2.335	5.750	2.010	-2.755	-4.640	-6.050	-0.535	13.715
82	-29.251	-120.706	-104.116	-79.116	-64.231	-70.696	-67.281	-71.021	-75.786	-77.671	-79.081	-158.566	-144.316
83	32.577	-38.878	97.712	82.712	97.597	1.132	4.547	0.807	-13.958	4.157	2.747	-31.738	-17.488
84	-30.915	-62.370	54.220	39.220	54.105	27.640	31.055	27.315	22.550	20.665	19.255	4.770	19.020
85	268.095	256.640	203.230	259.230	253.115	246.650	-50.935	-54.675	11.560	9.675	8.265	-76.220	-21.970
86	207.574	436.119	432.709	-62.291	-67.406	-73.871	-70.456	-74.196	-78.961	-30.846	-32.256	-46.741	17.509
87	-219.845	-191.300	-54.710	-29.710	5.175	38.710	122.125	118.385	93.620	-8.265	-9.675	95.840	170.090
88	-302.163	-123.618	22.972	17.972	42.857	46.392	79.807	86.067	86.302	94.417	93.007	53.522	67.772
89	-637.019	-558.474	-191.884	-206.884	-191.999	71.536	-195.049	-198.789	-183.554	-185.439	-186.849	98.666	112.916
90	6.621	175.166	261.756	306.756	371.641	425.176	448.591	424.851	420.086	388.201	386.791	-257.694	-193.444
COL EFFS	32.34	63.79	-32.80	-17.80	-32.68	-26.22	-29.63	-25.89	-21.13	-19.24	-17.83	-3.35	-17.60

14	15	16	17	18	19	20	21	22	23	24	25	ROW EFFECT	
18.875	34.795	46.350	34.550	-22.220	-32.415	-34.565	-42.395	-28.385	-37.175	-3.330	-14.235	-185.533	76
-8.712	-2.792	-1.237	16.963	-19.807	-30.002	-32.152	30.018	24.028	15.238	9.083	-1.822	-107.946	77
-8.619	25.301	57.856	55.056	39.286	60.091	57.941	-11.889	-17.879	139.331	29.176	39.271	-48.039	78
-32.523	33.397	24.952	-6.848	6.382	6.187	-5.963	-23.793	10.217	1.427	-4.728	4.367	315.865	79
-3.676	12.244	3.799	31.999	-34.771	5.034	22.884	-4.946	-20.936	-19.726	-0.881	3.214	-32.982	80
4.330	-35.750	-10.195	-5.995	-13.765	-21.960	-19.110	-20.940	-2.930	70.280	42.125	77.220	-20.987	81
-133.701	37.219	148.774	166.974	130.204	120.009	117.859	130.029	124.039	115.249	139.094	128.189	72.043	82
-26.873	-20.953	-19.398	38.802	-7.968	-8.163	-10.313	-18.143	15.867	27.077	-49.078	10.017	-109.785	83
9.635	-44.445	7.110	25.310	-11.460	-21.655	-23.805	-31.635	-37.625	-46.415	-52.570	-3.475	-66.293	84
-61.355	-45.435	16.120	44.320	-2.450	-22.645	-4.795	-12.625	11.385	2.595	-3.560	-14.465	-85.303	85
8.124	14.044	75.599	93.799	17.029	6.834	4.684	56.854	50.864	42.074	35.919	45.014	-44.782	86
160.705	26.625	-211.820	16.380	-10.390	-20.585	-22.735	-30.565	-36.555	-45.345	-51.500	-62.405	182.637	87
58.387	64.307	-34.138	-15.938	-52.708	-62.903	-65.053	-72.883	-78.873	-87.663	-113.818	-124.723	264.956	88
103.331	109.451	111.006	229.206	92.436	82.241	80.091	72.261	66.271	57.481	51.326	40.421	909.811	89
-202.829	-226.909	-145.354	-77.154	-133.924	-124.119	-126.269	-104.099	-110.089	-118.879	-165.034	-195.939	116.171	90
-8.21	-14.13	-15.69	-33.89	2.88	13.07	15.22	23.05	29.04	37.84	43.99	54.89	1344.87	

CHAPTER 4

Grain Price Reporting and Grain Price Quotations During the Ch'ing

4.1 Background to Ch'ing With Special Emphasis on Ming

Practically all grain price quotations which have survived in memorials and central government compilations of the Ch'ing period were ultimately derived from the type of price report discussed below.[1] The following reconstruction of the price reporting system therefore is primarily intended to assist the evaluation of grain price quotations (particularly those analyzed in Chapter 5) rather than to provide a rounded account of the aims and operation of the institutions to which price reporting became linked in the Ch'ing period. Thus the operation of these institutions, the public or 'price-stabilizing' granaries, is only mentioned in passing.

An important feature of government from the early Han to the mid-T'ang (2nd century B.C. to 8th century A.D.)

---

[1]Although district gazetteers frequently contain price quotations these are almost invariably found in the section on natural calamities. These disaster price quotations do not appear to have been derived from the regular type of price report discussed in this chapter. As I have suggested elsewhere (Wilkinson, 1969), disaster quotations were arrived at by multiplying the 'normal' price in a given district by a factor fixed by the intensity of the calamity. Not infrequently a fixed disaster quotation would be repeated again and again but this was by no means always sc.

was the attempt to regulate commodity markets. The blueprint for market control at the beginning of this period is contained in the Chou-li while its mature expression may be found in the T'ang Code and Statutes and their Japanese counterparts.[2] An integral part of the control system as it is described in the T'ang texts is the provision for regular price reports on three qualities of each commodity. These reports were to be based on price lists which were compiled under the direction of the market supervisor and posted every ten days in the market.[3] The ten-day lists were intended to set a fair standard for market prices while the reports which were submitted quarterly served two main purposes; first as a standard for fixing and later checking on all official purchasing and second as a means of establishing the value of goods involved in criminal process and hence the appropriate punishment.[4]

---

[2]See Li Chien-nung (1952), pp. 205-213 for markets in the early part of this period. Niida Noboru (1933) has brought together the relevant Chinese and Japanese texts plus many others, in the section "Statutes on customs and markets" pp. 713-721. Niida (1960) further commented on these texts in his important article on "Documents relating to the law of transactions discovered at Turfan," see note 5 below. Twitchett (1966), pp. 243-248 has conveniently translated many of the texts on markets contained in Niida (1933).

[3]The subordinate in charge of actually compiling the price lists (pu [illegible]) was probably the bookkeeper (chang-ku 掌固). See Twitchett (1966), p. 209. This position as well as Market Director no longer existed after the T'ang when officials came to rely more on the private sector; see below.

[4]i.e. (1) fan-mai 販賣 , mai-pu 買補 etc. and (2) p'ing-tsang 評贓 , chi-tsang 計贓 or ku-tsang 估贓 .

Until very recently there was no means of judging whether the T'ang regulations on price reporting were ever put into effect. In 1960 however striking confirmation as to their actual operation came with the publication by Niida Noboru of seventy T'ang price lists or fragments of price lists found amongst the materials brought back from Turfan by the Otani expedition.[5] Niida dated the lists to just before the An Lu-shan rebellion. The lists show that at this time prices for three qualities of each commodity were being recorded. Further confirmation as to the operation of the system comes from a comparison that Niida made between lists of prices paid by officials at Tunhuang and the Turfan price lists. The comparison shows (although not absolutely conclusively) that officials did indeed pay the 'middle price' (of the three reported) as they were required to by statute.[6] If price reporting was in

---

[5]See Niida (1960), pp. 808-826. The Otani Turfan materials are at Ryūkoku University, Kyoto. See also Ikeda On (1968).

[6]See Niida (1960), pp. 802-805. The Tunhuang official-purchasing list is in the Pelliot collection, Bib. Nat., Paris. The question of the "middle-price" (chung-teng chia-chih 中等價值) is a difficult one. The Japanese commentaries on the T'ang regulation which says that three prices are to be recorded for each commodity state that each commodity is to be divided into three qualities and for each quality three prices are to be recorded, making a total of nine prices in all for each commodity. Niida's analysis of the Turfan price lists shows that this may indeed have been the practice in T'ang China. What is not clear is the basis on which the three prices for each quality of a given commodity were to be decided. If the criterion was also quality this would strongly differentiate the T'ang system from that in operation in the Ch'ing when so far as I know only rice prices were regularly recorded for three qualities. During

operation at this relatively late date in these by no means central areas then there is every reason to suppose that it was carried out in more important centres.

Following the collapse of central control in the late 9th century the government gradually abandoned the attempt to regulate the time and places at which markets were held. It did not however give up the attempt to control merchant activities. Many of the duties of the defunct Market Director and his staff were taken over by police officers whose duties included keeping order in the market place, maintaining standard weights and measures (either directly or through the guilds), checking the activities of the guilds and brokers, registering visiting merchants and collecting various trade taxes and assessments. The tendency was increasingly to shift the responsibility for all these duties to the guilds and their representatives

---

the Ch'ing official purchasing was still to be conducted at 'middle prices' but the Ch'ing understanding of this regulation was as follows. Prices were divided into three categories not on the basis of the quality of the commodity but according to the state of the market. The three prices were referred to as prices at times of shortage (i.e., high prices, chi-chia 急價); prices at ordinary levels (huan-chia 緩價) and finally prices at times of glut (i.e. low prices, p'ing-chia 平價). Official purchases were to be made at the huan-chia which were sometimes referred to as 'medium' or middle prices. This allowance in the Ch'ing system for price fluctuation shows a much greater understanding of market forces than was apparent in the T'ang system. I have based this explanation of the 'middle price' during the Ch'ing upon the introductory memorials attached to a series of purchasing and hiring guidelines set out by the Board of Works in the 18th century. For full references to these documents see note 9.

as well as to the licensed brokers who by the Ch'ing were reporting on the movement of goods throughout the Empire and also collecting trade taxes.[7]

One measure of the growing responsibilities of these semi-official, semi-private brokers was that commodity price reporting appears to have been abandoned in the post-T'ang period; fair prices instead being now indirectly regulated through the official overseeing of the brokers.[8]

Standards for official purchases were still required however and as a result, certainly in the Ch'ing, occasional purchasing guidelines were issued as the need arose. Such guidelines took the place of regular commodity price reports and were issued by the Board of Works. They also included estimates of wage and transport costs.[9]

---

[7]For official market control during the Sung see Shiba (1968) especially pp. 32-49 and pp. 371-376 which include references to the standard works on the subject. For Ming-Ch'ing market regulations see Ta Ming lü, chüan 23, pp. 139b-142 and also Wada Sei (1957), vol. 2, pp. 847-851; Ta Ch'ing lü-li hui-t'ung hsin-tsuan, chüan 14, pp. 1-12 and also Kato Shigeshi (1954), pp. 545-551. The police officers mentioned in the above paragraph were during the Ming and Ch'ing organized under the 'Warden's Office' (ping-ma ssu 兵馬司).

[8]On the increasing role of the guilds and brokers see Kobayashi (1931); Shiba (1968), pp. 392-420 and Negishi (1932), pp. 193-261, Negishi (1951), pp. 202-204; 214-215.

[9]One such series of guidelines dating from the 18th century has survived in Japanese collections (Ch'in-ting Ho-nan kung-pu wu-liao chia-chih tse-li (1768) 欽定河南工部物料價值則例) and same title for the other provinces. Shen Chün (1940) published the Kiangsu guidelines in this series from a Tao-kuang reprint which suggests they were not updated at least in the 19th century. All yamen were required to keep a copy of these guidelines, see Ch'ien-ku pei-yao (1814 ed.), chüan 2, 34b.

The other purpose for submitting commodity price reports, the need to assess the value of goods involved in criminal process, continued to be required by statute but was met in practice either on an *ad hoc* basis or with the aid (especially in the Ming) of 'commodity-price-punishment scales' (*ku-tsang piao* 估贓表) which although occasionally updated tended to remain at fixed levels.[10]

Despite the emergence of indirect price control through the guilds in the post-T'ang period and the discontinuance of price reporting either as a means of budgeting for official purchases or as a means of assessing the value of stolen goods, the Ch'ing period was to see the development of a regular grain price reporting system which became an integral part of official grain purchasing and distribution policies. Before turning to the operation of this system however I shall briefly describe price reporting in the Ming in order to provide the background necessary to evaluate the Ch'ing achievement in this sphere. No attempt has been made to cover the Sung or Yuan for even less data on price reporting has survived from these periods than the little

---

[10] A Ming example of one of these scales is discussed below.

which I have been able to find for the Ming.[11]

One of the first tasks of the newly founded Ming dynasty was to prevent soldiers or officials from using force to acquire food, goods or labour from the populace. Accordingly one of the financial statutes in the Ming Statutes (issued in 1368) forbade soldiers and officials to use the excuse of 'hiring by consent' or 'purchasing by consent' for such practices. Instead they were to make purchases "according to the exact level of market prices" and moreover pay merchants on the spot.[12] The Statutes make no reference to recording or reporting prices although one of those dealing with punishments follows the T'ang Statutes in requiring that calculations of the value of goods involved in criminal process should be based on the original purchase price. How the price was to be

---

[11]The only direct evidence on price reporting during the Sung which I have seen is contained in the late 12th century work Regulations for implementing the Code, Ch'ing-yüan period (Ch'ing-yuan t'iao-fa shih-lei 慶元條法事類) which enlarges on the T'ang regulations by requiring that commodity prices be reported monthly and in the event of any change of price, every 10 days. Administrative units below the district town were also required for the first time to send in price reports. Quoted in Niida (1933), p. 717. In addition the 12th century author of Chiu-huang huo-min shu 救荒活民書 , Tung Wei 董煟 , states that one of the duties of magistrates is to take concern for rising and falling rice prices. He gives no indication that regular price reporting was undertaken however. See also Ikeda (1968) for material from Sung hui-yao chi-kao.

[12]Ta Ming ling (1368), chüan 1, p. 15. All references to the basic sources on early Ming administrative law in this chapter unless otherwise stated are to Yamane Yukio's edition of Kō Min seisho 皇明制書 (for the Koten Kenkyūkai), 1966 and 1967. The phrases 'hiring by consent' or 'harmonious hiring' 'purchase by consent' or harmonious purchase' (ho-ku 和雇 , ho-mai 和買) were euphemisms for abuses which had become notorious during the Sung whereby officials bought goods or hired labour without actually paying. See Hoshi (1966), pp. 423-424 for succinct definitions.

ascertained however is not mentioned.[13]

The first regulations on reporting prices were contained in a compendium of regulations guiding the activities of censorial officials first issued in 1371.[14] That the regulations should have been included in a work of this nature serves to emphasize that the early Ming regulations on price reporting fell not so much in the broad context of an attempt to control market prices as in the sphere of checking and controlling official dealings with the private sector which was left to a much greater extent than in previous periods to regulate itself. The regulations read in part:

> Market Prices:
> Administrations attached to prefectures, departments and districts must in the first ten days of each month check on the current prices of goods, verify them each in turn and then report them in due time. They must not report prices as either higher or lower thereby either bringing loss to the local government or harm to the people.
> Equipment required by the army: . . . materials must be payed for at current prices estimates for which must not be forcibly lowered.
> When higher officials purchase any form of materials the prefectural, departmental and district officials should settle the price according to the monthly price reports so as not to cause a loss for either the local government or for the people. Moreover they must not be permissive to the clerks and underlings, the heads of the *li* and the *chia* or shopkeepers etc., forcibly lowering prices and falling into corrupt practices.

The statutes and regulations of 1368 and 1371 noted above were succinctly summarized in a ruling on price report-

---

[13] *Ta Ming ling*, *chüan* 1, p. 52b.

[14] *Hsien-kang shih-lei* (1371), *chüan* 15, pp. 28-29.

ing in a compendium of statutes dealing with the organization of the central government and issued in 1393:

> Market Prices:
> In all market transactions amongst the people all commodity prices should be reported by the local government once a month to higher levels. In the event of official purchasing or army requirements these are to be conducted according to the current prices.[15]

In 1397 the first full edition of the Ming Code followed the T'ang Code in laying down the objects of market control by defining as crimes the unjustified raising or lowering of prices as well as the incorrect assessment of goods involved in criminal process. Significantly however the Ming statute differs from the T'ang statute in charging that the guild representatives be held responsible for preventing these abuses.[16] Despite this emphasis on control of unfair practices amongst merchants, as noted above the major thrust of the early Ming statutes on price reporting was more in the direction of controlling dealing between officials and merchants; price reporting was seen in the narrow light of an audit or checking tool, control of the market being left to the merchants themselves.

To what extent were the early Ming regulations summarized above put into operation or modified in the light of increasing administrative experience? Not a single Ming source has been found with data on the price reporting system in action while the little evidence that has been found suggests that price reporting as laid down in the statutes

---

15 Chu-ssu chih-chang (1393), chüan 3, pp. 139a–139b.

16 Ta Ming lü (1397), chüan 13, pp. 139b–140.

was simply not carried out. Thus a statute of 1437 states that when buying materials officials from a given Board are to meet with local officials who are to bring together guild members and shopkeepers there to settle the price between them. In other words face to face discussions had taken the place of price reports within the short space of forty years. This statute was still on the books towards the end of the dynasty.[17]

Turning to assessing procedures for goods involved in criminal process we find here too that there is no evidence that such procedures were based on current price reports. On the contrary early in the dynasty a commodity-price-punishment scale (ku-tsang piao 估贓表) was promulgated. Thereafter updates of the scale were few and far between. After 1407 it was repeated unaltered to the end of the dynasty.[18]

Not only do the regulations on price assessment for goods involved in criminal process as well as the regulations for official purchases appear to have become a dead letter, but all the regulations quoted from the basic compendia of the beginning of the dynasty were simply repeated in compilations such as the Collected Statutes or Monograph on the

---

[17]Nan-ching hu-pu chih (1595), chüan 18, p. 7b.

[18]A series of memorials on the long-overdue update of this scale is contained in Huang Ming t'iao-fa shih-lei tsuan (1531?), chüan 5, pp. 125a-130d (Koten Kenkyūkai reprint). The scale was reprinted without the memorials in the Collected Statutes which led Li Chien-nung to the mistaken belief that the scale reflects an official attempt to fix prices, see Li (1930). As it stands the price equivalents in the scale bear little relation to actual commodity prices.

Nanking Board of Finance.[19] This apparent non-evolution of administrative law should be compared with the very different situation during the Ch'ing.

Commodity price reporting appears to have been abandoned in practice during the Ming. Nor was it re-introduced during the Ch'ing except insofar as the occasional guidelines which have already been mentioned were promulgated by the Board of Works and other Boards. It remains to be seen therefore whether the regular reporting on grain prices which was undertaken in the Ch'ing as part of official grain purchase and price stabilization policy had any antecedents in the Ming. Since grain price reporting in the Ch'ing was intimately connected with the system of public granaries it is in this general area that we should expect to find regulations on grain price reporting in the Ming. Although public granaries existed during the Ming their use was primarily seen in terms of preparing for famine rather than of stabilizing grain prices.[20] I have been able to find no discussion of the difficulties of price control using these granaries; such discussions were very common in the Ch'ing. Nor has a single Ming regulation survived on reporting grain prices either in the context of granary sales and their timing or in any other context. Such regulations as we shall see

---

[19] Ta Ming hui-tien (1587), chüan 37; Nan-ching hu-pu chih (1595), chüan 18.

[20] On these granaries in the Ming see Hoshi (1963), pp. 453-494.

are extremely common during the Ch'ing. The operation of such granaries for price control purposes required all kinds of price reports and price summaries during the Ch'ing. Quotations of prices at every level of the system abound in Ch'ing writings, not only in hundreds of memorials but also in the works of private writers. Several thousands of the actual price lists have also survived. On turning to the Ming sources we do not find comparable traces of the system. There are, to be sure, a handful of price quotations from the northern borders found scattered in the Veritable Records.[21] There are also very occasional references to famine prices in private writings. Taken alone however these cannot be considered sufficient evidence for supposing that the system of regular price reports on major grains was operating in the Ming. The full significance of this negative conclusion is discussed at the end of the chapter.

4.2 Investigating Prices at the District Level

During the Ch'ing market control objectives, narrowly defined as policing the market area, checking on weights and measures and making sure that the guilds did not play the

---

[21]These quotations were gathered together and analyzed in Terada (1967 etc.). His data suggests that at least in the area of army purchase and supply close attention was paid to market prices. There is no trace in this data however of a regular reporting system.

market too blatantly, were inherited from previous dynasties. What was added in the Ch'ing was a national system of grain price reporting which enabled for the first time a much more effective implementation of traditional policies of grain distribution, as a means of famine prevention as well as consumer protection, through grain price stabilization. Since the price reporting system was central to all facets of these policies and since it was used for different purposes at different levels of government the discussion which follows centres round the price reporting system. The major reason for concentrating on the mechanics of price reporting however is that only by so doing can we hope to evaluate those price quotations which have survived from different levels of the reporting system.[22]

The lowest level of administration at which grain prices were gathered were the markets in or serving the district towns. The reasons are not hard to find. Unlike the Ming whose policy vacillated in this matter, during the Ch'ing public granaries were placed inside the district towns from the outset. These granaries (ch'ang-p'ing ts'ang 常平倉 price-stabilizing granaries) became the centre of the government's attempt to provide famine relief as well as control the level of grain prices in the markets of district towns

---

[22]Ch'üan Han-sheng and Wang Yeh-chien's work on grain prices (Ch'üan Han-sheng, 1957; 1959; 1960; 1962; 1965) contains no analysis of the nature of the price quotations which they gathered from memorials and other sources. Spence (1966), pp. 109-116 discusses an interesting sidelight on the system, namely special reporting on grain prices by the Emperor's bondservants. I attempted a preliminary outline of the report-system in Wilkinson (1969).

thereby providing urban consumer protection.[23] In order to decide when and at what price to buy the grain to restock the granaries which were usually replenished in the period following the harvest when prices were low, it was necessary to have constant price reports. Furthermore these reports were also needed in order to decide at what price to sell the grain (which was to be sold according to a fixed scale below current market prices).[24]

There are few detailed accounts of price reporting at the district level but one such account was found in a handbook for secretarial assistants in charge of financial matters which was probably compiled in about 1820 and which deals with conditions in Shantung. Under the heading "At what times should grain prices be raised?" it states:

> Information on grain prices is the responsibility of the town tipao who is to report them every ten days. As soon as the draft list of grain prices is completed and ready for submission it must be checked over again. Prices are not to be selected for inclusion on the list

---

[23]Lu Lien-tching (1932) summarizes the general outlines of the public granary system during the Ch'ing as depicted in the standard central government compendia. Ch'ü T'ung-tsu (1962), pp. 156-159 gives a succinct outline of the system from the point of view of famine relief while Hsiao Kung-ch'uan (1960), pp. 143-183 discusses the 19th century system in some detail and also covers the rural granaries. None of these authors relates the public granary system to price reporting or to the wider context of market control.

[24]Many Ch'ing sources were found discussing the problem of fixing these prices. A selection is given below.

Illustration of a financial secretary's handbook

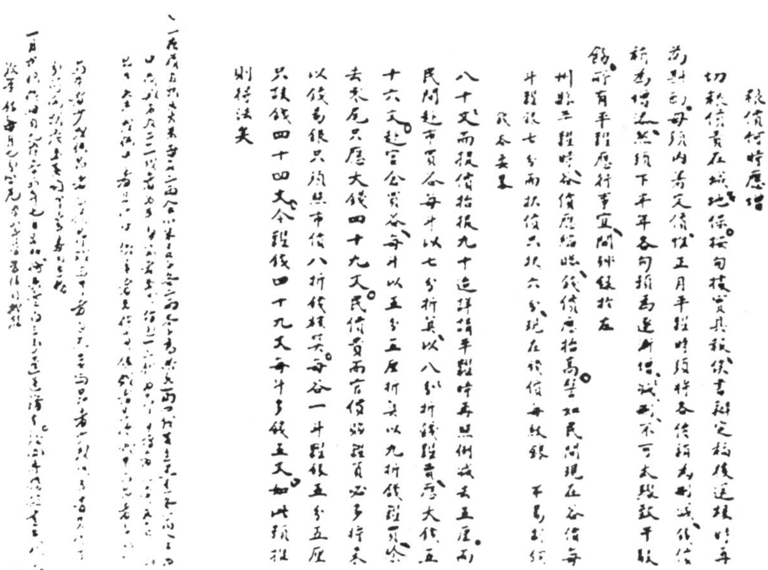

B A

The first part of the passage from handbook A is translated on pages 110 and 112 (see note 25 for reference). The passage from handbook B is translated in full on page 124. Both handbooks deal with Shantung conditions and were written not later than 1820. Such sources enable a slightly different perspective on local administration, in this case the business of price reporting. Without such glimpses we should know very little, for the more formal sources tell us next to nothing on how secretaries and their staffs actually made the system work.

> inside the yamen (i.e. arbitrarily without investigation). In the First Month when sales are made from the price-stabilizing granaries they are done so at prices slightly below the reported prices and the cash price of silver is raised slightly. In the second half of the year (i.e. after the harvest) prices are to be raised slightly every ten days. These adjustments should not be too violent. . . .[25]

Another and slightly earlier source from Fukien makes no mention of the tipao in the initial price investigations but places the responsibility on specially appointed clerks in the yamen. These are referred to as 'miscellaneous servitors' (ch'ai-i 差役); 'supervisory clerks' (kuan hsu ch'ai 管胥差); 'clerks with special assignment' or 'old and experienced clerks' (ching-ch'eng 經承); or in more general terms as 'special clerks' (chuan-shu 專書) or 'special servitors' (chuan-i 專役).[26] In some areas therefore it would appear that price gathering in the first instance was the responsibility of the omnicompetent and unpaid members of the police control system in the towns (the tipao) while in others it was left in the hands of specially appointed clerks in the yamen of the district magistrate. Whichever was the case the initial ten-day price lists as soon as they were gathered became the immediate responsibility of the tax secretaries (ch'ien-ku 錢穀), indeed the investigating clerks were no doubt

---

[25] Ch'ien-ku yao-lüeh, (c. 1820), pp. 1-2. For a detailed introduction to this type of handbook see Wilkinson (1970). A list of seven of these handbooks may be found in References Cited, Chinese manuscript sources, Handbooks for secretarial assistants in charge of financial matters.

[26] See Sheng-li, Fu-chien, (1873?) chüan 6, pp. 3-10b for reports on price reporting to the provincial governor of Fukien in 1781 and 1795.

drawn from the clerks in the office of revenue (<u>ch'ien-liang fang</u> 錢糧房) which came under the supervision of the <u>ch'ien-ku</u>. The <u>ch'ien-ku</u> (from one of whose handbooks I have just quoted on conditions in Shantung) undertook a large number of functions in the broad area of tax and revenue. Besides the price reports he was also responsible for routine crop progress reports; rainfall reports; percentage harvested etc. etc.[27] Coming with the magistrate as a specialist the tax secretaries were responsible to him and therefore acted as a countervailing force to local particularist interests which the yamen clerks frequently represented. In the case of price reporting there was every reason why the local grain guild might have wished to influence the investigating clerks and have them report prices lower than they were in an attempt to keep cheap official grain off the market. Whether or not the guilds were able to influence the reports depended upon the tax secretaries and ultimately of course upon the magistrate himself who was responsible to his superior yamen for the accuracy of all routine reports. He knew that higher levels could easily check and frequently did just that. Checks usually came about as the result of higher levels noticing anomalies thus the handbook for the eyes of <u>ch'ien-ku</u>

---

[27] Ts'ai Shen-chih (1941), p. 49 gives a full list of <u>ch'ien-ku</u> responsibilities.

only advises that when prices are raised or lowered they should not be done so too sharply in order to avoid attracting the attention and therefore the censure of higher levels.[28] But it was not to his advantage simply to fill out prices from previous months or years. In 1795 the yamen of the provincial treasurer of Fukien was struck by a long series of unchanging prices and ordered investigations and follow-ups. As a result those responsible for gathering the prices were ordered to enter their names on the reports along with the copyists in an effort to secure more scrupulous reporting.[29] Thus although there were strong forces both outside as well as inside the yamen to 'cook' the reports, they were not necessarily in concert and meanwhile there was always the possibility of a higher level check. These were the tensions which although not guaranteeing 100% accuracy at least prevented outright misrepresentation in the reports.

Granted that grain price investigations were conducted at the lowest level either by local policing officers working under district governments or by members of the staffs of district officials and granted also that the investigations were of prices in markets within or serving district towns the question still remains as to the nature of the prices collected. The best evidence on this point comes from the

---

[28] Ch'ien-ku yao-lüeh (c. 1820), pp. 2-3.

[29] Sheng-li, Fu-chien (1873?), chüan 6, pp. 3-10.

Fukien Provincial Precedents already mentioned. Circulars on price reporting from the provincial treasurer printed in the Precedents state that the investigating officers were to report on "the market selling price of upper, medium and lower grade rice in terms of cash." They were also to report on the local C/S rates and convert the cash prices of the grains into the standard government silver accounting unit, the *Kuping tael*. Local units of measure were also to be converted before the reports went up to higher levels to standard official bushels (*kuan shih* or *ts'ang shih* 官石, 倉石).[30] The district lists were to be made up every ten days and reported to the prefectural or department yamen in the form of a monthly report which was to be submitted before the 22nd of each month.[31] Besides rice prices the prices of the other major grains in a given district were also reported on. These included millet, wheat, field-peas, soy-beans, rye, buck-wheat etc. etc. Each ten-day report as well as monthly report had also to include by how much each grain price had risen or fallen in comparison with the price recorded in the previous ten-day or monthly report. The same applied to changes in the C/S rates. The above account is based on the Fukien Precedents and may not be accurate in every detail for other parts of the country. Thus the form for the Fukien

---

[30]See *Hu-nan sheng-li ch'eng-an* (1820), *chüan* 24, p. 33 for the reprimanding of a clerk who forgot to convert local *taels* to *Kuping taels* in the ten-day reports of 1767/3.

[31]*Sheng-li, Fu-chien*, *chüan* 6, p. 5.

reports as given in the Precedents while basically the same as found in actual reports from Szechuan, Shensi and Kiangsu over one hundred years later does in certain details differ. None of the later reports which I have seen for example carry the names of the copyists and investigators. Nevertheless the basic conclusions remain; the prices initially gathered were retail prices in cash which were converted to silver accounting units before being forwarded along with the original quotations to the prefectural and departmental yamen. In the next section we shall examine what became of these quotations as they were reported to higher levels. A district report is reproduced overleaf.

4.3 The Process of Summarization and Reporting

The district grain prices were sent up from the district yamen to the next higher yamen (prefectural or departmental) in the form of ten-day lists and monthly price reports. There they were checked and used as reference when later reports and requests for grain purchases and sales were made by the districts. At the same time the monthly reports had to be re-copied, stitched together and summarized, preparatory to being sent on up to the yamen of the provincial treasurer who assumed ultimate control and responsibility for the movement and sale of grain throughout the province. There is some evidence that district magistrates sent up the price lists in rough form and paid clerks in the higher

fig. 1

District town price report (Shen-mu, Shensi)

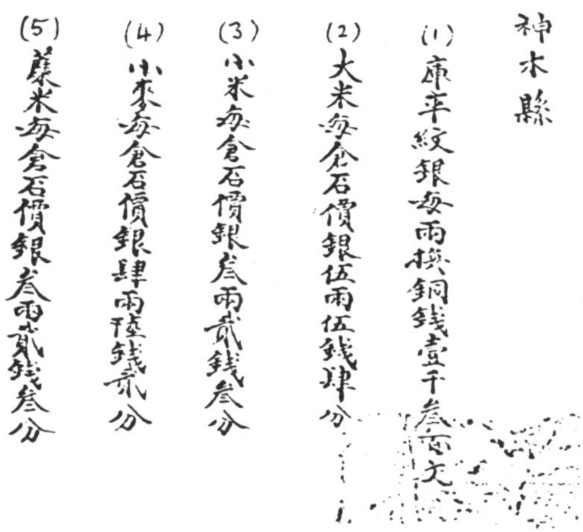
神木縣
(1) 庫平紋銀每兩換銅钱壹千叁百文
(2) 大米每倉石價銀伍兩伍钱肆分
(3) 小米每倉石價銀叁兩貳钱叁分
(4) 小麥每倉石價銀肆兩陸钱貳分
(5) 糜米每倉石價銀叁兩貳钱叁分

Translation

Line 1 One Kuping tael exchanges for 1,300 cash
Line 2 Each granary bushel of rice costs 5.54 taels
Line 3 Each granary bushel of millet costs 3.23 taels
Line 4 Each granary bushel of wheat costs 4.62 taels
Line 5 Each granary bushel of millet, proso costs 3.23 taels*

Portion of the seal of the provincial treasurer is shown at the bottom right hand corner. As an unusually poor district Shen-mu (town 51) reported few grains. This particular report is for the 4th month of 1904.

Scale: 175 by 225 cm. Characters are actual size but most of the seal and the blank border have been cut out.

* Millet, proso, glutinous (shu-tzu 黍子) and non-glutinous (mi-tzu 糜子) was an important crop in this part of Shensi. See Buck (1937), vol 2, p. 74.

Source: Shensi Reports

---

yamen to copy out the quotations in the correct form. The evidence comes from Kiangsu and also from Shantung.[32] Reports from every district town in Shensi and Szechuan at a later date however were each written in a different hand which strongly suggests that the district reports reached their final form at the district level.[33] The point is of some importance for if the reports were simply compiled at higher level yamen on the basis of local data expressed in local units of capacity and account there would have been a much greater possibility for error as the result of arbitrary decisions on conversion ratios owing to lack of knowledge of local conditions. In the light of my examination of several thousand district price reports I came to the conclusion that they were in fact written out at the district level and that the fees paid for clerical services to higher yamen were for their services in re-copying and eventually forwarding the copies of the reports to higher levels.

---

[32]The Shantung evidence is drawn from a handbook for tax secretaries which quotes a ruling of 1789 that blank forms are to be sent to the provincial capital along with a fee for copyists. See Ch'ien-ku chai-yao (1823?), chüan 2, no page number. The Kiangsu evidence comes from an account book of Fu-ning district yamen at the beginning of the 19th century as quoted by Ch'ü T'ung-tsu who writes that among the fees paid by the district magistrates of Fu-ning to clerks of superior yamen was a fee "for making reports on the price of grain...." (Ch'ü, 1962, p. 216, footnote 44). Ch'ü also quotes a late 19th century magistrate who said that such fees had become customary and were necessary simply to speed documents and reports on their way (ibid., p. 46). The Shantung evidence suggests however that the clerks at least at the provincial capital did actually do some copying.

[33]See References Cited, Chinese manuscript sources, Shensi Reports, Szechuan Reports.

The prefectural summaries (many of which survive in whole or in part in the memorials of provincial governors) were written on a single sheet of paper and stitched to the front of the bundle of district reports. They simply state the highest and lowest price recorded for each grain in the subordinate districts (as well as the highest and lowest C/S rates) and in addition the amount by which the highest price was higher or lower than the highest price in the previous month (see the following two pages for a reproduction of a prefectural summary and translation). The prefectural summaries therefore enabled the reader in the provincial treasurer's yamen to tell at a glance the range of prices in each prefecture. Their use at this level was also greatly enhanced by a simple gloss added at the beginning of the summary which stated whether the prices in a given prefecture were 'high', 'medium' or 'low'. Even at the provincial level such glosses were necessary for in provinces with fifty to one hundred districts it would have been impossible to remember for example that 2.0 taels in district A was a high price whereas for district B it might well have been a low price. In their function as a rapid index to the state of the province-wide market therefore the glosses attached to the prefectural summaries played a crucial role. As we shall see it was usually the glosses which attracted the attention of higher officials, not the prices themselves.

fig. 2.

1 鳳翔府屬小米小麥價中餘俱偏貴

2 庫平紋銀每兩換銅錢自[illegible]百肆拾[illegible]文至[illegible]千伍百玖拾[illegible]文

3 大米每倉石價銀自貳兩壹錢陸分至貳兩捌錢玖分

4 較上月減銀貳分

5 小米每倉石價銀自壹兩伍分至壹兩柒錢陸分

6 較上月增銀柒分

7 大麥每倉石價銀自伍錢柒分至壹兩

8 與上月相同

9 小麥每倉石價銀自壹兩壹錢捌分至壹兩肆錢

10 較上月減銀叁錢肆分

11 豌豆每倉石價銀自壹兩壹錢壹分至壹兩柒錢伍分

12 較上月減銀貳錢壹分

FIG. 2

Prefectural summary of subordinate district town grain price reports (Feng-hsiang prefecture, Shensi, 1904/4)

Translation

Line 1	In the districts subordinate to Feng-hsiang prefecture: millet and wheat prices, medium. The rest all high.
Line 2	One Kuping tael exchanges for between 1143 cash and one string 591 cash
Line 3	Each granary bushel of rice costs from 2.16 to 2.59 taels
Line 4	This is .02 taels lower than last month (i.e. the high price for the previous month had been 2.61 taels)
Line 5	Each granary bushel of millet costs from 1.05 to 1.76 taels
Line 6	This is .07 taels higher than last month (i.e. the high price for the previous month had been 1.69 taels)
Line 7	Each granary bushel of barley costs from .57 to 1.0 taels
Line 8	Same as last month
Line 9	Each granary bushel of wheat costs from 1.18 to 1.14 taels
Line 10	This is .34 taels lower than last month (i.e. the high price for the previous month had been 1.52 taels)
Line 11	Each granary bushel of field peas costs from 1.11 to 1.75 taels
Line 12	This is .21 taels lower than the last month (i.e. the high price for the previous month had been 1.32 taels

Original size of document: 175 by 225 cm.

The seal is that of the provincial treasurer of Shensi

Source: Shensi Reports

The bundles of district reports with their prefectural summaries were supposed to reach the provincial capitals not later than the fifth of the month succeeding the month to which they referred.[34] Once there they were copied out again ready to be sent to the Board of Revenue in Peking for reference purposes.[35] At the same time the governors and governors-general prepared their monthly memorials on grain prices within their provinces. These monthly price memorials (which began to be submitted regularly in the early 18th century) usually did no more than quote certain of the prefectural summaries. They thus give the range within selected prefectures especially within the prefecture of the provincial capital. Only selected grains were included. In evaluating price quotations found in these memorials therefore it is important to remember what they were based on. They carried selections from the prefectural summaries which gave the range for a given grain in the prefecture as found in the monthly district price reports which were themselves based on the ten-day market price lists. The monthly memorials of the governors were only intended to give the Emperor and the central government the broad outlines of an extremely complex subject, the state of the grain market in the different provinces of the Empire. More-

[34] Sheng-li, Fu-chien, chüan 6, p. 5b. This is a useful point for it is not always clear how to date a price quotation when only the date of the memorial is given.

[35] This practice was not introduced until 1763. See note 45 below for references and further discussion.

ever since they gave ranges within prefectures (and very frequently only the range for an entire province) unaccompanied by the distribution within the range these memorials can only be used with extreme care. Even the Emperor appears often to have scanned the original reports or at least the full prefectural summaries rather than limit himself to the information contained in the memorials. Great care was exercised by the 18th century Emperors in looking over the memorials and price lists in search of inconsistencies and in this sense they provided a final check on the entire system. Some idea of the care which they exercised in this regard may be seen in the following example.

In the grain price lists submitted by the governor of Shantung in 1772 the gloss 'rising prices' had been added in most cases. This led the Emperor to remark, "the harvests in Shantung have been good this year, how can the prices be rising?" An investigation was ordered and it was found that a former governor of the province had thirty years previously laid down definitions of what constituted high, rising, medium etc. prices. Thus although changing prices had been recorded the old glosses had been retained leading, as the Emperor noted, to the absurd situation that the prices which thirty years previously would have been high and which now, owing to the general rise in prices could be considered low, were still being glossed as 'high'.[36] By good fortune

[36] Ch'ien-ku t'iao-li (1817), ts'e 54, chüan 6, pp. 35a-36b. Shorter version in Kao-tsung shih-lu, chüan 919, pp. 13b-15b.

we have in another source an instruction promulgated a few years later by the provincial treasurer of Shantung updating the instructions for the price glosses in that province. They were jotted down in the handbook of a tax secretary working in Shantung at that time:

> Monthly grain price reports
>
> When rice is 2.8 taels per _shih_, millet and corn each 2.0 taels, kaoliang and unhulled millet each 1.4 taels, soybeans and black beans each 1.8 taels then the gloss should be 'medium price'. If they are 0.2 or 0.3 taels less then the gloss should be 'medium low price'. If they are even lower then the gloss should be 'low price.' If the prices are higher then the gloss should be 'rising price.' If even higher then the gloss should be 'expensive.'
>
> If half the prices are high or medium high and the other half are low or medium low or if all the prices are medium then the gloss should be 'medium prices.' If they are all expensive then the gloss should be 'expensive.' If they are all low then the gloss should be 'low prices'. If there are more which are high and medium high than there are low or medium low than the gloss should be 'medium high prices' (ditto if they are all medium high.) If there are more which are low or medium low of if they are all medium low than the gloss should be 'medium low prices.'
>
> They are to be reported at the appropriate times following careful investigation.
>
> 1778. Issued by the provincial treasurer for circulation to lower levels.[37]

Other examples of the 18th century Emperor's keen eye for anomalies in the price report glosses, rather than in the quotations themselves, could easily be multiplied.[38]

---

[37] _Ch'ien-ku chai-yao_ (1823?), _chüan_ 2, no page number. The grains mentioned at the beginning of this passage with the exception of rice are in the original given as _hsiao-mi_ 小米, _mai-tzu_ 麦子, _ku-tzu_ 谷子 and _kao-liang_ 高粱.

[38] See _Chu-p'i yü-chih_, _passim_ for the early part of the century and _Kao-tsung shih-lu_, _chüan_ 917, pp. 16b-17b; _chüan_ 1254, pp. 8a-8b for example, for the later part of the century.

Their trenchant comments often improved vigilance at lower levels and brought about reforms in the system, yet even without their interest the entire system had built-in checks at every level. In the 19th century when the Emperors gave less attention to such matters the system continued to function. In the 18th century the Emperor played a crucial role in extending an essentially prefectural and provincial reporting system by requiring that the central government also receive the reports. Such centralization on a routine basis for the entire Empire had not existed in the Ming but once it was established in the 18th century it continued right down to the end of the Empire. Before discussing the uses to which these new sources of price information were put I shall briefly describe the stages by which the price reporting system was set up.

Although the entire system as outlined above was operating by the later part of the 18th century it is not certain when it began to operate on a regular basis for the first time. There is no mention of price reporting in the Ming sources for the public granaries, nor do the early Ch'ing sources on the price-stabilizing granaries carry any regulations on the subject. By the 1690's the central government had developed sufficiently to start coping on a regular basis with grain distribution problems (rather than concentrating more on capital and army supplies as well as the occasional major natural calamity) but a preliminary scanning of the Veritable Records suggests that it was not yet doing so on the basis of regular market reports.

The first glimpse of regular reporting that we have are the reports of the Kiangnan textile commissioners. Their reports to the Emperor from the late 1690's on appear to have developed from routine enquiries of the Emperor's health after the Emperor began to request them to add to these enquiries information on rice prices.[39] Whether or not price reporting up to the provincial level already existed at this time must remain a moot point; I have been able to find no regulations on the subject in the early editions of the various standard government compendia.[40] References to price quotations in memorials submitted by provincial governors up to the end of the K'ang-hsi reign, while not plentiful, certainly exist.[41] Whether or not therefore we should follow Spence in assuming that the textile commissioners reported on grain prices to enable the Emperor "to check personally on the veracity of the similar reports sent through the normal channels by the provincial governors," must I think wait until we have more evidence that "normal channels"

---

[39]This interesting view is being developed by Dr. Silas Wu and is confirmed by Dr. Spence's research (personal communication from the latter).

[40]I checked the 1670 edition of the <u>Liu-pu tse-li</u>; the 1690 edition of the Collected Statutes as well as <u>Tse-li lei-pien</u>(Ch'ing continuation), 1703 edition. All with negative results.

[41]Opening of the Palace Museum archives will no doubt enable more definite conclusions on this matter. Meanwhile publication of a selection of early Ch'ing memorials on grain prices from the museum's archives has been announced.

were operating at this time. Until more evidence is forthcoming it seems more reasonable to regard the price memorials of the Kiangnan commissioners as forerunners of the regular provincial governors' price memorials.[42]

Whatever the origins of the system we certainly find that by the third decade of the 18th century provincial governors are sending in regular memorials on grain prices based on prefectural reports.[43] Their reports were not as full however as those which were submitted in the first half of the Ch'ien-lung period and after. Then for the first time governors appear to have begun to attach the prefectural summaries to their monthly price memorials.[44] In 1763 the full system came into operation when the governors were required to have the original district reports copied out and sent to the Board of Revenue in Peking.[45] Although price reporting was under the control of the Board of Revenue the

---

[42]See Spence (1965), p. 110.

[43]See Chu-p'i yü-chih, passim.

[44]This statement is based on the numerous rescripts of the Ch'ien-lung Emperor which mention "price-lists" (liang-chia tan 糧價單). Judging from the quotations from these lists they were in fact the prefectural summaries. See for example Kao-tsung shih-lu (1738), chüan 69, pp. 19-20; ibid. (1739), chüan 93, pp. 11a-11b; ibid. (1742), chüan 163, pp. 1b-2; ibid.(1747), chüan 290, p. 4b; ibid. (1772), chüan 909, pp. 18b-19b; ibid. (1772), chüan 917, pp. 16b-17b.

[45]"At the time each governor sends in his monthly memorial on grain prices he should take each departmental and district grain and legume price quotation and should make detailed lists of them to be sent to the Board (of Revenue)," Shih-li, p. 7609.

various editions of the Regulations of the Board of Revenue were slow to reflect changes in the system. Thus the 1763 statute already quoted was not carried in the Regulations until the edition of 1791.[46] Nor should this surprise us for price reporting was in the first instance connected with the district public granaries whose activities were overseen by the prefectural and provincial yamen. The Regulations are mainly concerned with links at the next higher level i.e. between the provinces and the centre. They carry regulations therefore on the memorializing and summarizing procedures rather than on the actual details of investigating the prices in the district markets. The same of course applies to the Collected Statutes which contain only passing references to price reporting.[47] As a district and provincial matter price reporting is dealt with much more fully in Provincial Precedents, handbooks for provincial and district tax secretaries etc.

During the 19th century the system as described above continued to operate in all essentials although without innovations.[48] Several thousand district reports have survived over a long series of years in the later part of the

---

[46]Hu-pu tse-li (1791), chüan 28, "Regulations for price-stabilizing granaries."

[47]Shih-li, p. 7609 and p. 7424.

[48]Even in 1861 the reports seem to have been reaching the central government, see Mu-tsung shih-lu (1861), chüan 2, pp. 15a-15b.

century.[49] While right up to the fall of the Empire all the districts in at least two provinces were still sending in monthly price reports.[50]

4.4 The Function of Price Reports

Having established that market reports in the form of retail grain price reports were compiled from about 1700 to 1900 and having shown how and where these prices were gathered, summarized and reported at district, intermediate, provincial and central government levels, it remains briefly to consider the uses to which the system was put and with what effect. As before the discussion is essentially based upon documents and sources which date from the period when the system was working at its best, namely c. 1720 to 1800.

As we have seen at the district level grain price reporting was carried out as a means of effecting the price

---

[49] Liu I-cheng (1930) published a table of rice prices based on the prefectural and departmental summaries submitted by the provincial treasurer of Kiangsu for the 8th, 9th, 33rd and 34th years of Kuang-hsü (1882/3; 1907/8), months one through twelve for each of these years. He also included a table of rice prices based on district reports from all the districts attached to sub-prefectures and departments subordinate to Suchow prefecture for the same years and months. According to Liu the documents upon which these tables were based were in the archives of the Kiangsu Provincial Library (Lung-p'an-li kuo-hsueh t'u-shu-kuan tang-an k'u 龍蟠里國學圖書館檔案庫) which at that time contained a complete series of these documents for every month from 1882 to 1908. For reasons of space however Liu was only able to publish the first two years and last two years of the series. The present whereabouts of these documents which were not listed in the catalogues of the day is unknown.

[50] These are the reports which are analyzed in Chapter 5 and also in Chapter 3. See References Cited, Chinese manuscript sources, Shensi Reports; Szechwan Reports.

stabilization policy connected with the public purchase of grain during months of glut and its storage until lean months when it was sold below current market prices. The granaries in which the grain was stored however served a second and related purpose (famine relief) and it is this purpose which had received most attention in the secondary literature.[51] The two purposes may be seen as complementary; in times of famine the granaries were used to supply relief while in more normal times they were used to stabilize urban grain prices. Neither purpose was new in the Ch'ing. What was new in the Ch'ing period was the ability to place the old price stabilization theory on a firm basis (the market price reports) and put it into practice. Those evaluations therefore which mainly on the basis of 19th century sources conclude that the granaries only had enough grain in them to provide temporary relief for mild disasters only tell half the story. Furthermore in the light of the large number of special expedients used in large-scale disasters it could be argued that the district granaries, in their role as relief stores, were only intended to provide temporary relief for mild disasters. Not only were there many other forms of local relief, including 'persuasion' brought to bear on grain merchants and local wealthy by the officials

---

[51]See references cited in note 23.

but also many forms of incentive were provided to encourage charity in times of need.[52] In a major disaster the provincial and national levels combined to provide relief which went beyond what the district granaries could supply. The role of the district granaries should therefore not be seen exclusively in terms of the percentage of surplus grain which they held at a given time. During the Ch'ing they were more than merely relief granaries.[53] Their function was also to provide grain at reduced prices during normal years when prices shifted according to regular seasonal forces. Price stabilization meant the attempt to provide some sort of year round security for urban dwellers who would otherwise have been adversely affected by seasonal shifts in the prices of staple grains. To provide this sort of service during normal years did not require vast grain reserves. It only required an adequate knowledge of market prices, relatively small reserves and the ability to prevent each individual from buying more than a small quantity of grain at one time.

The expedients used for providing against major disasters were related to the district granaries in that their employment was frequently based upon the summaries

---

[52]During the Ch'ing the language of chivalry of a previous age was used for those who gave grain in times of need. Those who performed such charitable acts are often referred to in their biographies as i-hsia 義俠 or hao-hsia 豪俠 (see jen-wu sections of district gazetters, subsection i-hsing 義行).

[53]See Abe Takeo (1957), pp. 506-515 for a functional division between emergency relief, price-stabilizing and military granaries.

of the district price reports which were as we have seen regularly sent to higher levels of administration. The summaries were also used for planning movements of grain in more normal times. Thus the funds for the purchase of grain for the district granaries were kept by the provincial treasurer to whom all reports and prefectural price summaries were sent. There the reports were checked for inconsistencies and then on the basis of them funds for grain purchases throughout the province were allocated. Not only was the movement of grain within a province decided on the basis of the reports and possible emergencies planned for when prices appeared to be unusually high, but also grain purchases from other provinces were planned on the basis of price reports received laterally from those provinces. Thus a regulation from the later 18th century states that,

> "Kiangsi, Hukuang and other rice producing provinces are to send reports of rice prices in districts accessable to water transport to Fukien and other (rice deficient) provinces. If Fukien needs to buy rice then it can budget on the basis of these reports."[54]

A constant complaint made against official grain purchasing was that prices tended to be set below market prices.[55]

---

[54]<u>Ch'ien-ku pei-yao</u> (1850?) <u>chüan 9</u>. This handbook for tax secretaries in Fukien should not be confused with Wang Yu-huai's more general handbook of the same name.

[55]Wang (1958), p. 14 has shown that the prices at which Fukien officials bought grain in Taiwan lagged behind market prices with the result that in this instance at any rate price reports were apparently not used for budgeting grain purchases from grain surplus areas.

Part of the reason for making market price reports was to provide a means of checking such abuses. Nevertheless complaints of collusion were levelled against clerks and local headmen responsible for the original investigations upon which the price reports were based at the same time that charges were levelled against officials conducting grain purchasing. No doubt in periods or places of weak or corrupt government the objectivity of the price reports suffered badly.[56]

While open to abuse and neglect at every level the entire system of price reporting was as we have seen subject to checking and scrutiny at each level. Information in the price reports could easily be checked against expectations of the likely range of prices in a given district as well as against the information contained in the monthly rain and snowfall reports, progress of the harvest reports, reports on the percentage harvested, annual audits of accounts, annual reports of granary holdings, statements of account at transfer of office and many other types of regular and special reports.[57]

At the highest level the entire system of price reports, grain purchase and price stabilization was overseen by the Board of Revenue which received all the district

---

[56]See Ho (1959), pp. 48-49 for an excellent short discussion of the influence of weak government on statistics gathered at the lowest levels.

[57]All requests for purchases or sale of grain were checked against the regular reports.

reports as these were forwarded by the yamen of the provincial treasurers. In the 18th century too the Emperor became involved in this review and planning process. The Ch'ing Emperors, especially the K'ang-hsi, Yung-cheng and Ch'ien-lung Emperors as is well known, took an active and amazingly close interest in all matters of government especially in those areas affecting the peace and prosperity of the metropolitan, the Central Yangtze and the Kiangnan regions. So firmly routinized had the system of grain price reporting become by the 19th century that it continued to operate long after scrupulous central review had become a thing of the past. Decisions at provincial and local levels were taken within the context of generalized procedures laid down in the great compilations of the central government which were modified in the light of local conditions in the compendia of regulations and administrative statutes kept in all local yamen.[58]

4.5 Conclusions

Government accounting was done in units of silver and as a result the grain price quotations had to be converted from the original cash units to standard official silver

[58] These Provincial Precedents (sheng-li 省例) and their relation on the one hand to the central government compilations and on the other to the handbooks of regulations used by financial and legal secretaries are discussed in Wilkinson (1970).

units of account. These conversions were made at the district level. In order to provide some check on these conversions and subsequent buying and selling all districts had to include cash/silver exchange rates with the grain price reports.[59] The range of C/S rates was also entered in the prefectural summaries.[60] The monthly price memorials of the provincial governors, which were only intended to give a general idea of the state of the market to the Emperor, did not as a rule include C/S rates.[61] In evaluating these memorials it was the descriptive gloss which seems to have caught the Emperor's eye, not the actual prices.

The problem for the price historian is that he must take into account that the adjusted price quotations, owing to the wide variations in C/S rates between places, may effectively mask price differentials. For a high silver price for example could conceivably reflect the low purchasing power of silver in terms of cash rather than the scarcity of a given grain. This problem, which has its counterpart in European price history,[62] is discussed in Chapter 5 where

---

[59] "For the purpose of greater clarity" as the Fukien regulations put it, see Sheng-li, Fu-chien, chüan 6, p. 3. The Shensi exchange rates introduced in Chapter 3 were recorded in district grain price reports using exactly the same formula as found in the Fukien regulations. See also Ch'ien-ku yao-lüeh (c. 1820), pp. 2-3.

[60] See line 2 of the illustration of a prefectural summary, fig. 2.

[61] An interesting exception is contained in the memorial of the governor of Kiangsu, Ch'iao Shih-ch'en, in 1733 reporting on special procedures set up to check grain prices. He quotes the original cash prices per sheng and then gives their silver equivalents per shih (see Chu-p'i yü-chih, p. 3727).

[62] See Braudel and Spooner (1967), p. 392.

a series of grain prices expressed in both cash and silver units is analyzed.

The major finding of this chapter is that there developed during the Ch'ing dynasty a system of grain price reporting. The price quotations surviving from the different levels of the system have to be handled with great care for their accuracy depended upon the efficiency of non-specialized clerks. Their performance was no doubt directly related to the general level of administrative efficiency at the district yamen as well as to the efficiency of the institutions to which grain price reporting was connected, the public granaries.

A secondary and tentative finding of this chapter is that the system of grain price reporting which was found to be operating in the 18th century was not in operation in the Ming or earlier periods. I say tentative for it is always possible that new evidence may come to light or that evidence which I have overlooked be brought forward to show that such a system was indeed operating in the Ming. Meanwhile it can only be recorded that no trace of a regulation on grain price reporting was found in a Ming source.

The significance of the 18th century system of reporting on grain prices (as opposed to commodity price reporting which had been abandoned after the T'ang) was that it formed an integral part of the old public granary system which was now provided with a type of information allowing a much more effective use of the granaries for price stabilization as well as for famine relief. In the absence of a full-scale study of the operation of these granaries in the 18th and 19th centuries however this conclusion too must remain tenative.

Having established that the vestiges of grain price quotations found in memorials to the central government during the Ch'ing period were in fact based upon a regular system of reporting on market prices of grain, we return to Shensi in the following chapter in order to utilize a series of original grain price reports which have survived from each of the district towns in the province. The present chapter will have achieved its purpose if it enables us to approach the Shensi reports with some degree of confidence that they represent market conditions; had no attempt been made to evaluate them there would have been no certain way of knowing just what they were. The reports themselves simply state the prices, nothing more.

CHAPTER 5

Shensi Grain Markets, 1900-1910

5.1 Introduction

This chapter focuses on the scope and nature of the market for wheat, rice, and millet and field peas in Shensi between the years 1900 and 1910. The analysis of these markets centres on the differentials in prices over geographic areas for these grains. The prices where reported from the ninety district towns in Shensi every month to the provincial capital as part of the price reporting system outlined in the previous chapter.

The opening section serves to introduce the main crops, cultivated acreage, yields, harvest fluctuations, population and transport costs within the province at this time. Typical prices derived from the price data analyzed in the body of the chapter are used to construct a system of weights to calculate total agricultural production in terms of kilograms of wheat equivalent per person per year (kw/p/y). The section closes with a brief consideration of the technical problems involving the nature of the data from which the price quotations were drawn.

The cultivated acreage in Shensi (total area, 195,800 sq. km.) in the first decade of this century was in the neighborhood of 4 million hectares of which just over 50%

was sown to winter wheat (see table 1); 6% to rice; 6% to barley; 9% to millet, corn, _kaoliang_ etc.; 10% to miscellaneous grains, legumes etc. and finally 15% to the major cash crop, cotton.[1]

Map 1

Crop areas & Geographic Zones in Shensi, c. 1900

(based on Buck, 1937, vol iii, pp.21-27).

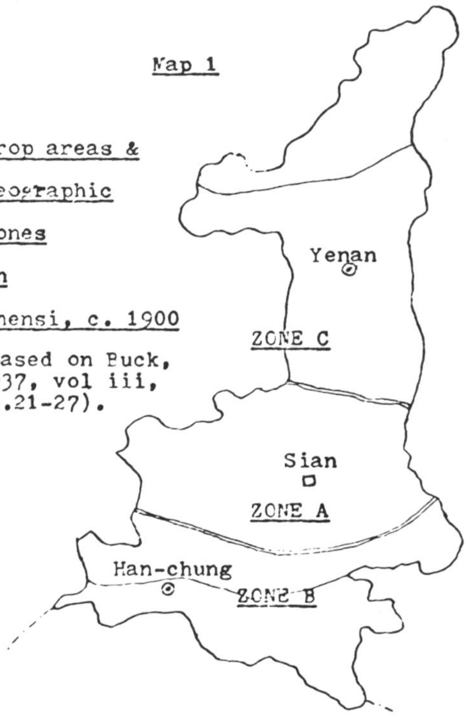

---

[1] See Perkins (1969), pp. 233-237; 241-265. All acreage, production and yield statistics have been converted to the metric system. Available estimates of cultivated acreage are open to considerable margins of error, the present figures are no exception. Nevertheless they were based on the comparison of the best estimates. They take into account double cropping and inter-planting practices in the province.

Table 1

Estimated Crop Acreage, Yields and Production in Shensi (c. 1900-1910)

Crop	Cultivated Acreage in Hectares	Yield (kg./hect.)	Production (Metric Tons)
Wheat	1,900,000	900	1,710,000
Rice	220,000	2100	462,000
Barley	280,000	1125	315,000
Millet	130,000	1200	156,000
Corn	180,000	1200	216,000
Kaoliang	50,000	1275	63,750
Peas			
Beans			
Oats	450,000	1125	506,250
Buckwheat			
Soybeans	50,000	750	37,500
Peanuts	5,000	1500	7,500
			3,474,000
Cotton	630,000	150	94,500
Tobacco	17,000	1125	19,125
Opium	?		
	3,910,000		

Source: Recalculated to metric system from data in Perkins (1969), pp. 233-237; 241-265; 270ff.

Rice was grown in the southern part of the province (see map 1) which partly falls in Buck's Szechwan rice area. The centre of wheat production, the main crop, was the Wei valley or broadly the geographic zone A on map 1. The tip of zone C fell in Buck's spring wheat area but the remainder of this zone was the poorest area in the province, growing maize, millet etc. as main crops. The province thus divides into three more or less well defined geographic zones; zones A and B each centres on its own river valley while each is also separated from the other by the Ch'in-ling range. Zone C has poor land and next to no rivers suitable for navigation and was the most backward and cut off part of the province. It should be noted that each geographic zone overlapped with crop areas (see map 1).

Long-term changes in productivity are difficult to measure owing to lack of information. The semi-annual reports to the Board of Revenue on amounts harvested do however give some indication of the deterioration in the latter part of the 19th century (see Table 2). The number of districts reporting harvests of over 80% (column A) had dwindled almost to zero by 1880. Those reporting 70-80% harvests also declined in the same period (column B). After 1860 more districts were reporting less than 60% harvests than even 60-70% harvests.[2] Some indication of why harvests were declining is given in Table 3 which is based on reports to

---

[2]Feuerwerker (1969), pp. 5-6 offers the view (in assessing this type of data) that these figures merely reflect increasingly effective efforts by the provinces to resist central government taxation by claiming exemption from the land tax because of poor harvests. This view would carry more weight were it not for the fact that the central government successfully doubled the land tax in the 19th century. Nor did the major effort to raise taxes fall on the land tax; the increase in all other forms of taxation was much greater (they rose by 12 times between 1783 and 1908). See Wang Yeh-chien's unpublished dissertation "Land Taxation in the Late Ch'ing" quoted in Perkins (1969), p. 176. Corroboration for the declining harvest data also comes from the data on calamities in Table 3 whose effects are well documented in literary sources.

Table 2

Percentage of districts in Shensi reporting different amounts harvested, 5-year intervals, 1821-1910

	Summer harvests (70 districts reporting)				Autumn harvests (90 districts reporting)			
	A	B	C	D	A	B	C	D
	80%+	70-80%	60-70%	below 60%	80%+	70-80%	60-70%	below 60%
1821	18	42	40	-	32	40	18	10
1825	60	33	7	-	42	38	18	2
1830	33	33	27	7	34	33	26	7
1835	-	6	64	30	33	29	28	10
1840	35	50	13	2	1	29	47	23
1845	29	40	28	3	1	21	61	17
1850	-	-	-	-	12	41	35	12
1855	-	-	-	-	5	37	38	20
1860	66	30	4	-	-	-	-	-
1865	-	12	42	46	2	21	37	40
1870	2	5	24	69	1	17	25	57
1875	15	18	50	17	2	18	47	33
1880	5	31	45	18	-	16	37	47
1885	2	19	34	45	1	15	42	42
1890	-	9	38	53	-	5	35	60
1895	-	9	49	42	-	4	26	70
1900	2	4	23	71	1	10	31	58
1905	3	18	45	34	-	3	60	37
1910	3	17	26	54	-	8	29	63

Source: recalculated from table in Li Wen-chih and Chang Yu-i (1957), p. 764 which was based on the original semi-annual harvest reports to the Board of Revenue.

the Board of Revenue of natural and man-made disasters. During the 40's and 50's of the 19th century there were very few disasters in Shensi but after the 70's which saw rebellion and the worst famine in the history of the province there were large numbers of districts reporting disasters in all years except '82 and '83, '94, and'95, '04 and '05. The cumulative effect of these bad years is amply attested in many accounts of the poverty in the province by Chinese and western observers alike. One such account must suffice. It was written by Francis Nichols, agent of the famine relief fund of New York's Christian Herald, who described conditions north of Sian in 1901:

> To get a better idea of the ravages of famine throughout the province of Shensi, I passed five days...in the town of San Yuan (town 9) about thirty miles north of Sian... We made excursions from San Yuan out across the plain of Sian. The country gave evidences of a former dense population. Every quarter of a mile a mud village rose out of the white, treeless desert, which stretched away to the north, east, and west like a limitless ocean. The vast plain was silent. Along the old roads, all worn and sunken, we met no travellers. No farmers were in the fields. In some of the villages were half-starved men and children, the only survivors of communities that had perished. The plain was silent because its inhabitants were dead. Only at rare intervals was a house with a roof visible anywhere... as a last resort before abandoning all hope the starving villagers had sold the shelter of their homes.

Nichols goes on to describe the fall in the population of San Yuan itself which had been the commercial centre of the province. He reckoned the population had fallen from about 50,000 to less than 20,000 as a result of the three years of famine.[3]

---

[3]See Nichols (1902), pp. 243-248.

Table 3

Percentage of total districts (90) in Shensi reporting crop disasters due to drought, flood, war, hail, frost, locusts, 1846-1910

Year	percent of districts	drought	flood	war	hail	frost	locusts
1846	2	X					
1848	5						
1862	34			X			
1870	1			X			
1873	51			X			
1876	80	X					
1877	90	X					
1881	57	X		X			
1882	5		X		X		
1883	1		X				
1884	21		X		X	X	
1885	60	X		X			
1886	13		X		X		
1887	13		X		X		
1888	13		X		X		
1889	33		X		X		
1890	11		X		X		
1891	22	X	X		X		
1892	33	X	X		X	X	
1893	33	X					
1894	1				X		
1895	6		X		X		
1896	20		X		X		
1897	11	X	X		X		
1898	75	X	X		X		
1899	43	X	X		X	X	X
1900	67	X			X	X	
1901	68			X			
1902	32		X		X	X	
1903	25		X		X		
1904	1		X				
1905	0						
1906	40		X		X		
1907	11	X	X		X		
1908	14	X	X		X	X	
1909	26		X		X		
1910	1		X				
	Total:	14	23	6	22	6	1

Source: With the exception of the entries for 1876 and 77 this table was recalculated from the data in Li Wen-chih and Chang Yu-i (1957), pp. 733-735. For 1876 & 77 see <u>ibid</u>, p. 746.

The total population in the province is given in the official annual population reports to the Board of Revenue as 12 million in 1861 (the last year for which we have figures in this particular series from Shensi). However since this figure had been submitted virtually unchanged since 1819 considerable doubt arises as to its reliability.[4] In view of the long chain of man-made and natural disasters which afflicted the province, the estimates made in the 1930's which put total population at the end of the 19th century at about 9 or 10 million, would appear much more likely.[5] Before deciding one way or the other however we can test the degree of plausibility for the different estimates by using the data on crop acreages, yields and production summarized in Table 1. Assuming for the moment that these represent fairly reliable estimates we can test the various total population estimates by calculating kg. of grain equivalent/person/year (total grain equivalents produced divided by total population estimate equals kg. of grain equivalent/person/year or k/p/y) and comparing the different k/p/y resulting from different

---

[4]The annual provincial totals in the Board of Revenue archives were printed by Lo Erh-kang in an appendix to Yen Chung-p'ing (1955), pp. 362-374. P. T. Ho (1959), p. 283 gives a total of 12 million for Shensi in 1850 based on the Lo figures.

[5]The best of these estimates was made by the National Agricultural Research Bureau and Nanking University (reprinted in Li Wen-chih and Chang Yu-i (1957), vol. 3, pp. 907-908). See also Perkins (1969), p. 212.

assumed total populations with likely levels of k/p/y based on information on k/p/y of similar societies or derived from surveys of North China itself.[6] In measuring the likely range of k/p/y we are of course not only testing total population estimates but also expressing the level of agricultural development in Shensi at this time in standard units of grain equivalent i.e. in terms allowing of ready comparisons with other societies. Finally we shall be providing some basis for judging the standard of living in the province at this time.

In order to calculate total grain output in the province at this time it is necessary to have some means of converting the different crops into a common unit. Since wheat was the most widely produced crop it was selected and all output of the other grains has been converted to wheat equivalents using the following formula:[7]

$$\frac{\text{total production of given grain X typical price of that grain}}{\text{typical price of wheat}}$$

---

[6]See Clark and Haswell (1967), esp. pp. 53-77 for applications of this approach and also Buck (1937) for North China surveys.

[7]This method differs from Buck's where all grains were counted equally. The reason for using prices of grains to calculate wheat equivalents rather than calorific values is that a grain such as millet has almost the same calorific equivalent as milled rice but sells at much lower prices since it is much less palatable (see Clark and Haswell, 1967, p. 60). In estimating production therefore due allowance is made for those grains which are considered more valuable. This method was considered particularly suitable for China since producers frequently produced the expensive grain for the market to a greater extent than the cheaper but technically almost equally nutritious grains.

'Typical' prices for the different grains were obtained from the price reports analyzed in the body of this chapter using the same data analysis methods as for the C/S rates (see Chapter 3, note 7). In cases where the reports provide insufficient quotations for calculating typical prices the system of weights given in Clark and Haswell (1967) was used.[8] Although the fit between typical prices in terms of cash and silver was not always exact, it was usually near enough to allow selection of prices in terms of only one unit of account; in the event, taels.

Table 4

System of Weights (based on typical prices in Shensi, 1900-1910)

	Typical Price (in Taels)	Weights
Wheat	2.28	100
Rice	3.75	161
Millet	2.12	93
Field peas	1.96	86
Beans		86
Oats		60
Buckwheat		63
Barley	1.45	63
Corn	1.45	63
Kaoliang		63
Soybeans		130
Peanuts		110
Cotton		294
Tobacco		800

Source: Shensi Reports and Clark & Haswell (1967), pp. 222-223.

[8] *Ibid.*, pp. 222-223.

The prices in the Shensi Reports are given for a measure of capacity (the 'granary bushel' <u>ts'ang-shih</u> 倉石) the definition of which is discussed below in the section on weights and measures. Here it need only be noted that the prices per 'granary bushel' were converted into units of weight (kg.) due allowance being made for the different weights of the same measures of different crops.

We are now in a position to estimate total production in terms of wheat equivalents by combining the data in Table 1 with that in Table 4:

Table 5

<u>Total Estimated Agricultural Production in Shensi in Tons of Wheat Equivalent, c. 1900</u>

Grain	Tons of Wheat Equivalent	Per Cent of Food Crops	Per Cent of All Crops
Wheat	1,710,000	48	39
Rice	792,850	22	18
Barley	200,300	6	5
Corn	180,000	5	4
Millet	145,000	4	3
Kaoliang	53,000	1	1
Misc. Grains	435,200	12	10
Soybeans	48,750	1	1
Peanuts	8,250	.2	
	3,573,450		
Cotton	614,250		14
Tobacco	153,000		3.5
Grand Total	4,340,700		

Source: See Table 1 and Table 4.

Dividing these estimates of total agricultural production in tons of wheat equivalent by different estimates of total population we obtain the following estimates of kg. of wheat equivalent/person/year (kw/p/y):

Table 6

Total Product from Agriculture in Shensi, 1900-1910, Expressed in kg. of Wheat Equivalent/Person/Year

Population Estimate (in millions)	Food Crops	Non Food	Total
9	397	85	482
10	357	77	434
11	325	70	395
12	298	64	362
13	275	59	334

Source: Tables 4 and 5.

The above estimates of agricultural production in terms of kw/p/y only include important staple crops (important crops defined as those occupying one per cent or more of the crop area in all the localities covered in Buck's surveys).[9] The only important crop not included was the potato (Irish and sweet). Potatoes only supplied averages of 7.3% of total calories consumed in the Spring wheat area, 1.1% in the winter wheat-millet area and 3.2% in the Szechwan rice area.[10] Since these estimates were for the

[9] See Buck (1937), vol. 3, Preface, n.p.

[10] See Buck (1937), vol. 3, pp. 75-76.

years 1929-33 they would probably have to be adjusted downward for the years 1900-1910 as the period 1910-30 was one of increasing potato consumption.[11] Given the comparatively small contribution of the potato in these areas to total calories consumed however I have not attempted an estimate of potato production in terms of kw/p/y on the assumption that such an estimate would have relatively little influence on the figures for total production of the important crops.

It should be emphasized that the estimates of kw/p/y are based on data for normal years; crop failure or devastation would have caused much lower kw/p/y. Nor do the estimates as they stand take any account of the uneven distribution, not only between localities within the province but also between farms within each locality. (For example for the period 1929-33 Buck gave 156 kw/p/y for small farms in the winter wheat-millet area and 456 kw/p/y for very large farms in the same area.)[12] Nevertheless it is hoped that despite these and other drawbacks (notably the large margin of error in the crop acreage, yield and total product

---

[11]See Buck (1937), vol. 3, p. 81.

[12]See Buck (1937), vol. 1, p. 286. Buck's "production of grain equivalent per capita in kilograms" is similar to what I have termed kw/p/y. It should not be confused with his "production per man-equivalent in kilograms of grain-equivalent" which was designed to express productivity of farm labour not production per capita.

estimates) the kw/p/y as calculated above can serve to give us some indication of the level of development of the agricultural sector in Shensi at this time.

For reasons explained below and in the discussion of population distribution in the province the lower estimates of total population of 9 or 10 millions would appear less plausible than the upper estimates of 11 or even 13 millions. If we accept 11 million as the lower estimate and 13 million as the upper estimate this would give an estimated range of food crop production of between 275 and 325 kw/p/y or all-crop production estimate of between 334 and 395 kw/p/y. These estimates may be compared with those made by Buck thirty years later. The Buck estimates were made for rural population only. I have accordingly re-adjusted them on the basis of Buck's estimates of rural, urban population distribution estimates.[13]

Table 7

Total Production of Food and Non-Food Crops in kg. Grain Equivalent Per Capita, 1929-33.

Size of Farm	small	med. small	med. large	large	very large	average
Spring Wheat Area	73	128	153	181	234	171
Winter-Wheat-Millet Area	138	182	241	311	405	202
Szechwan rice area	187	338	548	614	1226	612
		Average of All Farms				445

Source: Adjusted from data in Buck (1937), vol. 1, p. 286.

[13] See Buck (1937), vol. 1, p. 365.

If we take the averages for all farms in each of the three areas and allow that 1/5 of Shensi be considered in the Szechwan rice area; 1/10 in the Spring wheat area and the remaining 7/10 in the Winter wheat-millet area, then we can derive an estimate of average agricultural production of +/-280 kg. of grain/person/year.[14]

We now have therefore comparable estimates for 1900-1910 and 1929-1933. Assuming that there were no new factors of production in Shensi between these years, k/p/y appears to have fallen from approx. 364 to 280. Even if we take the highest estimate of total population in 1900-1910 (rather than the average of 11 and 13 millions) and calculate k/p/y on that basis there still appears to have been a fall in agricultural production per capita; from 334 k/p/y to 280 k/p/y. In view of the evidence of declining production due to poor harvests and devastation from the later 19th century it is hard to avoid the conclusion that in this province at any rate production per capita was falling continually from about 1860 right through to 1933.

The above estimates of agricultural production are in a form (k/p/y) which allows of easy comparison with other societies. Such comparisons enable us to draw some conclusions

---

[14]The fact that Buck's calculation of k/p/y did not allow for the greater value of rice would not have altered this general conclusion. Also to be taken into account is the move to cheaper crops, of which the potato was only one, see note 9 for reference.

as to the standard of living in the province at this time. In summarizing data on k/p/y from many different countries Clark and Haswell reach the conclusion that minimum subsistence requirements for large-bodied people (adult males 60 kg.) in cold climates (both apply to Shensi) would stand at about 290 k/p/y(including minimum textile requirements).[15] De Vries placed the subsistence minimum at a little below 300 k/p/y (both per head of total population).[16]

We may conclude therefore that production in normal years in Shensi c. 1900 was only barely enough to provide slightly above minimum subsistence requirements for an estimated total population of 12 to 13 million people. During the next thirty years that margin fell even to levels slightly below minimum subsistence requirements. Some localities were undoubtedly better off than others but in aggregate in this predominantly agricultural society most people had hardly enough to remain alive even in normal years.

We must now turn to the problem of the size of urban population supported at the estimated level of agricultural production at this time in Shensi. The argument begins with the construction of likely ranges of urban population based on population data from about 37 towns in Shensi c. 1910. These estimates are then used to project total population

---

[15]See Clark and Haswell (1967), pp. 53-77.

[16]*Ibid.*, pp. 61-62.

estimates on the basis of various assumptions as to population distribution. These total population estimates as well as the estimates for urban population are then compared with the total population estimates presented above. Finally on the basis of these estimates the amount of grain marketed to the urban sector are calculated.

The largest concentration of towns was in zone A which contained 35 district towns of which 5 may have contained populations of 10,000 to 20,000, but most of which had no more than 3 to 5,000 inhabitants.[17] There were also three larger higher administrative centres, two of which may have had populations of 20,000 to 30,000 (nos. 29 and 53) while the third, the provincial capital of Sian, had between 300 and 400,000 inhabitants. In the southern part of the province (zone B) there were 20 district towns most of which had populations between 3 and 5,000. The two administrative centres of Han-chung and Hsing-an (Nos. 40 and 65) had between 30 and 50,000 inhabitants. Finally in the northern part of the province (zone C), the 20 district towns and administrative centres were all small, many having less than 1000 inhabitants. A low estimate of the population

---

[17] Urban population figures in this paragraph are taken from Shina shōbetsu zenshi (1918), vol. 7, part 2, 'Towns' (Tokai 都会), pp. 26-140 which contains descriptions of 42 of the 90 towns in the province, including population estimates of 37 of them which were made on the basis of the direct observations of the research teams.

of the 90 district towns and higher administrative centres, based on these estimates for the towns in the three zones, would therefore give a total urban population of about 650,000 people. A somewhat higher estimate would place the total not above 750,000. Granted this range of urban population we can now calculate likely ranges for mixed rural-urban and rural populations and thus arrive at a total population estimate. Part of Buck's survey dealt with the distribution of population in city (i.e. administrative centre) and country. Using his percentages for population distribution in the winter wheat-millet area (6% urban; 10% mixed; 84% rural)[18] and using our estimate of 650,000 to 750,000 for urban population we get the following estimates for total population distribution:

Table 8

Estimates of Urban Population in Shensi, c. 1900

1. Minimum Estimate	
6% urban	650,000
10% mixed	1,083,000
84% rural	9,100,000
Total	10,833,000
2. Maximum Estimate	
6% urban	750,000
10% mixed	1,250,000
84% rural	10,500,000
Total	12,500,000

18See Buck (1937), p. 365. The spring wheat area estimate of urban population (18%) applies to the N-E, not to Shensi.

If we accept Buck's estimate that half the population of the mixed centres were not engaged in agriculture then the amount of grain equivalents required to support the different urban population estimates will be

1. minimum estimate: 650,000 + 541,500 x 387 kw/p/y
   = 461,000 tons of wheat equivalent

2. maximum estimate: 750,000 + 625,000 x 348 kw/p/y
   = 478,500 tons of wheat equivalent

Or if we take only the urban population estimates (administrative centre populations) the results are:

1. minimum estimate: 650,000 x 387
   = 221,550 tons of wheat equivalent

2. maximum estimate: 750,000 x 348
   = 261,000 tons of wheat equivalent

Since the price quotations analyzed in the second half of this chapter are from markets in the administrative centres we shall be concerned with the marketing of approx. 221 to 260,000 tons of wheat equivalent.

Transport within the province was extremely slow and expensive owing to the lack of navigable rivers (see Map 2 for main transport routes). The longest river connection open most of the year was provided by the R. Han which linked Mien (No. 45) with P'ing-li (No. 66), a distance of 850 km. From P'ing-li it was possible to continue down stream to Hankow (500 km.) and so eventually to Shanghai. The direct route from Shanghai via Hankow to Sian branched off in Hupei from the route to Hanchung and Mien and went up the R. Tan as far as Shang-chou (No. 78) and so overland by mule to

Map 2

Land routes and navigable rivers in Shensi, c. 1900

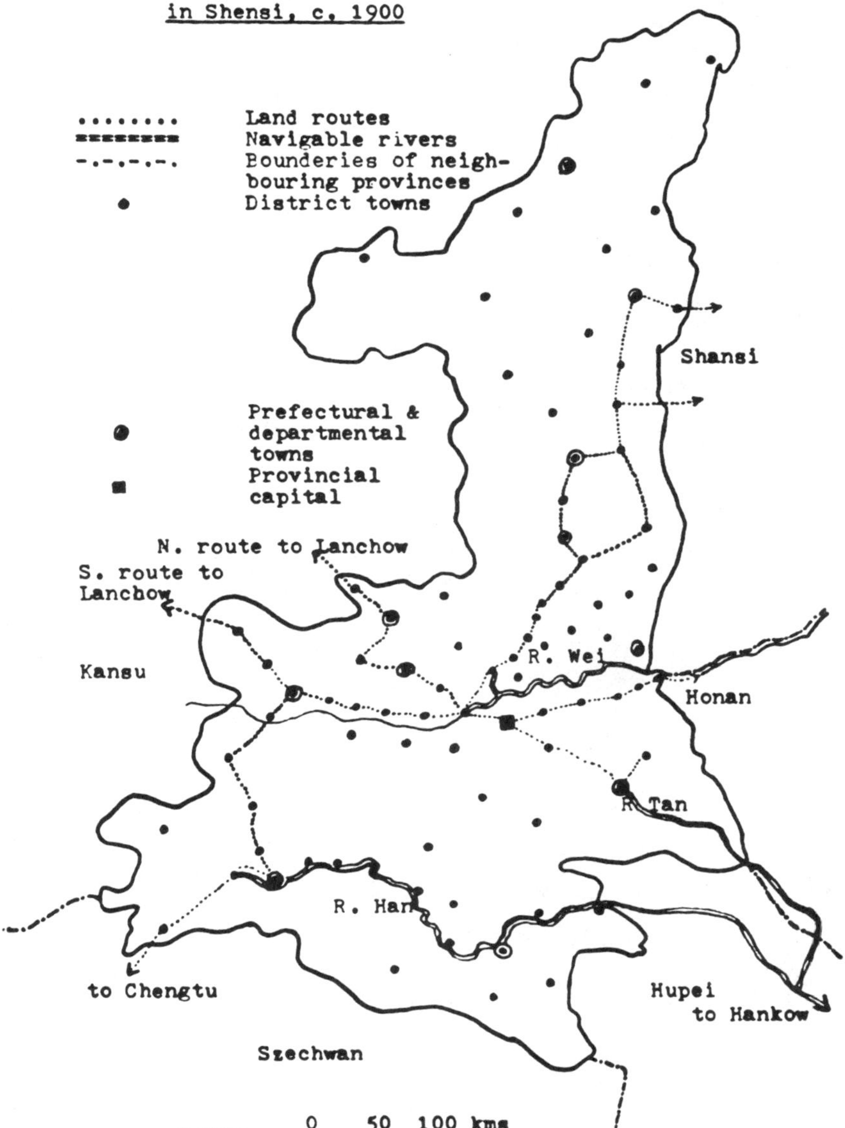

the provincial capital. The R. Wei was navigable from T'ung-kuan (56) to Hsien-yang (12) a distance of 250 km. Apart from these river connections all other transport within the province was by land; by human carrier, by pack animal or by cart. Carrying on the shoulder or pushing a wheel-barrow were the most frequently used means of transport, followed by carts (drawn by between one and eight animals), followed by pack animals (donkey, horse, mule and camel in order of capacity).[19] These were the means of transport used to bring produce to the markets of the district towns. In 1929-1933 none of the districts surveyed in Shensi reported the use of mechanical power (truck or steam boat) and we can definitely assume therefore that in 1900-1910 the means of transport were essentially as they had been for many centuries. Apart from the numerous mule tracks, the legacy of the past was visible still in the great imperial high-ways (great ruts sunk in the loess, rather than flagged roads) which linked the provincial capital to Peking and towards the west, to Lanchow. The following table summarizes time spent under average travel conditions from Sian to select centres within the province and also to major cities outside. For normal speed of travel within the province 40-50 kms. per day was the upper limit.

---

[19]See Buck (1937), pp. 351-357. Also Kingsmill (1897), pp. 29-45.

Table 9

Time Taken From Sian, c. 1900

Sian to	Feng-hsiang (29)	4 days
	Han-chung (40)	11 days
	Yenan (18)	7 days
	Yu-lin (48)	12 days
	T'ung-kuan (53)	4 days
	Peking (via T'ai-yuan)	29 days
	Hankow (via Shang-chou (78) and R. Tan	23 days
	Shanghai (via Hankow)	27 days
	Tientsin (via T'ai-yuan and Pao-t'ou)	33 days
	Chengtu (via Han-chung)	30 days
	Lanchow (via N. route)	18 days
	Lanchow (via S. route)	13 days

Two surveys are useful for supplying details on transport costs at this time. The first was undertaken in the form of a circular sent out to the members of the Royal Asiatic Society (RAS), China Branch, in 1890. The replies contain a great deal of valuable information on trade routes, transport costs etc. The second survey was done by the graduating classes of the Tōa Dōbun Shoin in their summer data-gathering tours. The Japanese students were not as interested in trade as the members of the RAS, nevertheless their data often supplements the RAS survey as it was gathered and presented in a more systemmatic form.[20]

---

[20] See Kingsmill (1897) pp. 1-214 for RAS survey and Shina shōbetsu zenshi (1918), vol. 7, part 3, pp. 141-317 for the Tōa Dōbun Shoin survey.

The following table of transport costs in terms of the amount of cash required to carry one ton for the distance of one kilometre was calculated on the basis of data drawn from the two surveys.

Table 10

Transport Costs in Shensi, c. 1900
(In Cash per Ton km.)

Human carrier (80 catties per day covering maximum of 40 km. at a charge of 350 cash) =	220 cash
Pack animal (240 catties per day covering maximum of 40 km. at a charge of 700 cash) =	140 cash
Cart (800 catties per day covering 40 km. at a charge of 1600 cash) =	100 cash
Boat (downstream, carrying between ½ and 20 tons and covering 100 km. per day) =	6 cash
Boat (upstream, carrying same amounts as downstream but covering approx. 70 km. at increased charges)	16 cash

Source: See note 20.

Ton km. are converted into kg. of grain equivalent below in the discussion of price differentials. Buck's survey data on relative transport costs was used as an independent check on the above estimates.[21] The ratios tally well with the exception of boat transport costs which are much lower than those given by Buck. The reason is probably that the Shensi estimates were based on a quotation

[21] See Buck (1937), vol. 1, pp. 352-355.

for long hauls which were much cheaper. The upstream estimate is probably nearer the truth.

It should be emphasized that the above estimates are only approximate. Transport costs varied greatly according to season, direction, type of goods etc. Another important variable was distance covered; the above rates were calculated from data for day hauls (one chan 站 or approx. 40-50 km. under Shensi conditions). Rates for longer distances would have led to slightly lower estimates.

Long-Term Grain Price Movements in Shensi

Data on long-term grain price movements in Shensi is almost totally lacking. A search through (1) gazetteers, (2) central government compendia and collections of memorials and (3) archive collections of memorials in the Palace Museum, Taipei revealed the following results. The gazetteers yielded no more than 30 quotations for the three hundred year period 1600-1900. Moreover these quotations were for disaster years. Memorial collections and central government compendia were found to contain even fewer quotations. Monthly price memorials were simply not included in such collections and compendia. The only exception being the Vermilion Endorsements and Edicts (of the Yung-cheng period, 1723-1735) which contains summaries of seven monthly price memorials from Shensi. Seven out of a total of 136 submitted from Shensi in this period. The archives in the Palace Museum,

Taipei contain 43 monthly price memorials from Shensi between approximately 1700 and 1800 but they are not yet available while the Museum's 19th century memorials have not yet been catalogued. Presumably amongst the much larger archive collections in Peking there are many thousands of price memorials and reports. These too are unavailable. The sum total of price quotations available at the present time therefore are totally inadequate for tracing long-term movements of prices.

Without further ado therefore we shall turn to the series of district town grain price reports for the years 1900-1910 which I have termed the Shensi Reports. The physical appearance of these reports has already been discussed in Chapter 3, section 1, while their institutional background was the subject of Chapter 4.

5. 2 The data

The reports from each of the 90 towns in Shensi at this time were submitted in the 25 months listed in the following table to which is appended the number of towns reporting on on each grain (for the original Chinese dates see chapter 3, table 1).

Table 11

	1900	1902	1903	1904	1905	1906	1908	1909	1910
Jan				✓					✓
Feb					✓				
March						✓			
April									
May		✓	✓					✓	
June	✓				✓		✓		
July			✓					✓	
August			✓					✓	
Sept	✓		✓		✓			✓	
Oct			✓					✓	
Nov			✓			✓		✓	
Dec			✓					✓	

Grain	Number of towns reporting
Wheat	90
Millet	88
Field peas	82
Rice	73
Barley	72
Soybeans	30
Black beans	9
Millet, proso	8
Corn	8
Buckwheat	5

All 12,000 quotations were transcribed from the reports (see reproduction of a report below)[22] but in the event the price quotations of wheat, millet, rice and field peas were selected as being those crops best represented in the reports. They were also, as we have seen, important crops in Shensi at this time. The prices of the selected grains (along with the cash/silver exchange rates were

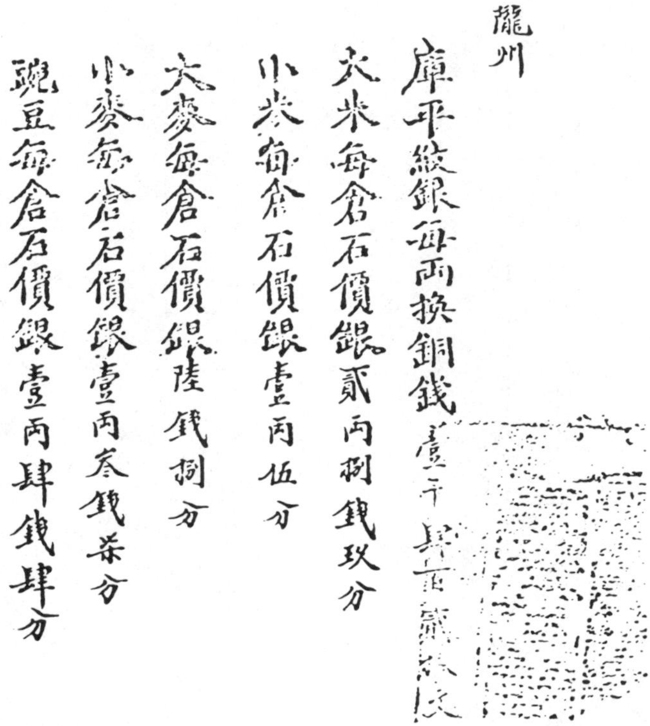
隴州
庫平紋銀每兩換銅錢壹千肆百貳拾伍
大米每倉石價銀貳兩捌錢玖分
小米每倉石價銀壹兩伍分
大麥每倉石價銀陸錢捌分
小麥每倉石價銀壹兩叁錢柒分
豌豆每倉石價銀壹兩肆錢肆分

---

[22]See Chapter 4, fig. 2 and fig. 3 for reproduction and translation of two of the Shensi Reports.

then punched onto IBM cards ready for sorting and analysis on the IBM 91/360 at the Princeton University Computing Center. Before setting out the results of this analysis three problems relating to the data remain to be discussed; the problem of weights and measures, of units of account and of different varieties and qualities of the grains.

1. Weights and Measures

Each of the 12,000 entries in the reports records prices for 'granary bushels' (ts'ang-shih 倉石). The definition of this granary bushel is appended in a note at the end of each bundle of 90 reports which was added in the yamen of the provincial treasurer. The note reads:

> In each of the reports submitted by the subordinate administrative units the granary bushel referred to is in accord with the granary peck promulgated by the Board (of Revenue). It is not the same as the old granary peck used in past years in Shensi for grain procurrance (ts'ai-mai chiu ts'ang-tou 採買舊倉斗). Seven of the old grain purveyance pecks (liang-tao chiu ts'ang-tou 糧道舊倉斗) now make up one granary bushel as used in the reports.

In other words the enlarged granary bushel (or the enlarged peck) which had come to include various additional fees in Shensi had now had these accretions removed in order to bring it into line with the standard granary bushel of the Board of Revenue. This reform was promulgated at the national level at the very beginning of this century. One reformed granary peck was now to be equal to the equivalent of 10.75 litres. Thus one reformed granary bushel (the measure used in the reports) was equal to the equivalent of 107.5 litres.[23] The only exception amongst the reports in this respect are 28 entries from the reports from Lin-t'ung (town no. 5) which record prices for 'capital tribute bushels' (<u>chin ching shih</u> 進京石). These bushels had come to include allowances for shipping and meltage charges and were therefore larger (but by differing amounts) than the standard statutory measure.[24] The Lin-t'ung quotations have been adjusted downwards to allow for the larger measure.

In order to convert granary bushels of different grains into kilograms the following steps were taken. 1 granary bushel (107.5 litres) = 3 western bushels (3 x 35 litres). Assuming one western bushel of wheat weighs 60 lbs. then one granary bushel of wheat weighs 180 lbs. or 80 kg. Since rice weighed slightly less than wheat, however, one granary bushel of rice was taken as 75 kg. Thus to convert granary bushels of wheat to metric tons, multiply by 13.3. To convert granary bushels of rice to metric tons, multiply by 12.5. All other grains were converted at the rate of 13.3 granary bushels to the ton.

2. <u>Units of Account</u>

The prices throughout the reports (with the exceptions noted in Chapter 3, section 1) were expressed in <u>Kuping</u>

---

[23] See Wu Ch'eng-lo (1957), p. 189; chart 27 facing p. 250.

[24] See Wu Ch'eng-lo (1957), p. 189.

taels. The note at the end of each bundle of 90 reports states that all prices were converted from 'market taels' (shih-p'ing 市平 i.e. shih-p'ing liang 市平兩) to the standard treasury or accounting unit, the Kuping tael. What the note does not state however is that the original prices, as we saw in Chapter 4, were collected as retail prices in terms of cash. To have said so in the reports would have been to have stated the obvious. Moreover each report also included the monthly C/S rate for each place. In Chapter 2 we saw that one of the characteristic features of the Chinese monetary system was that the C/S rates were not in fixed ratio and thus prices in terms of cash did not move in harmony with prices in terms of silver. An example taken at random from the Shensi reports illustrates the point:

Place/Month	Price in taels (per bushel of wheat)	Price in Cash (per bushel of wheat)
30/20	3.60	4112
31/20	3.60	4248
54/20	3.60	4612
44/19	3.60	5436

Were we only to look at the column of prices in taels we would receive the erroneous impression that the price of one bushel of wheat in all four district towns was the same. When the quotations in taels are adjusted back to their original form as prices in terms of cash (by multiplying each quotation by the C/S rate of that month and place) we immediately see that this was very far from being the case; wheat prices in these places differed substantially.

We see this phenomenon more systematically illustrated in Table 12, in which typical prices of one granary bushel of wheat from all 90 district towns are ranked in terms of cash and <u>taels</u>. Although there is a certain degree of matching there are also some large discontinuities. The provincial capital for example, ranks 54th highest for <u>tael</u> price of wheat but 28th highest for cash price of wheat. Town 89 ranks 82nd for <u>tael</u> price of wheat but 32nd for cash price. In both the provincial capital and in town 89 the purchasing power of <u>taels</u> was very high. Other things being equal wherever the purchasing power of <u>taels</u> was high (i.e. in those places characterized as forming high plateaus of C/S rates in Chapter 3) the cash price of commodities was correspondingly high. This was a period as we saw in Chapter 2 when cash was depreciating more rapidly than <u>taels</u>; prices expressed in <u>taels</u> therefore tend to appear more steady than in fact they were, for differentials were absorbed in the fluctuating C/S rates.

Prices in terms of <u>taels</u> were a convenient abstraction for any budgeting or accounting (such as that of the government) which had to straddle many different localities each with its differing cash currency.[25] From the point of view of the urban dweller or peasant however it was the cash price

---

[25]See <u>Kao-tsung shih-lu</u> (1745), <u>chüan</u> 16, p. 17 for the comments of the Emperor Ch'ien-lung on the conveniences of <u>taels</u> as opposed to cash as a unit of account for the government.

Table 12

Cash	Places	Rank	Places	Tael
6215	44	1	44	4.50
5719	27	2	27	4.18
5365	45	3	80	3.87
4977	80	4	78	3.79
4943	63	5	63	3.68
4831	23	6	45	3.37
4767	78	7	39	3.36
4731	38	8	43	3.15
4696	88	9	69	3.12
4502	39	10	38	3.03
4311	37	11	42	3.02
4297	79	12	88	2.96
4272	18	13	51	2.94
4269	2	14	1	2.91
4229	69	15	40	2.88
4153	1	16	24	2.87
4124	43	17	16	2.84
4109	40	18	41	2.84
4080	41	19	11	2.76
3751	24	20	37	2.72
3645	42	21	52	2.72
3499	50	22	65	2.70
3494	51	23	79	2.68
3413	87	24	23	2.67
3399	11	25	2	2.66
3290	16	26	19	2.60
3286	65	27	61	2.55
3267	3	28	17	2.53
3248	52	29	49	2.52
3224	70	30	48	2.51
3208	61	31	64	2.50
3208	89	32	18	2.43
3159	82	33	46	2.39
3147	64	34	53	2.37
3098	74	35	50	2.33
3094	49	36	81	2.33
3042	26	37	82	2.32
3041	25	38	68	2.30
3033	68	39	47	2.30
3017	81	40	7	2.25
2968	46	41	87	2.24
2915	17	42	85	2.20
2915	19	43	26	2.18
2888	48	44	36	2.16
2861	53	45	15	2.16
2854	47	46	70	2.16
2817	67	47	67	2.14
2707	7	48	74	2.13
2696	90	49	77	2.13
2657	85	50	54	2.11
2613	66	51	13	2.08
2558	77	52	76	2.04
2521	54	53	5	2.03
2484	15	54	3	2.02
2481	36	55	66	2.02
2479	5	56	75	1.99
2415	13	57	14	1.98
2374	4	58	4	1.98
2340	14	59	8	1.94
2326	75	60	90	1.91
2315	76	61	33	1.90
2285	33	62	22	1.88
2275	8	63	25	1.85
2259	22	64	12	1.84
2245	12	65	30	1.84
2216	34	66	34	1.80
2210	71	67	60	1.78
2180	60	68	32	1.77
2170	32	69	71	1.76
2169	62	70	83	1.75
2151	30	71	6	1.71
2140	58	72	58	1.70
2105	28	73	31	1.68
2090	83	74	9	1.66
2037	86	75	56	1.65
2010	21	76	86	1.65
1988	6	77	62	1.59
1977	31	78	73	1.58
1927	56	79	29	1.55
1921	73	80	35	1.54
1850	9	81	28	1.53
1829	55	82	89	1.53
1797	35	83	55	1.52
1787	29	84	59	1.49
1768	59	85	10	1.48
1746	10	86	21	1.46
1708	72	87	57	1.45
1692	57	88	72	1.45
1682	84	89	84	1.38
1547	20	90	20	1.31

Typical prices of wheat per granary bushel in cash and in taels ranked in 90 district towns, Shensi, 1900-1910

Source: Shensi Reports

which directly affected his standard of living, not the accounting price in taels. Accordingly I have adjusted all quotations back into terms of cash by multiplying each quotation by its appropriate C/S rate (tael price of wheat times cash price of taels equals cash price of wheat). For purposes of comparisons between price levels in different places however I have used the tael quotation on the assumption that taels being much more easily transported were much more likely to have a more uniform value than cash which was so heavy as to make transport almost prohibitively expensive.[26] The cash quotations are useful for reference purposes and also for assessing changes over time.

3. Varieties and Qualities of Grains

All of the grains in Shensi were grown in many different varieties and qualities. Although differentials in prices with respect to different grades of grain form one important aspect of agricultural price analysis we simply do not have the information for this type of analysis. This lack is not as serious as it might seem perhaps in view of the fact that medium grades (see Chapter 4, note 6) were supposed to be stored, not fancy grades. As a result

---

[26] 280 strings of cash weighed approximately one ton, see Chapter 2, note 9.

the prices recorded were presumably for medium grades. Since the Chinese language has different nouns for the grains in their husked and unhusked state there is also no confusion between prices for husked and unhusked grains. Prices in the reports were for husked grains. The uniformity of the documents from which the price quotations were drawn insures some degree of uniformity in the prices themselves (in the present case, as we saw in Chapter 4, the prices were retail selling prices in markets within or serving the district towns). This uniformity of the documents also introduced uniformity as regards measures and units of account; the same held true we may infer, but to a lesser extent, with regard to the varieties and qualities of each grain whose price was recorded.

5.3 Price Differentials Between Places

In this section the price quotations of wheat, rice, millet and field peas from each town are examined in order to establish the degree to which there existed in Shensi at this time an articulated grain market for any of these grains either coterminous with the province or within any part of it. The criteria used for assessing the degree of articulation are as follows:

1. The major producing areas of any of the four crops should have lower price levels for those crops than any of the other areas. Prices moving away from the producing areas should rise as a function of transport costs over the distance from those areas.

2. Major consumption centres should have higher price levels than the surrounding towns if these were on transport routes. Prices in these towns should decline as the distance between them and the centre grows.

3. Price differentials between nearby towns should not be larger than the transport costs between them.

Typical Prices

The same methods of data analysis as used for the C/S rates were used for the grain price quotations and for the same reasons (see Chapter 3, note 7). Each quotation was arranged on a two-way table by months (in columns) and by places (in rows). Month effects and place effects were calculated and taken out. Next a value typical of the data as a whole was calculated and removed leaving a series of residuals for each place in each month.[27] Thus the residual of a given place in a given month + place effect of that place + month effect of that month + general effect = original price of that place in that month. Place effect of a given place + general effect = price typical of that place in all months. The weights calculated in the first part of this chapter were done so on the basis of a price typical of all places in all months i.e. the general effect. The typical

[27]The original data and two-way table elementary analysis may be found in the appendices to this chapter.

prices, which are the basis of the discussion that follows, are prices typical of a given place in all months and were obtained in the manner described above.

(i) Wheat

As the single most important crop in Shensi (accounting for 48% of all food crops in tons of wheat equivalent or 39% of all crops,(see Table 5) wheat prices are dealt with first. Typical prices of wheat in terms of cash and taels per bushel for the 90 district towns of Shensi are arranged by place number in Table 13. The testing of the above criteria is based (for the wheat market) on the data summarized in this table. The argument is graphically presented (for wheat) on maps 3, 4 and 5.

The major producing area for wheat was in the Wei valley (broadly zone A).[28] Averaging of typical prices by zone (see Map 3) shows that the price level of wheat in terms of taels in the north and in the south (zones B and C) was almost equal at 2.85 in marked contrast to the lower average typical prices in the wheat producing areas of the Wei valley at 1.89. These averages for whole zones however tend to obscure significant discontinuities. For example the 15 towns in the far south have a price level of 2.71

[28] See Shina shōbetsu zenshi (1943) (SSZ,2), p. 592.

Table 13

Typical prices of one granary bushel of wheat in cash and in taels, 90 district towns, Shensi, 1900-1910

Place	Price in cash	Price in taels	Place	Price in cash	Price in taels
1.	4253	2.91	46.	3068	2.39
2.	4369	2.66	47.	2954	2.30
3.	3367	2.02	48.	2988	2.51
4.	2474	1.98	49.	3194	2.52
5.	2579	2.03	50.	3599	2.33
6.	2088	1.71	51.	3594	2.94
7.	2807	2.25	52.	3348	2.72
8.	2375	1.94	53.	2961	2.37
9.	1950	1.66	54.	2621	2.11
10.	1846	1.48	55.	1929	1.52
11.	3499	2.76	56.	2027	1.65
12.	2345	1.84	57.	1792	1.45
13.	2515	2.08	58.	2240	1.70
14.	2440	1.98	59.	1868	1.49
15.	2584	2.16	60.	2280	1.78
16.	3390	2.84	61.	3308	2.55
17.	3015	2.53	62.	2269	1.59
18.	4372	2.43	63.	5043	3.68
19.	3015	2.60	64.	3247	2.50
20.	1647	1.31	65.	3386	2.70
21.	2110	1.46	66.	2713	2.02
22.	2359	1.88	67.	2917	2.14
23.	4931	2.67	68.	3133	2.30
24.	3851	2.87	69.	4339	3.12
25.	3141	1.85	70.	3334	2.16
26.	3142	2.18	71.	2310	1.76
27.	5819	4.18	72.	1808	1.45
28.	2205	1.53	73.	2021	1.58
29.	1887	1.55	74.	3198	2.13
30.	2251	1.84	75.	2426	1.99
31.	2077	1.68	76.	2415	2.04
32.	2270	1.77	77.	2658	2.13
33.	2385	1.90	78.	4867	3.79
34.	2316	1.80	79.	4397	2.68
35.	1897	1.54	80.	5077	3.87
36.	2581	2.16	81.	3117	2.33
37.	4411	2.72	82.	3259	2.32
38.	4831	3.03	83.	2190	1.75
39.	4602	3.36	84.	1782	1.38
40.	4209	2.88	85.	2757	2.20
41.	4180	2.84	86.	2137	1.65
42.	3745	3.02	87.	3513	2.24
43.	4224	3.15	88.	4796	2.96
44.	6315	4.50	89.	3308	1.53
45.	5465	3.37	90.	2796	1.91

Source: Shensi Reports

Map 3

Wheat price zones in Shensi, 1900-10

Source: Shensi Reports

while the towns lying between them and the centre (on the approaches to and in the Ch'in-ling mountains have an average of 2.91. This ridge of high prices indicates that there was no movement of wheat from centre to south. The same holds true of the north; although the towns in the extreme north had higher levels than those nearer the centre (average of 2.86 compared with 2.25) upon closer scrutiny we find many troughs and ridges in the price lines indicating a break in the possible flow of wheat from centre to north. This becomes clearer if the typical prices in the towns on the transport routes to the north are listed (see also Table 14 for transport costs per granary bushel km.).

Places (going north)	Prices
10.	1.48
11.	2.76
86.	1.65
85.	2.20
84.	1.38
83.	1.75
19.	2.60
18.	2.43
22.	1.88

By the time we have passed place 85 we have already entered a different price zone. The type of continuity called for by the second part of criterion one, that prices should rise in direct proportion to the distance from the major producing centres, is not fulfilled. Without testing the other criteria we can therefore conclude that there was at this time in Shensi no province wide wheat market.

Although it would be possible to test the criteria for each zone within the province I decided to select zone A for wheat and zone B for rice, as being the production centres for these crops, and also those zones best served by cheap transport facilities. If we find no trace of a grain market larger than a single town and its hinterland in these zones then it is unlikely that the northern part of the province (zone C) will be any different in this respect. We now turn therefore to the examination of the wheat markets in the 44 towns of Zone A.

Zone A has been divided into seven sub-zones (see Map 4) with the major consumption centre, the provincial capital, in the middle. The price level is highest in the middle (2.15), declines in the two sub-zones on either side of the middle (2.03 and 2.05) and declines still further in the sub-zones beyond (1.70 and 1.82). In the sub-zones to the north and north-west levels are 1.77 and 1.73. Zone A therefore falls into three well-defined groups of sub-zones; (1) the middle, (2) the two near sides and (3) the two far sides and the northern sub-groups. The first part of criterion two is satisfied but we must now test the correlation between the distance from the consumption centre and declining price level in greater detail.

Map 5 shows in schematic form towns on major transport routes leading to Sian, the distances between them, C/S rates and prices of one granary bushel of wheat in cash and in <u>taels</u> in each of them.

Map 4

Wheat prices in centres of wheat production, Shensi, 1900-1910

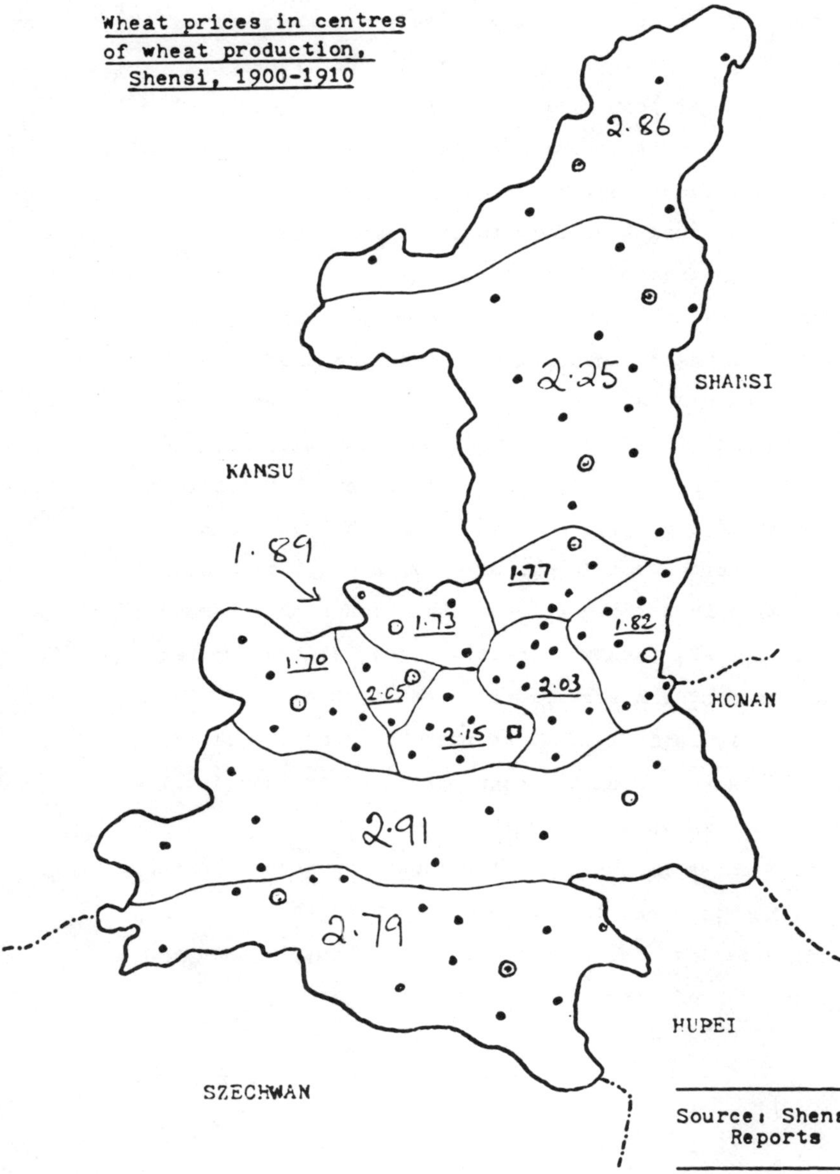

Source: Shensi Reports

Map 5

Typical prices of one granary bushel of wheat in cash and in taels in towns on major routes to Sian, c. 1900

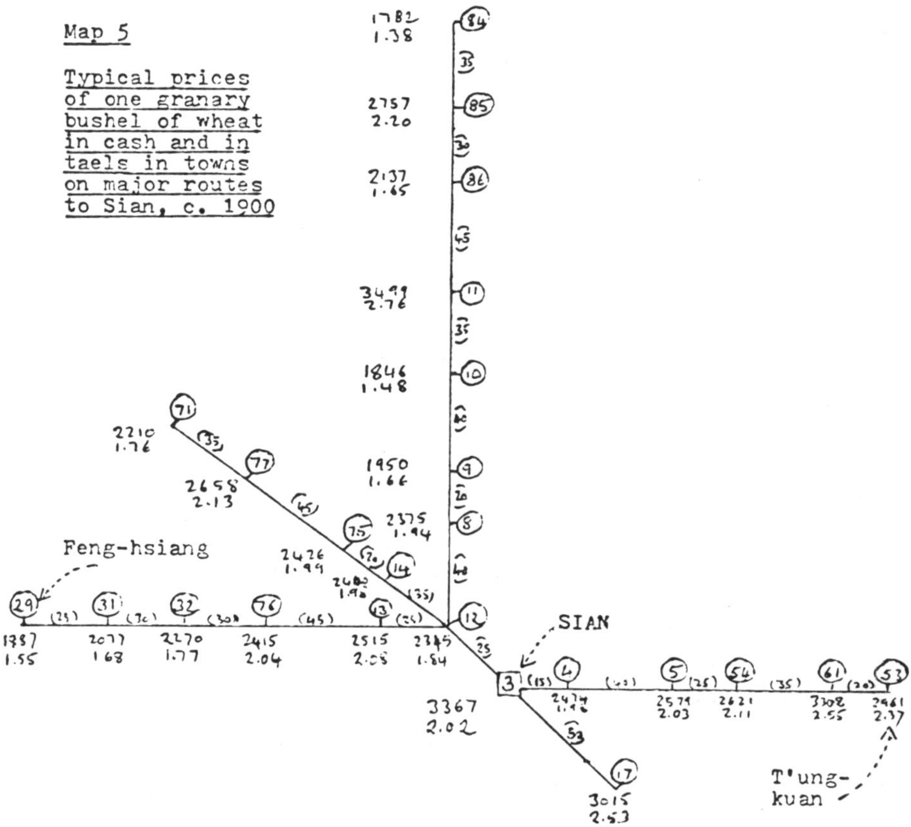

Key

(4) town number
(40) km.
(5) town number

2474 price in cash
1.98 price in taels

Source: Shensi Reports

Moving in towards Sian from Feng-hsiang (29) prices rise gradually as far as Hsing-p'ing (13) then fall at Hsien-yang (12) only to rise again at Sian. Moving in towards Sian from Pin-chou (71) prices rise then fall all the way to Hsien-yang (12). Moving south from Lo-ch'uan (84) prices rise and fall alternately to Ching-yang (8) then fall to Hsien-yang. Moving towards Sian from T'ung-kuan (53) prices rise then fall from Hua-yin (54) all the way to Lin-t'ung (5) before rising to Sian. Thus Sian was open to supply from Hsien-yang (12) as well as from Lin-t'ung (4), both of whose prices were lower than those in Sian. None of the other places beyond were in a position to supply Sian with wheat owing to the ridge of high prices at towns 13, 14, 8 and 5. The major city in the province was supplied with its most important staple from a market area with a radius of about 25 km. around it.

The wheat market in Shensi far from being coterminous with the boundaries of the province or even with the limits of one of the zones within the province was not even as large as the sub-zone which contained the major consumption centre. With regard to its wheat market the largest city in the province was no different from the smallest town in that the market areas of both were confined to their immediate neighbourhoods. This statement must now be tested for the towns in the Sian plain using criterion three.

Criterion three, that price differentials between near-by towns should not be larger than the transport costs between them, is easily tested. The average difference between C/S rates in towns within the neighbourhood of the capital was very small; only 40 cash (see Map 5). Only the provincial capital stood out from the other towns, for reasons explained in Chapter 3, with a C/S rate 400 cash higher. As a consequence of the near uniformity of C/S rates amongst these towns quotations for wheat in cash showed very similar differentials as quotations in taels and for this reason I have calculated transport costs in taels only. The average difference between wheat prices in taels was .13 if we exclude those towns (beyond 10, beyond 54 and 17) which stood sharply differentiated from their neighbours. The average differential from 3 to 4 to 5 was only .05 taels, no doubt a reflection of the use of the cheap river transport available here (see Map 2). None of the differentials between these towns was larger than the transport costs between them, even by the most expensive means of transport, human carrier (see Table 14 below).

Table 14

Transport Costs per Granary Bushel of Wheat in Taels Over Selected Distances

Distance (km.)	5	10	15	20	30	40	50
Human carrier	.062	.12	.196	.25	.37	.49	.62
Pack animal	.039	.078	.12	.16	.23	.31	.39
Cart	.028	.056	.084	.11	.17	.23	.28
Boat	.005	.01	.015	.02	.03	.04	.05

Source: Calculated from data in Table 10 (converted at province typical C/S rate of 1345).

Criterion three is fulfilled in that the differentials between C/S rates and prices of wheat in towns for 180 km. to the west, for 160 km. to the north-west, for 85 km. to the north and for 55 km. to the east of Sian were not greater than the transport costs between those towns. We may conclude that although there was no long distance trade supplying the major consumption centre (as we saw from the non-fulfillment of criterion two) there was sufficient trade over short hauls between these towns to create a single price region somewhat smaller than the entire zone but nevertheless larger than any of the sub-zones with which we began. Demand for wheat within these towns was largely met by the supply available in their neighbourhoods; each was a centre of consumption to be sure but each was also its own centre of production.

One important consideration has been omitted from the previous argument which has been based entirely on typical prices extracted from an incomplete series covering ten years. Stability of price levels over time should be tested to see if major producing regions showed greater stability than major consumption centres. Movements of price levels over time are also an important part of any price analysis for price regions are liable to change yearly or even monthly largely as the result of variations in production.[29] Unfortunately however I have not been able

---

[29]See Shepherd (1963), pp. 214-217.

to find a way to make comparisons over time and for the following reasons. The price quotations were taken from incomplete data; the longest unbroken series of months (from 1909-1910) only covers a portion of the harvest year (see Table 11). Other months for which we have quotations in the Shensi Reports are in scattered years over the previous decade. It is hard to see any way to calculate even annual averages and at the same time allow for seasonal fluctuation, on the basis of the Shensi data. When we consider the problem of monthly changes we must also remember that although the prices collected were market prices the whole object of collecting them was to prevent monthly fluctuation by selling grain cheaply before the harvest and buying it at slightly higher prices after the harvest. Even granted that these activities were only 50% effective their result would have been to minimize monthly and seasonal changes in price levels. For these reasons I have not attempted to test the degree of change over time in price zones. I have assumed that since each month each grain was reported on by the same number of towns the typical prices used in the analysis so far do reflect typical price levels in the different towns. The difficulties of measuring seasonal change are perhaps suggested by the plot of month effects for each of the 25 months over all 90 towns which was calculated for wheat prices (see fig. 1). Apart from the enormous rise in prices as the result of the province wide droughts of 1899, 1900 and 1901 (see first three points on plot representing 1900/5,

fig. 1 Plot of month effects of wheat prices (taels)

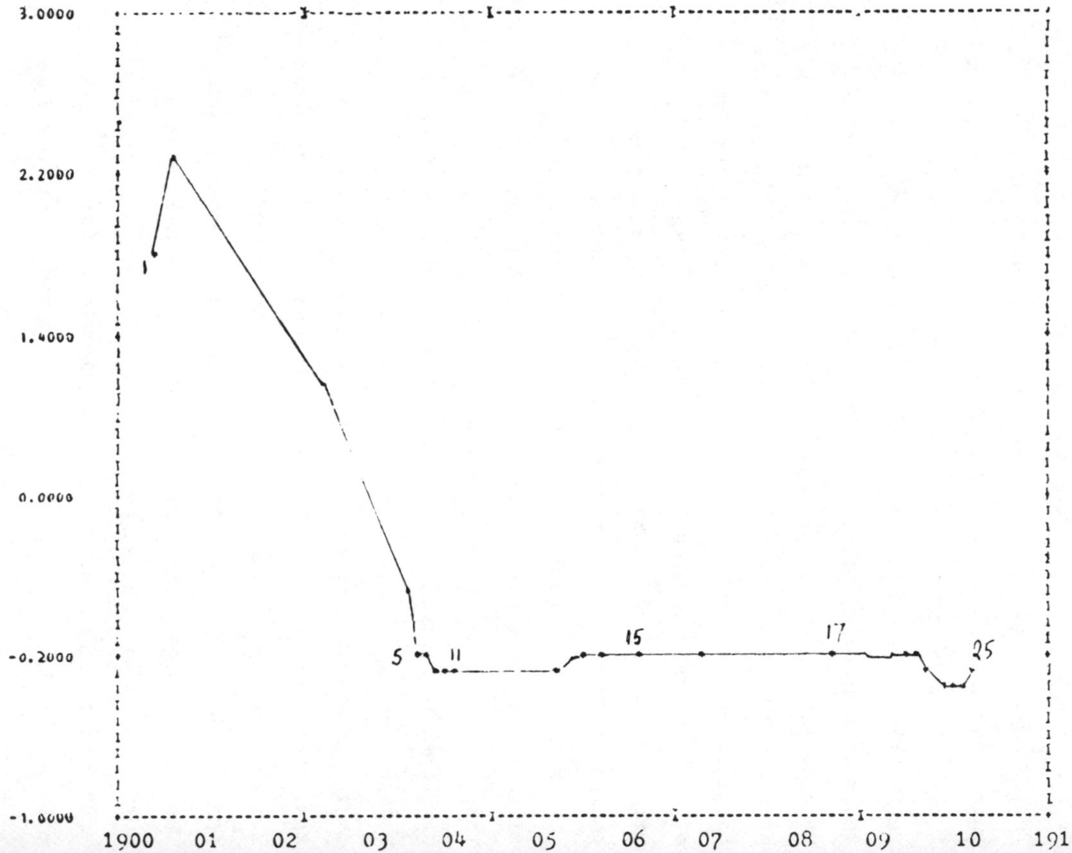

1900/8 and 1902/4) the month effects show little or no change over the remainder of the months. Plots of month effects for the other grains are substantially the same and are therefore not reproduced.

Before drawing further conclusions as to the nature of the Shensi grain market we must turn to the examination of typical prices of the second most important crop in the province, rice (accounting for 22% of food crops in kw/p/y or 18% of all crops in kw/p/y, see Table 5).

(ii) Rice

Seventy-three out of ninety towns reported on rice prices. Typical rice prices for these towns are given in cash and in taels in Table 15. The argument which follows is based on these typical prices which are summed up graphically in Maps 6 and 7.

The major producing area for rice was zone B centered on the Han valley. The secondary producing area was zone A while zone C produced practically no rice since it had for the most part too dry and cold a climate. Only 11 out of the 23 towns in zone C reported on rice prices. Rice in these towns was imported from the centre of the province in very small quantities.

Average typical prices in each zone are presented in Map 6. As we should suspect the highest prices were in the north, 4.70 taels and 4.33 taels. Lowest prices were in the south (zone B) which had an overall average of 3.38 taels.

Table 15

Typical prices of one granary bushel of rice in cash and in taels, 90 district towns, Shensi, 1900-1910

Place	Price in cash	Price in taels	Place	Price in cash	Price in taels
1.	4462	3.05	46.	5250	4.14
2.	6160	3.73	47.	6341	4.96
3.	6026	3.57	48.	3721	3.14
4.	--	--	49.	5076	3.87
5.	5181	4.13	50.	6196	4.06
6.	2607	2.17	51.	5415	4.43
7.	7189	5.88	52.	6505	5.30
8.	5072	4.18	53.	6477	5.19
9.	4402	3.77	54.	4455	3.54
10.	3503	2.90	55.	3942	3.13
11.	5446	4.41	56.	3948	3.25
12.	4261	3.41	57.	5617	4.51
13.	4930	3.29	58.	5727	4.30
14.	3813	3.17	59.	--	--
15.	3203	2.72	60.	5294	4.17
16.	5414	4.66	61.	5739	4.48
17.	4253	3.54	62.	4379	3.11
18.	--	--	63.	4849	3.67
19.	--	--	64.	4014	3.12
20.	--	--	65.	4872	3.10
21.	--	--	66.	3172	2.35
22.	4881	4.04	67.	4841	3.50
23.	--	--	68.	3555	2.61
24.	--	--	69.	4736	3.41
25.	11,647	6.66	70.	4455	2.89
26.	--	--	71.	5573	4.42
27.	10,603	7.40	72.	2840	2.30
28.	4955	3.41	73.	3485	2.79
29.	3906	2.53	74.	6468	4.28
30.	3397	2.84	75.	--	--
31.	3214	2.65	76.	3618	3.09
32.	3664	2.90	77.	--	--
33.	3213	2.62	78.	6666	5.05
34.	4124	3.22	79.	5857	3.55
35.	--	--	80.	6632	5.01
36.	3501	2.93	81.	5017	3.75
37.	5866	3.61	82.	4814	3.37
38.	7097	4.41	83.	4815	3.89
39.	5343	3.93	84.	--	--
40.	5377	3.66	85.	4156	3.29
41.	5476	3.75	86.	3695	2.76
42.	4526	3.64	87.	--	--
43.	5073	3.81	88.	--	--
44.	8304	5.98	89.	--	--
45.	5689	3.49	90.	--	--

Source: Shensi Reports

Map 6

Rice prices in

Shensi, 1900-10

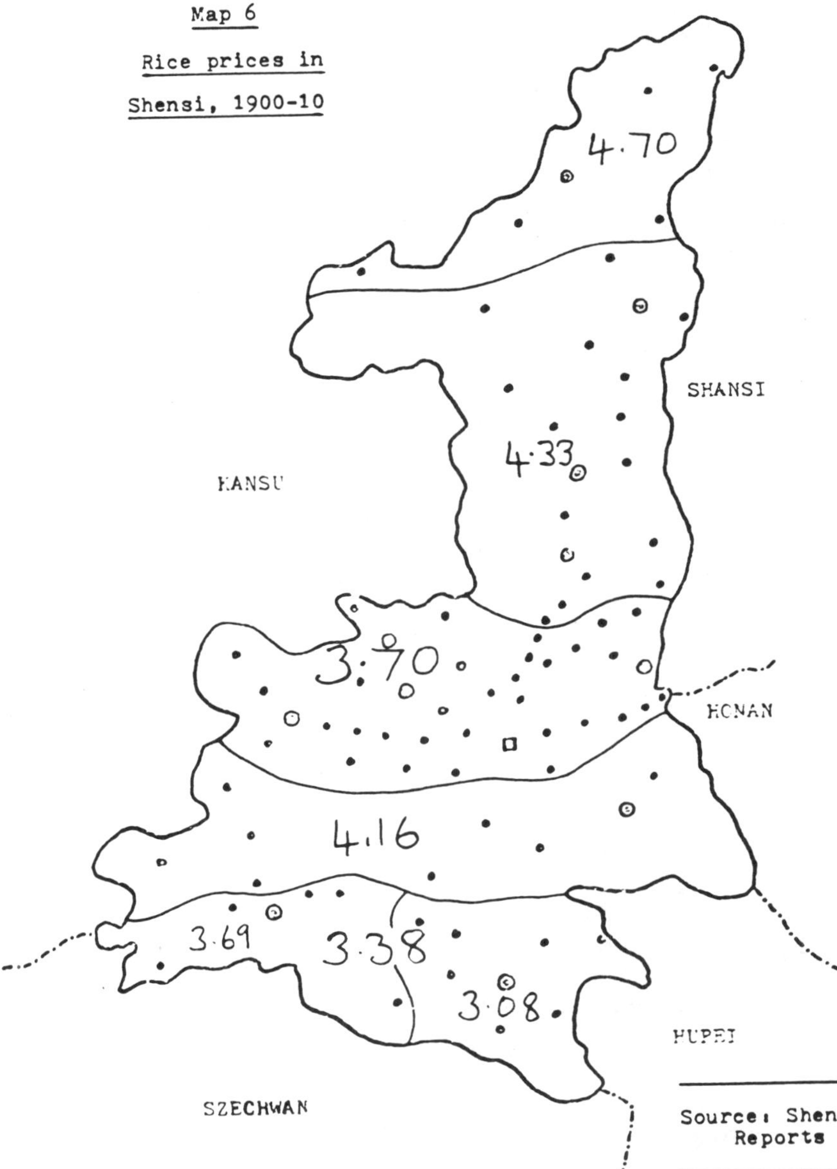

Source: Shensi Reports

In the towns in the Ch'in-ling range prices rose to 4.16 taels while in zone A, the secondary producing area, the average was the second lowest in the province, 3.70 taels. As in the case of wheat we find that the first part of criterion one is satisfied, prices in major producing areas are lower than in all other areas and also, as in the case of wheat, we find the second part of criterion one is not satisfied; prices moving away from the major production centres do not rise as a function of transport costs over the distances from those centres. This may be seen for example in the prices of rice in the towns along the major transport route from the south through the Ch'in-ling range to the centre:

Place	Price
44	5.98
36	2.93
47	4.96
30	2.84

It may also be seen in the prices of rice in the towns along the main route from the centre of the province to the north:

Place	Price
10	2.90
11	4.41
86	2.76
85	3.29
84	--
83	3.89
19	--

We may conclude as we did in the case of wheat that these price zones over the whole province imply different supply and demand conditions in the different zones rather than a well-integrated market covering the whole province. In the case of rice however not only is this true of the entire province but it is also true even of the major rice producing zone, to the analysis of whose prices we now turn.

Typical rice prices in towns in the Han valley close to the river Han are summarized, with distances between them in schematic form in Map 7 below.

Map 7

Typical Rice Prices in Towns Along R. Han

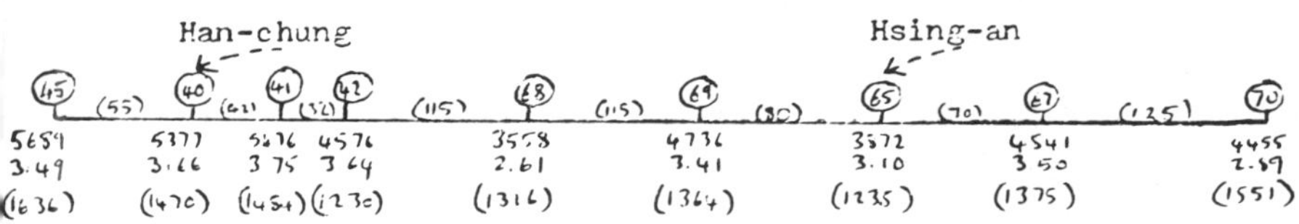

town number: (45) km.: (55) C/S rate: (1636)

price in cash: 5659 price in taels: 3.49

Source: Shensi Reports

The chief production and collection point for the upper Han valley was the prefectural city of Han-chung (40) while the chief production and collection point for the lower Han valley was the prefectural city of Hsing-an (65). The typical rice price levels in these two cities as well as the price levels in the other cities along the Han show few consistent relations with neighbouring towns. In the case of Han-chung, 55 km. to the west at Mien (45) the price level was lower; 42 km. to the east at Ch'ien-ku the price level was higher. Going down the river prices fell to 3.64

at Yang (42) but south of the river at Hsi-hsiang, the second most important production centre in the upper Han valley, the price level was even higher at 3.81. The lowest prices were at Shih-ch'uan (68) a town not noted for its rice production which stood moreover incongruously between the higher price levels of Yang (42) and Tzu-yang (69), 115 km. to the west and east respectively. Hsing-an (65) had lower prices than either the next town upstream or the next town downstream. It is possible therefore that criterion one is fulfilled for Hsing-an which as a major production centre had lower prices than the neighbouring towns while in the case of Han-chung this criterion is fulfilled as far as the next town downstream is concerned. Although a few towns did have price differentials lower than the transport costs between them (criterion three) none of the differentials were lower than river transport costs; few were lower than cart transport costs and most were only lower than pack animal transport costs. It is hard to avoid the conclusion that little rice can have flowed between the towns for all lay on the river Han, which, as we have seen (Map 2), was navigable for most of the year; thus each town was its own production centre and the rice market was coterminous only with the area surrounding each town.

Turning to rice price differentials in zone A we find a much more structured market:

Place	Price
29	2.53
31	2.65
32	2.90
76	3.09
13	3.29
12	3.41
3	3.57

Price levels rise step by step all the way from Feng-hsiang (29) to Sian (3); they also rise by steps from Li-ch'uan (14) to Hsien-yang (12) to Sian (from 3.17 to 3.14 to 3.57 taels) as well as rising from Lan-t'ien (17) to Sian (from 3.54 to 3.57 taels). With the exception of the Lan-t'ien/ Sian differentials the remainder show strong correlations with cart and pack animal transport costs. We conclude that the provincial capital rice market was much more extensive than its wheat market and as we shall see much more extensive than its market for millet or field peas. Throughout the province the largest marketing area that we have found so far for any crop was for a luxury staple, namely rice, which, in the areas where it was a normal staple (zone B) had markets not much larger than the hinterlands of the towns which produced it.

(iii) Millet and Field Peas[30]

Typical prices of millet are given in Table 16,

---

[30]Field peas (wan-tou 豌豆) were by no means the most important legume grown in Shensi. They were used approximately half and half for human consumption and animal feed. Grown as a winter crop they were often interplanted with wheat or barley, harvested at the same time and ground together with them into a meal. See Buck (1937), vol. 2, p. 66. Unfortunately the Shensi Reports only cover prices of the various types of soybean (a much more important legume than field peas) in a fragmentary manner (see Table 11).

Table 16

Typical prices of one granary bushel of millet in cash and in taels, 90 district towns, Shensi, 1900-1910

Place	Price in cash	Price in taels	Place	Price in cash	Price in taels
1.	3667	2.49	46.	2870	2.21
2.	4505	2.71	47.	3075	2.35
3.	3245	1.94	48.	2436	2.07
4.	2562	2.19	49.	3345	2.47
5.	2995	2.37	50.	3464	2.26
6.	2264	1.85	51.	2844	2.35
7.	3285	2.65	52.	2813	2.29
8.	2398	1.97	53.	3041	2.42
9.	2031	1.72	54.	3056	2.42
10.	1909	1.53	55.	2316	1.83
11.	2420	1.91	56.	2218	1.80
12.	2434	1.89	57.	2057	1.65
13.	2903	2.44	58.	2355	1.77
14.	2599	2.09	59.	2058	1.64
15.	2319	1.93	60.	2403	1.86
16.	3379	2.83	61.	3273	2.51
17.	3024	2.48	62.	1944	1.36
18.	3905	2.13	63.	--	--
19.	2454	2.11	64.	2807	2.17
20.	1593	1.25	65.	2786	2.22
21.	2117	1.42	66.	1688	1.26
22.	2118	1.80	67.	2135	1.54
23.	3806	2.12	68.	--	--
24.	2511	1.86	69.	2250	1.65
25.	2804	1.65	70.	3668	2.36
26.	2764	1.90	71.	2308	1.73
27.	4384	3.03	72.	1419	1.13
28.	2133	1.45	73.	1948	1.52
29.	2067	1.69	74.	2969	1.98
30.	2708	2.19	75.	2448	2.01
31.	2153	1.72	76.	2418	2.02
32.	2509	1.94	77.	2513	2.00
33.	2552	2.01	78.	5355	4.10
34.	2342	1.80	79.	3568	2.16
35.	1843	1.49	80.	4861	3.70
36.	2394	2.03	81.	3481	2.60
37.	3936	1.83	82.	4220	2.98
38.	3876	2.44	83.	2212	1.76
39.	3693	2.70	84.	1693	1.30
40.	3636	2.44	85.	2720	2.15
41.	4024	2.68	86.	1724	1.30
42.	4057	3.27	87.	3462	2.23
43.	3514	2.61	88.	4803	2.95
44.	4364	3.05	89.	3877	1.78
45.	4335	2.69	90.	2854	1.98

Source: Shensi Reports

Table 17

Typical prices of one granary bushel of field peas in cash and in taels, 90 district towns, Shensi, 1900-10

Place	Price in cash	Price in taels	Place	Price in cash	Price in taels
1.	4016	2.72	46.	2521	1.94
2.	—	—	47.	2806	2.15
3.	2795	1.67	48.	--	--
4.	2181	1.78	49.	--	--
5.	2664	2.08	50.	2962	1.96
6.	1903	1.55	51.	--	--
7.	3015	2.42	52.	--	--
8.	2456	2.01	53.	2874	2.28
9.	2090	1.76	54.	2337	1.86
10.	1954	1.56	55.	1751	1.38
11.	4415	1.46	56.	1895	1.52
12.	2204	1.72	57.	1821	1.44
13.	2659	2.19	58.	--	--
14.	2328	1.90	59.	1946	1.55
15.	2018	1.67	60.	2337	1.81
16.	2537	2.10	61.	2774	1.79
17.	2152	1.76	62.	2295	1.58
18.	4398	2.36	63.	3554	2.58
19.	—	—	64.	1996	1.51
20.	1637	1.29	65.	2485	1.96
21.	2177	1.48	66.	1807	1.31
22.	2047	1.71	67.	2171	1.58
23.	4455	2.40	68.	2343	1.69
24.	2259	1.68	69.	2351	1.68
25.	3811	2.19	70.	2611	1.69
26.	3184	2.23	71.	2543	1.93
27.	5066	3.61	72.	1698	1.35
28.	2594	1.75	73.	2097	1.66
29.	1884	1.54	74.	3752	2.46
30.	1910	1.54	75.	2353	1.93
31.	1949	1.57	76.	2168	1.81
32.	2233	1.71	77.	3184	2.55
33.	2176	1.71	78.	3501	2.68
34.	2568	1.96	79.	2707	1.64
35.	2000	1.60	80.	3192	2.41
36.	2830	2.36	81.	3071	2.30
37.	3069	1.87	82.	2620	1.83
38.	--	--	83.	1789	1.42
39.	3828	2.78	84.	1458	1.11
40.	3480	2.33	85.	2057	1.65
41.	3236	2.14	86.	2067	1.55
42.	2884	2.32	87.	3643	2.35
43.	3681	2.73	88.	4066	2.50
44.	4201	3.03	89.	3692	1.64
45.	4189	2.58	90.	2469	1.64

Source: Shensi Reports

typical prices of field peas in Table 17. Neither crop was grown for the market to the extent that wheat and rice were. I decided therefore to select only one area to examine their prices in any detail, namely the greater Sian plain. Typical prices of both millet and field peas are presented graphically on the next page.

Unlike the price levels for wheat and rice, the millet and field pea price levels of Sian were lower than those of Lin-t'ung (4) and Lan-t'ien (17) to the east and south-east. The field pea price level in Sian was also lower than in neighbouring towns to the north and north-west (Hsien-yang, 12) and to the west (Hsing-p'ing, 13). Millet price levels were only lower in Hsien-yang (12) which was itself surrounded away from Sian by a ridge of high millet price levels (Kao-ling, 6, was not on a direct transport route to Hsien-yang or Sian). We conclude therefore that the Sian field pea market alone of all the markets examined was no larger than the limits of the immediate Sian hinterland. The Sian millet market was only slightly more extensive in that it included the environs of Hsien-yang (12) within its price orbit. Either production of field peas and millet in the neighbourhood of Sian was unusually large (which would also be suggested by the rising field pea price levels going east from Sian as far as Hua-yin (61) 115 km. away) or the demand for these subsidiary crops in the capital city of the province was unusually low. I found no evidence to support either or both of these possibilities.

Map 8

Typical prices of one granary bushel of millet and one granary bushel of field peas in taels in towns on major routes to Sian, c. 1900

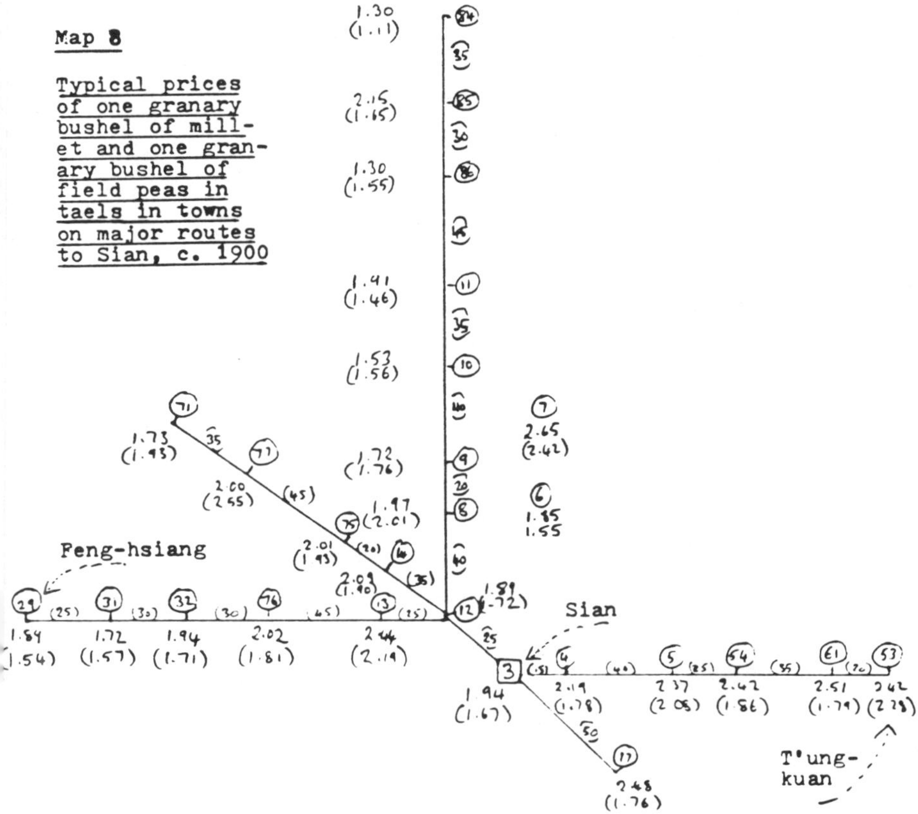

Key

(4)	town number
(40)	km.
(5)	town number
2.19	price in taels (millet)
(1.78)	price in taels (field peas)

Source: Shensi Reports

The discussion of millet and field pea price levels closes with a comparison of differentials between price levels of all crops in the 23 towns on main transport routes leading to Sian (see Table 18).

In the previous pages we have shown that although there was no grain market in Shensi covering the entire province and although even the Han valley cannot be regarded as having an integrated market for its major crop, rice, the main consumption centre in the province, Sian, was able to draw wheat not only from its own environs but also from Hsien-yang (12) and Lin-t'ung (4). It drew rice from a much larger region (from Feng-hsiang (29) in the west and from Li'ch'üan (14) in the north-west). It drew millet from its own environs and Hsien-yang (12). It drew field peas from its own environs only.

The largest near uniform price region (implying short distance trade between towns, not long distance trade supplying consumption centres) was also in the greater Sian plain (Wei valley) and we can sum up its extent from the information presented in Table 18.

The greater Sian plain wheat price zone (limits placed at those towns the difference between whose price levels was greater than the transport costs by the most expensive means between them) extended from Feng-hsiang (29) in the west to Hua-chou (54) in the east (215 km.); from Pin-chou (71) in the north-west to Sian (60 km.) and from Hsien-yang (12) in the north to Sian (25 km.).

Table 18

Differences in typical prices between towns on major routes leading to Sian

Differentials from west to Sian*

Place	Wheat	Rice	Millet	F/peas	Distances (km.)
29					
31	+.13	+.12	-.03	+.03	25
32	+.09	+.25	+.22	+.14	30
76	+.27	+.19	+.08	+.1	30
13	+.04	+.20	+.42	+.38	45
12	-.24	+.12	-.55	-.47	25
3	+.18	+.16	+.05	-.05	25

Differentials from north-west to Sian

Place	Wheat	Rice	Millet	F/peas	Distances (km.)
71					
77	+.37	--	+.27	+.62	35
75	-.14	--	+.01	-.62	45
14	-.01	--	+.08	-.03	20
12	-.14	+.24	-.2	-.18	35
3	+.18	+.16	+.05	-.05	25

Differentials from north to Sian

Place	Wheat	Rice	Millet	F/peas	Distances (km.)
84					
85	+.82	--	+.85	+.54	35
86	-.55	-.53	-.85	-.1	30
11	+1.11	+1.65	+.61	-.09	45
10	-.28	-1.51	-.38	+.1	35
9	+.18	+.27	+.19	+.2	40
8	+.28	+1.01	+.25	+.25	20
12	-.1	-.77	-.09	-.29	40
3	+.18	+.16	+.05	-.05	25

Differentials from east to Sian

Place	Wheat	Rice	Millet	F/peas	Distances (km.)
53					
61	-.18	-.71	+.09	-.49	20
54	-.44	-.94	-.09	+.07	35
5	-.08	+.59	-.05	+.22	25
4	-.05	--	-.18	-.3	40
3	+.04	--	-.25	-.11	15

Source: see maps 5 and 7 and table 14

* Difference in typical prices of wheat between towns 29 and 31 for example, is .13 taels. The addition sign indicates that the price level in town 31 is .13 taels higher than in town 29. Distances are likewise marked from the previous town to the town in question.

The greater Sian millet price zone extended from Hsien-yang (12) in the west to T'ung-kuan (53) in the east (160 km.); from Pin-chou (71) in the north-west to Sian (160 km.) and from T'ung-kuan (11) in the north to Sian (160 km.). Finally the greater Sian plain field pea price zone extended from Hsien-yang (12) in the west to Hua-chou (53) in the east (105 km.); from Ch'ien-chou (75) in the north-west to Sian (80 km.) and from Chung-pu (85) in the north to Sian (235 km.).

It should be stressed that we have considered only those towns on the main transport routes crossing the greater Sian plain. As we have seen differences between the C/S rates of these towns was small at an average difference of 40 cash.

The price data presented and analyzed above has enabled us to demonstrate that in a province untouched as late as 1910 by changes in transportation, marketing and urban development which were already apparent in certain provinces to the south and east, the price levels of wheat and rice in the 90 towns of Shensi divide into six or five broad zones which correspond with what we know concerning the production of these crops at that time. These zones however show no inter-relation and therefore we concluded that there was no province wide grain market nor indeed any market larger than a single zone. Upon closer inspection of price differentials within zones we were able to extend this by saying that there was in fact only one zone within the entire province which had grain markets larger than the limits of a single town. This zone was in the central part of the province and contained the main consumption centre (the provincial capital with a population larger by a factor of six to ten than any other town in the province). This zone also contained the major crop producing area in the province. The only signs of a long distance trade to Sian in any of the grain prices examined were found in the price levels of rice in the towns to the west of Sian. Rice was a luxury crop in Shensi and when we turned to a widely consumed, cheap legume (field peas) we found that the Sian market for this crop was coextensive with the immediate environs of the city itself.

A more detailed analysis of the Shensi Reports taking account of changes between months and also covering a larger number of towns would not, I think, alter the main outlines of the picture presented above. A province which may be regarded as one of China's richer poor provinces, chronologically in this century but economically at any time in the past two or even three centuries, exhibited a cellular grain price structure, each cell coterminous with the boundaries of each of the 90 districts and at the centre of each cell, stood the district town which was at once the economic and administrative centre of its hinterland. The only exceptions to this structure were the marketing regions for wheat and rice in the plain which contained the provincial capital where we found for the first time grain markets larger than the hinterland of a single town.

APPENDIX 1

Original Data: Prices per Granary Bushel in Taels, 90 District Towns, Shensi, 1900-1910

ORIGINAL DATA: WHEAT PRICES (SILVER), 1900 TO 1910, SHENSI

PLACE \ MONTH	1	2	3	4	5	6	7	8	9	10	11	12	13
1	3.60	3.00	3.72	2.50	2.50	2.70	3.20	3.20	3.20	3.20	3.50	2.90	3.10
2	3.64	2.92	2.75	2.10	2.11	2.11	2.56	2.56	2.56	2.61	2.61	2.12	2.32
3	4.59	5.19	3.22	1.90	1.89	1.90	1.88	1.85	1.66	1.68	1.70	1.28	1.92
4	4.82	5.87	2.53	2.56	1.93	1.44	1.64	1.58	1.50	1.67	1.61	1.22	1.60
5	4.62	7.13	3.79	3.13	2.14	1.76	1.76	1.60	1.50	1.50	1.50	1.40	2.20
6	4.92	7.00	3.00	1.68	1.50	1.38	1.20	1.20	1.32	1.20	1.20	1.02	1.64
7	7.50	7.20	7.10	3.42	2.16	1.69	1.88	1.98	1.71	1.80	2.07	1.53	1.98
8	4.90	7.00	3.65	2.45	1.82	1.61	1.47	1.40	1.54	1.68	1.75	1.26	2.38
9	4.20	6.20	3.57	1.82	1.62	1.49	1.49	1.23	1.23	1.23	1.30	1.17	1.82
10	4.54	8.10	3.24	2.70	1.30	1.13	1.13	1.13	1.13	1.23	1.13	1.20	1.35
11	5.90	6.30	8.50	5.30	3.50	3.60	3.40	3.40	3.30	3.30	3.40	2.30	2.20
12	4.34	5.60	3.85	1.36	1.47	1.26	1.40	1.26	1.26	1.26	1.40	1.29	1.75
13	5.70	8.20	3.85	2.29	1.92	1.62	1.62	1.62	1.62	1.62	1.47	1.47	1.85
14	5.11	9.10	4.20	2.24	1.75	1.75	1.40	1.40	1.05	1.04	1.40	1.33	1.54
15	3.73	4.23	3.00	1.60	1.70	1.80	1.80	1.80	1.80	1.60	1.60	1.72	1.82
16	5.81	8.40	4.90	2.80	2.31	2.10	2.52	2.52	2.31	2.10	2.24	1.96	2.80
17	4.96	8.00	4.07	3.50	3.50	2.70	2.70	2.70	2.75	2.76	2.76	1.95	1.55
18	5.94	5.40	4.95	3.83	3.37	2.93	2.70	2.70	2.70	2.70	2.70	2.25	2.16
19	5.77	5.98	5.47	4.50	4.60	4.40	4.00	3.90	3.80	3.60	3.50	2.30	2.00
20	1.98	3.00	0.89	0.85	1.05	1.15	1.23	1.23	1.23	1.23	1.23	1.15	1.15
21	6.50	7.20	2.30	2.40	2.30	2.10	1.60	1.50	1.50	1.40	1.10	1.20	1.10
22	4.04	4.80	4.32	4.20	4.00	3.68	3.16	2.72	2.16	1.95	1.72	1.88	1.72
23	6.31	6.31	5.11	4.11	4.11	3.31	3.31	3.31	3.31	3.31	3.31	3.31	3.31
24	3.50	4.75	3.25	3.25	3.25	3.25	3.25	3.25	3.25	3.25	3.25	3.25	3.25
25	4.75	5.50	4.00	2.40	3.40	2.20	2.00	2.00	2.00	2.00	1.80	2.00	2.00

14	15	16	17	18	19	20	21	22	23	24	25	
2.70	2.05	2.33	2.60	2.45	2.45	2.45	2.45	2.45	2.45	2.45	2.45	1
2.54	1.97	1.95	2.72	2.45	2.62	2.62	2.26	2.26	2.26	2.79	2.79	2
1.69	1.99	2.16	1.79	1.82	1.84	1.76	1.70	1.69	1.69	1.77	1.77	3
2.05	2.15	2.30	1.86	1.96	1.70	1.53	1.51	1.67	1.79	1.99	1.73	4
2.10	2.23	2.15	1.72	1.85	2.38	1.82	1.68	1.62	1.73	1.68	1.73	5
1.52	1.64	1.83	1.70	1.70	1.58	1.51	1.45	1.45	1.58	1.58	1.52	6
2.37	2.70	2.60	2.20	2.25	1.98	1.98	1.80	1.80	1.98	2.02	1.98	7
1.82	1.96	2.24	1.96	1.89	1.89	1.61	1.40	1.40	1.61	1.68	1.75	8
1.49	1.69	1.88	1.62	1.46	1.50	1.30	1.23	1.17	1.23	1.37	1.30	9
1.35	1.62	1.50	1.25	1.35	1.19	1.19	1.19	1.19	1.19	1.19	1.19	10
2.30	2.30	2.30	2.20	2.40	2.10	2.10	2.00	2.00	2.00	2.10	2.20	11
1.96	1.89	2.10	1.82	2.03	1.89	1.54	1.61	1.54	1.54	1.61	1.54	12
2.16	2.13	2.17	1.91	1.95	1.95	1.95	1.78	1.78	1.78	1.98	1.98	13
1.96	1.89	2.31	1.68	2.10	2.10	1.89	1.89	1.89	1.89	1.89	1.89	14
1.82	1.92	1.82	1.80	2.00	2.00	2.30	2.30	2.30	2.30	2.30	2.30	15
2.59	2.80	2.59	2.45	2.94	2.94	2.94	2.94	2.80	2.80	2.80	2.80	16
2.18	1.35	2.57	2.57	2.12	2.00	2.00	2.68	2.00	2.00	2.00	2.00	17
2.03	1.93	2.25	2.34	1.80	1.80	1.80	1.71	1.71	1.71	1.71	1.71	18
1.90	1.80	1.70	2.00	1.75	1.50	1.45	1.45	1.50	1.50	1.50	1.50	19
1.16	1.50	1.26	1.59	1.02	0.87	0.82	0.81	0.81	0.82	0.82	0.82	20
1.10	1.00	1.30	1.80	1.20	1.20	1.10	1.10	1.00	1.00	0.80	0.70	21
1.80	1.48	1.56	1.76	1.19	1.19	1.19	1.19	1.12	1.12	1.12	1.12	22
2.31	1.81	1.81	2.16	1.56	1.56	1.56	1.35	1.35	1.35	1.35	1.35	23
3.25	3.25	2.00	2.50	2.00	2.00	2.00	2.00	2.00	2.00	2.00	2.00	24
1.80	1.60	1.48	2.10	1.40	1.10	1.00	1.00	1.00	1.00	1.00	1.00	25

	1	2	3	4	5	6	7	8	9	10	11	12	13
26	3.85	5.15	4.95	4.55	3.55	2.95	2.55	2.55	2.35	2.35	2.25	1.85	2.15
27	2.85	4.80	3.50	4.20	4.20	4.20	4.20	4.20	4.20	4.20	4.20	4.20	4.20
28	3.57	2.74	2.12	1.44	1.37	1.31	1.31	1.31	1.29	1.29	1.52	1.08	1.08
29	4.55	4.74	2.13	1.42	1.30	1.18	1.14	1.25	1.09	1.12	1.21	1.02	1.25
30	5.03	5.27	3.09	1.42	1.37	1.37	1.37	1.37	1.30	1.30	1.42	1.58	1.50
31	4.08	5.10	3.00	1.50	1.20	1.14	1.20	1.20	1.14	1.08	1.14	1.26	1.44
32	4.90	5.28	3.42	1.56	1.18	1.15	1.21	1.14	1.14	1.14	1.14	1.19	1.49
33	5.59	5.66	2.53	1.58	1.27	1.24	1.49	1.56	1.46	1.43	1.45	1.42	1.64
34	5.75	5.25	2.50	1.50	1.40	1.40	1.40	1.40	1.20	1.20	1.30	1.40	1.50
35	4.12	4.56	2.15	1.16	1.25	1.25	1.25	1.25	1.25	1.25	1.25	1.02	1.13
36	3.76	3.68	2.56	2.08	2.08	2.08	2.08	2.08	1.88	1.76	1.84	2.52	2.68
37	3.12	3.12	2.44	2.48	2.48	2.48	2.48	2.48	2.48	2.48	2.60	2.76	2.76
38	2.33	2.23	3.63	3.23	3.13	3.13	3.13	3.13	3.13	3.13	3.13	3.23	3.33
39	3.39	3.29	3.43	2.88	2.88	2.88	2.88	3.13	3.21	3.21	3.70	3.83	3.83
40	2.81	2.54	3.24	2.34	2.50	3.03	3.03	3.03	2.98	2.92	3.30	3.70	3.50
41	2.36	2.06	2.33	1.85	1.85	2.04	2.27	2.39	2.57	2.93	3.23	3.63	3.93
42	3.11	3.22	3.46	2.73	2.73	2.73	2.73	2.73	2.73	2.73	2.73	3.11	3.15
43	3.33	2.54	3.67	2.48	2.48	2.48	2.48	2.68	2.68	2.88	3.20	4.11	2.86
44	4.80	4.80	5.00	3.00	3.00	3.90	4.20	4.20	4.80	4.80	5.40	5.40	5.40
45	3.50	2.60	2.30	1.90	2.90	3.30	3.30	3.30	3.30	3.30	3.30	3.20	3.30
46	4.36	2.00	2.30	1.69	1.78	1.78	1.94	2.11	2.58	2.58	2.91	2.90	3.16
47	3.30	4.10	3.00	1.60	1.50	1.50	1.50	1.90	1.90	1.90	1.90	2.80	2.90
48	3.67	4.00	2.10	4.02	4.02	4.02	4.02	4.02	4.02	2.00	2.00	2.05	2.28
49	3.75	4.88	4.56	1.56	4.44	4.44	4.31	4.31	4.31	4.31	3.19	2.56	2.56
50	3.65	3.25	2.90	3.90	3.60	3.10	2.95	2.95	2.95	2.95	2.95	2.20	2.20

14	15	16	17	18	19	20	21	22	23	24	25	
1.95	1.75	1.85	2.75	1.60	1.55	1.50	1.20	1.50	1.50	1.50	1.65	26
4.20	3.80	3.30	4.30	3.90	3.90	3.90	3.60	3.60	3.60	3.60	3.60	27
1.07	1.12	1.45	1.01	1.36	1.38	1.38	1.38	1.38	1.38	1.38	1.38	28
1.25	1.29	1.26	1.33	1.60	1.77	1.62	1.37	1.29	1.36	1.28	1.47	29
1.49	1.45	1.54	1.93	2.04	1.79	1.80	1.72	1.68	1.71	1.83	2.04	30
1.38	1.62	1.66	1.56	1.71	1.80	1.80	1.56	1.56	1.56	1.56	1.56	31
1.36	1.53	1.77	1.62	1.60	2.10	2.00	2.35	2.25	1.95	1.70	1.80	32
1.53	1.81	1.62	1.61	1.89	2.29	1.81	1.81	1.84	1.79	1.83	1.90	33
1.70	1.70	1.62	1.30	2.10	2.10	2.10	1.60	1.60	1.60	1.60	1.80	34
1.13	1.43	1.36	1.22	1.57	1.57	1.57	1.32	1.32	1.16	1.16	1.39	35
2.16	1.92	1.68	1.84	2.16	2.12	2.04	1.72	1.72	1.72	1.72	1.72	36
2.56	2.56	1.80	2.60	2.60	2.60	2.60	2.36	2.36	2.36	2.48	2.48	37
3.23	2.93	2.53	2.63	2.63	2.63	2.63	2.43	2.43	2.43	2.43	2.43	38
2.73	2.23	2.28	4.33	4.53	4.00	3.15	3.15	3.15	3.15	3.15	3.15	39
2.49	1.84	1.98	2.91	3.76	2.81	2.32	2.32	2.32	2.32	2.32	2.32	40
2.37	1.89	1.81	3.13	3.25	2.95	2.47	2.47	2.65	2.83	3.13	2.95	41
2.76	2.21	1.99	2.88	3.11	3.15	2.99	3.53	2.53	2.79	2.95	2.95	42
2.71	2.44	2.79	3.48	3.48	3.48	3.23	3.11	2.33	3.41	3.41	3.64	43
3.30	3.00	3.30	6.60	5.70	3.60	3.60	4.50	4.50	4.80	4.80	4.80	44
3.30	2.50	2.50	3.30	3.70	3.50	3.40	3.10	2.40	2.90	2.90	3.10	45
2.57	1.72	1.69	2.43	3.69	2.46	2.00	2.00	2.00	2.00	1.45	1.84	46
2.60	2.10	1.80	1.60	2.70	2.50	2.50	2.20	2.20	2.20	2.20	2.20	47
2.28	1.70	2.57	2.20	2.05	2.05	2.05	2.05	2.05	2.05	2.00	2.00	48
2.19	1.81	1.43	1.87	1.50	1.50	1.50	1.50	1.56	1.56	1.56	1.56	49
2.00	1.60	2.00	2.25	1.75	1.75	1.40	1.40	1.40	1.40	1.40	1.40	50

	1	2	3	4	5	6	7	8	9	10	11	12	13
51	5.14	3.88	3.75	4.62	4.62	4.00	4.00	4.00	4.00	3.40	3.40	3.00	2.62
52	3.73	4.93	4.03	3.83	3.83	3.43	3.43	3.13	3.13	3.13	3.13	2.93	2.68
53	3.78	5.40	3.87	2.34	2.34	2.25	2.70	2.07	2.07	1.80	1.71	1.89	2.07
54	4.53	5.36	3.80	2.73	2.10	2.06	2.16	2.07	2.06	2.06	2.10	1.28	1.37
55	3.61	4.59	2.82	2.30	1.38	1.12	1.18	1.05	0.99	0.99	0.99	0.98	1.71
56	3.80	4.60	3.80	2.20	1.50	1.50	1.50	1.20	1.20	1.10	1.10	1.10	1.40
57	3.92	4.87	3.65	1.98	1.26	1.21	1.21	1.21	1.21	1.21	1.21	0.88	0.88
58	3.11	4.46	4.30	2.62	1.75	1.55	1.35	1.35	1.35	1.35	1.25	1.28	1.28
59	3.70	4.50	3.59	1.80	1.45	1.35	1.35	1.35	1.35	1.25	1.25	1.05	1.20
60	3.64	4.27	4.34	2.59	1.75	1.75	1.75	1.75	1.40	1.40	1.40	1.19	1.68
61	4.90	5.60	4.20	3.15	2.80	2.80	2.80	1.96	1.96	1.96	1.96	1.89	2.45
62	3.64	4.17	4.65	2.19	1.75	1.48	1.48	1.48	1.48	1.48	1.48	1.35	1.35
63	3.60	3.60	3.48	2.58	2.58	2.58	2.58	2.58	2.88	2.88	3.00	4.80	4.92
64	3.22	2.87	2.67	2.27	2.27	2.32	2.32	2.32	2.32	2.42	2.42	2.64	2.54
65	2.25	2.37	2.15	1.82	1.82	1.82	1.82	1.82	1.82	1.82	1.82	3.00	3.00
66	2.60	2.90	1.50	1.30	1.30	1.30	1.30	1.30	1.40	1.55	1.60	2.00	2.10
67	2.00	2.17	2.03	1.70	1.70	1.70	1.70	1.70	1.70	1.74	1.74	1.51	1.15
68	2.56	2.00	2.00	1.52	1.52	1.60	1.68	1.92	1.92	1.92	2.16	3.04	3.04
69	3.64	3.46	2.88	2.44	2.62	2.64	2.56	2.56	2.62	2.76	2.78	3.74	3.83
70	2.12	2.12	2.12	1.60	1.60	1.60	1.60	1.60	1.60	1.60	1.60	1.30	1.30
71	5.50	7.40	6.30	2.10	1.50	1.50	1.80	1.70	1.70	1.70	1.60	1.10	1.00
72	3.25	4.89	3.56	2.00	1.56	1.56	1.34	1.34	1.34	1.34	1.34	1.16	0.89
73	4.54	4.54	3.60	2.16	1.32	1.19	1.15	1.10	1.12	1.12	1.26	1.05	1.33
74	6.72	8.54	4.20	2.45	2.45	2.45	2.10	2.10	2.10	2.10	2.10	1.75	1.75
75	4.52	6.60	4.62	2.44	1.82	1.68	1.50	1.56	1.62	1.62	1.86	1.50	1.86

14	15	16	17	18	19	20	21	22	23	24	25	
2.32	2.32	2.09	3.00	2.20	2.00	2.00	2.00	2.10	2.10	2.10	2.10	51
2.63	2.48	2.68	2.58	1.88	1.88	1.48	1.58	1.58	1.58	1.58	1.58	52
2.16	2.16	2.07	2.25	2.16	2.25	2.25	2.16	2.16	2.16	2.16	2.16	53
1.80	2.00	1.95	1.97	1.67	2.02	1.80	1.79	1.68	1.63	1.67	1.68	54
1.44	1.77	1.58	1.44	1.44	1.51	1.31	1.25	1.25	1.18	1.25	1.38	55
1.35	1.75	1.70	1.40	1.30	1.50	1.60	1.60	1.60	1.60	1.30	1.30	56
1.00	1.41	1.41	1.21	1.23	1.23	1.23	1.23	1.14	1.14	1.14	1.27	57
1.28	1.71	1.67	1.67	1.60	1.60	1.50	1.50	1.30	1.30	1.30	1.70	58
1.02	1.32	1.50	1.30	1.20	1.20	1.20	1.20	1.20	1.20	1.20	1.20	59
1.54	2.03	1.89	1.54	1.33	1.47	1.47	1.40	1.40	1.40	1.40	1.40	60
2.45	2.52	2.45	2.10	2.10	2.38	2.38	2.38	2.38	2.38	2.38	2.38	61
1.46	1.83	1.46	1.36	1.40	1.40	1.24	1.24	0.93	0.93	0.93	0.93	62
4.62	3.60	3.24	3.72	3.60	3.84	3.84	3.84	4.08	4.08	4.32	4.32	63
2.52	2.52	2.48	2.05	2.00	2.00	2.00	2.00	2.00	2.30	2.30	2.30	64
3.00	2.88	2.52	2.78	2.78	2.78	2.78	2.78	2.78	2.78	3.13	3.13	65
2.20	2.20	2.20	1.73	2.00	2.00	2.00	2.00	2.00	2.00	2.00	2.00	66
1.18	1.91	2.06	1.21	2.45	2.56	2.56	2.65	2.65	2.65	2.65	2.65	67
2.08	1.76	1.84	2.48	2.32	2.32	2.32	2.00	2.08	2.16	2.36	2.36	68
3.72	3.28	2.76	2.96	2.96	3.08	3.04	2.88	2.88	2.88	2.96	2.96	69
2.00	2.00	2.00	2.00	2.60	2.60	2.60	2.60	2.60	2.60	2.60	2.60	70
1.30	1.60	1.60	1.51	1.62	1.62	1.51	1.29	1.29	1.26	1.54	1.66	71
0.89	1.11	1.29	1.70	1.07	1.38	1.07	1.07	1.07	1.07	1.03	1.03	72
1.39	1.64	1.82	1.27	1.55	1.72	1.55	0.98	0.98	1.43	1.48	1.51	73
1.40	1.75	1.75	1.96	1.61	2.10	1.75	1.75	1.75	1.75	1.75	1.75	74
1.04	1.98	2.04	1.80	1.86	1.98	1.80	1.74	1.74	1.68	1.68	1.80	75

	1	2	3	4	5	6	7	8	9	10	11	12	13
76	5.70	6.60	3.90	1.62	1.62	1.62	1.62	1.62	1.62	1.62	1.62	1.44	1.74
77	5.90	7.07	5.60	1.52	1.38	2.38	2.10	2.10	2.10	2.10	2.10	1.82	1.61
78	4.17	4.17	3.38	2.38	2.38	2.74	3.73	3.85	4.05	3.59	3.59	2.99	2.94
79	3.14	3.14	3.42	1.92	1.82	1.94	2.09	2.93	3.01	3.07	3.18	2.21	2.46
80	4.30	4.85	3.66	2.38	2.58	2.66	2.76	2.92	3.10	3.15	3.30	3.62	3.76
81	2.73	2.74	2.50	2.45	2.45	2.45	2.45	2.45	2.45	2.45	2.45	2.45	2.45
82	2.33	2.75	2.83	1.90	1.70	1.70	1.70	1.70	1.90	2.00	2.00	2.00	2.00
83	2.45	2.85	4.90	4.30	4.10	2.50	2.50	2.35	2.35	2.35	2.25	1.95	1.90
84	0.97	1.03	2.45	2.45	2.45	1.55	1.55	1.55	1.32	1.22	1.22	1.22	1.22
85	1.24	3.50	4.80	3.40	3.10	2.90	2.70	2.70	2.70	2.40	2.40	2.35	2.35
86	3.50	4.00	8.00	3.20	3.20	2.40	2.20	2.20	2.20	2.10	2.10	1.40	1.20
87	5.02	6.97	4.50	4.42	3.30	3.70	2.85	2.85	2.85	2.25	1.95	2.25	2.40
88	5.39	4.62	4.58	4.27	4.13	3.64	3.29	3.08	3.01	2.94	2.94	3.08	3.08
89	5.20	5.50	3.80	3.00	2.60	2.10	3.00	1.30	1.20	1.20	1.20	1.50	1.40
90	3.90	4.70	4.10	3.10	2.80	2.10	1.70	1.60	1.60	1.70	1.70	2.00	2.00

14	15	16	17	18	19	20	21	22	23	24	25	
1.98	2.04	2.25	1.80	1.86	1.86	1.86	1.86	1.86	1.86	1.86	1.86	76
1.61	1.96	1.89	1.75	1.83	1.83	1.83	1.73	1.73	1.87	1.87	1.87	77
2.94	2.94	3.47	3.70	3.88	3.71	4.03	4.03	4.03	3.99	4.34	4.34	78
1.96	1.85	2.15	2.69	3.01	2.77	2.63	2.42	2.53	2.57	2.06	2.75	79
3.59	3.59	3.93	3.83	4.35	4.35	4.35	4.40	4.45	4.42	4.52	4.55	80
2.45	2.08	1.80	1.79	1.81	1.81	1.81	1.81	1.81	1.81	1.83	1.88	81
2.00	2.40	2.20	2.40	2.40	2.40	2.30	2.30	2.30	2.30	2.30	2.40	82
1.63	1.39	1.33	1.12	0.97	1.00	0.95	0.77	0.78	0.78	0.85	0.99	83
1.22	1.32	1.00	1.00	1.04	1.00	1.00	1.00	1.00	1.00	1.00	1.00	84
2.27	2.21	2.10	2.00	1.10	1.20	1.10	1.10	1.10	1.10	1.10	1.20	85
1.00	1.15	1.15	1.20	1.05	1.05	1.05	0.95	0.95	0.95	0.95	1.10	86
2.10	1.72	1.80	1.95	1.40	1.40	1.40	1.40	1.40	1.40	1.40	1.40	87
3.08	2.17	2.52	3.01	2.59	2.17	2.17	2.17	2.17	2.17	2.17	2.17	88
1.40	1.30	1.30	1.60	1.05	1.05	1.05	1.05	1.05	1.05	1.05	1.05	89
1.80	2.00	2.40	1.80	1.60	1.40	1.30	1.30	1.30	1.30	1.50	1.50	90

ORIGINAL DATA: RICE PRICE (SILVER), 1900 TO 1910, SHENSI

PLACE \ MONTH	1	2	3	4	5	6	7	8	9	10	11	12	13
1	3.50	3.10	3.80	2.96	2.96	3.26	3.45	3.45	3.45	3.45	3.75	3.20	3.55
2	4.54	4.32	3.58	3.42	3.43	3.43	3.84	3.84	3.84	4.18	4.18	3.57	3.28
3	5.52	7.38	2.86	3.00	3.67	4.54	4.47	4.03	3.23	3.25	3.34	2.74	3.24
4	0.0	0.0	0.0	0.0	0.0	0.0	0.0	0.0	0.0	0.0	0.0	0.0	0.0
5	7.71	10.35	4.33	3.81	4.55	4.00	4.00	4.00	4.00	3.50	3.00	3.00	3.50
6	5.18	7.70	2.04	1.68	1.68	1.68	1.68	1.68	1.68	1.68	1.68	1.80	1.89
7	8.75	8.40	8.00	5.85	6.30	6.30	8.10	8.10	7.20	5.31	5.85	4.50	4.77
8	7.65	8.40	3.65	3.15	5.25	2.05	4.20	4.90	4.20	4.20	3.50	2.94	4.20
9	6.50	11.40	3.57	3.38	4.94	5.07	5.20	4.55	3.90	3.38	2.93	2.92	3.25
10	5.11	9.00	3.78	3.62	3.62	3.62	3.62	3.62	2.70	2.70	2.70	3.00	3.00
11	7.60	8.10	8.50	6.00	5.80	5.80	5.70	5.60	5.30	5.30	5.30	4.30	4.10
12	4.90	7.00	3.50	2.10	3.85	4.90	3.50	3.50	3.66	2.94	3.50	2.31	2.80
13	7.44	8.86	3.92	2.95	2.95	3.03	3.03	3.92	4.17	4.17	2.92	3.26	2.82
14	5.60	10.85	4.90	2.45	1.75	1.75	1.75	1.75	1.75	1.75	1.75	2.80	2.80
15	3.99	4.69	2.40	1.85	1.85	2.15	2.45	2.45	2.70	2.30	2.30	2.55	2.55
16	6.30	9.80	4.90	3.92	4.76	5.25	5.75	5.53	4.83	3.85	4.06	3.29	3.22
17	5.15	8.00	4.05	4.40	4.40	3.64	3.64	3.64	3.80	3.83	3.85	2.50	2.97
18	0.0	0.0	0.0	0.0	0.0	0.0	0.0	0.0	0.0	0.0	0.0	0.0	0.0
19	0.0	0.0	0.0	0.0	0.0	0.0	0.0	0.0	0.0	0.0	0.0	0.0	0.0
20	0.0	0.0	0.0	0.0	0.0	0.0	0.0	0.0	0.0	0.0	0.0	0.0	0.0
21	0.0	0.0	0.0	0.0	0.0	0.0	0.0	0.0	0.0	0.0	0.0	0.0	0.0
22	5.80	5.64	6.52	5.24	4.88	4.72	4.04	3.96	3.36	3.36	3.36	3.68	3.68
23	0.0	0.0	0.0	0.0	0.0	0.0	0.0	0.0	0.0	0.0	0.0	0.0	0.0
24	0.0	0.0	0.0	0.0	0.0	0.0	0.0	0.0	0.0	0.0	0.0	0.0	0.0
25	5.90	7.00	6.00	7.00	7.00	7.00	7.00	7.00	7.00	7.00	7.00	7.00	7.00

14	15	16	17	18	19	20	21	22	23	24	25	
3.05	2.05	2.50	2.70	2.60	2.60	2.60	2.60	2.60	2.60	2.60	2.60	1
3.28	2.76	3.14	3.86	3.48	3.75	3.75	3.71	3.71	3.71	3.71	3.71	2
3.34	3.21	3.20	3.33	3.23	3.57	3.61	3.73	3.70	3.34	3.68	3.67	3
0.0	0.0	0.0	0.0	0.0	0.0	0.0	0.0	0.0	0.0	0.0	0.0	4
3.50	3.97	4.50	3.75	3.90	4.31	4.08	4.32	4.32	4.22	4.80	4.22	5
1.89	1.89	2.08	2.21	2.14	2.34	2.34	2.34	2.34	2.34	2.34	2.34	6
5.94	5.65	5.50	5.20	5.85	5.40	5.40	5.85	5.85	5.85	5.40	5.94	7
3.50	3.50	3.50	3.35	4.90	4.20	4.20	4.20	4.20	4.55	4.55	4.55	8
3.77	3.19	3.25	3.25	3.57	3.57	3.90	4.23	4.30	3.45	3.70	3.77	9
3.02	3.02	3.25	2.11	2.16	2.16	2.16	2.16	2.16	2.16	2.16	2.16	10
4.20	3.90	3.60	3.40	3.40	3.30	3.30	3.30	3.30	3.30	3.30	3.30	11
2.66	2.80	2.80	3.50	3.78	3.78	3.50	3.50	3.50	3.15	3.15	3.15	12
3.40	3.12	3.57	3.19	3.00	3.00	3.00	2.86	2.86	2.86	2.96	2.96	13
3.08	2.80	3.36	3.50	3.71	3.71	3.71	3.71	3.71	3.71	3.71	3.71	14
2.70	2.35	2.30	2.45	2.65	2.65	3.00	3.00	3.00	3.00	3.00	3.00	15
3.64	3.64	4.20	4.41	4.90	4.20	4.90	4.90	4.90	4.90	4.90	4.90	16
2.35	2.96	3.10	3.00	3.45	3.47	3.47	3.42	3.42	3.42	3.42	3.42	17
0.0	0.0	0.0	0.0	0.0	0.0	0.0	0.0	0.0	0.0	0.0	0.0	18
0.0	0.0	0.0	0.0	0.0	0.0	0.0	0.0	0.0	0.0	0.0	0.0	19
0.0	0.0	0.0	0.0	0.0	0.0	0.0	0.0	0.0	0.0	0.0	0.0	20
0.0	0.0	0.0	0.0	0.0	0.0	0.0	0.0	0.0	0.0	0.0	0.0	21
3.80	3.33	4.04	4.60	4.00	4.00	4.00	4.00	4.00	4.00	4.00	4.00	22
0.0	0.0	0.0	0.0	0.0	0.0	0.0	0.0	0.0	0.0	0.0	0.0	23
0.0	0.0	0.0	0.0	0.0	0.0	0.0	0.0	0.0	0.0	0.0	0.0	24
7.00	6.10	6.10	6.70	6.40	6.20	6.20	6.20	6.20	6.20	6.20	6.20	25

	1	2	3	4	5	6	7	8	9	10	11	12	13
26	0.0	0.0	0.0	0.0	0.0	0.0	0.0	0.0	0.0	0.0	0.0	0.0	0.0
27	4.20	6.90	5.60	6.50	7.98	7.98	7.98	7.90	7.90	7.90	7.90	7.90	7.90
28	5.23	3.92	2.92	2.87	2.89	2.92	2.92	2.92	2.85	2.85	2.89	3.81	3.35
29	5.35	6.00	2.03	2.10	2.28	2.26	2.78	2.71	2.68	2.53	2.52	1.77	1.99
30	6.01	5.98	3.09	1.95	2.55	2.55	2.55	2.55	2.52	2.52	2.24	2.27	2.26
31	5.10	6.60	3.00	1.86	2.16	2.16	2.82	2.82	2.58	2.40	2.40	2.16	2.16
32	5.28	6.73	2.94	2.69	2.36	2.29	2.38	2.28	2.29	2.60	2.60	2.18	2.61
33	6.12	6.61	2.11	1.99	2.22	2.29	2.59	2.23	2.33	2.07	2.05	1.80	2.32
34	6.50	6.25	3.25	2.70	2.70	2.70	2.70	2.70	2.50	2.50	2.50	3.15	3.15
35	0.0	0.0	0.0	0.0	0.0	0.0	0.0	0.0	0.0	0.0	0.0	0.0	0.0
36	4.72	4.60	2.84	2.60	2.60	2.60	2.60	2.80	2.80	2.80	2.80	3.40	3.56
37	4.40	4.44	2.92	3.04	3.04	3.04	3.04	3.04	3.04	3.04	3.16	3.88	3.88
38	4.32	4.32	3.67	3.47	3.41	3.57	3.67	3.67	3.77	3.87	3.87	4.77	4.87
39	4.70	4.66	3.57	3.20	3.30	3.40	3.40	3.40	3.40	3.90	4.40	3.45	3.70
40	3.45	2.94	3.48	3.03	3.46	4.20	4.20	4.20	3.72	3.64	3.89	4.05	3.83
41	3.19	2.59	3.55	2.71	3.31	3.55	3.85	3.25	3.31	3.79	4.09	3.80	4.10
42	3.58	3.76	3.99	3.31	3.31	3.31	3.31	3.20	3.20	3.30	3.25	3.72	3.94
43	4.02	3.30	5.30	3.14	3.14	3.15	3.15	3.06	3.12	3.33	3.66	4.11	3.60
44	6.00	6.50	5.00	5.20	5.70	6.60	6.00	6.00	5.70	5.70	6.30	5.70	6.30
45	5.00	3.90	3.60	1.90	3.10	3.60	3.60	3.60	3.60	3.60	3.60	3.20	3.30
46	6.91	3.69	3.07	3.80	4.36	4.36	4.36	4.36	4.36	4.36	2.68	4.20	4.60
47	3.60	4.70	3.80	3.70	3.50	3.50	3.50	3.80	3.80	3.80	3.80	5.70	5.70
48	3.90	3.50	3.00	4.25	4.25	4.25	4.25	4.25	4.25	3.60	3.60	3.05	3.50
49	4.25	5.63	5.19	5.13	5.00	5.00	4.88	4.88	4.88	4.88	4.88	4.19	4.19
50	4.35	4.50	3.65	5.00	5.00	5.00	5.05	5.05	5.05	5.05	5.05	5.00	5.00

14	15	16	17	18	19	20	21	22	23	24	25	
0.0	0.0	0.0	0.0	0.0	0.0	0.0	0.0	0.0	0.0	0.0	0.0	26
7.90	7.50	7.10	7.20	6.90	6.90	6.90	6.70	6.70	6.70	6.70	6.70	27
3.33	3.48	2.30	3.67	3.53	3.57	3.57	3.57	3.57	3.57	3.57	3.57	28
2.22	2.15	2.53	2.40	2.56	2.63	2.48	2.42	2.37	2.31	2.28	2.62	29
2.61	2.03	2.40	2.91	2.94	3.15	3.13	3.00	2.99	2.85	2.85	3.40	30
2.04	2.22	2.99	2.40	2.70	2.88	2.76	2.64	2.64	2.64	2.64	2.64	31
2.58	2.49	2.22	3.12	2.70	3.10	2.93	3.20	3.00	3.75	3.40	3.40	32
2.04	2.46	3.10	2.14	2.56	3.01	2.93	2.93	2.83	2.75	2.74	3.00	33
3.15	3.15	3.10	3.30	3.60	3.60	3.60	3.20	3.20	3.20	3.20	3.30	34
0.0	0.0	0.0	0.0	0.0	0.0	0.0	0.0	0.0	0.0	0.0	0.0	35
3.44	2.44	2.40	2.52	2.88	2.88	2.88	2.88	2.88	2.80	2.68	2.68	36
3.72	3.72	2.80	3.84	3.84	3.84	3.84	3.64	3.64	3.64	3.88	3.88	37
4.87	4.37	4.57	4.77	4.67	4.67	4.67	4.67	4.67	4.67	4.67	4.67	38
3.70	2.95	2.95	4.50	5.48	5.48	4.23	4.23	4.23	4.23	4.23	4.23	39
3.02	2.01	2.18	4.35	3.73	3.86	3.48	3.48	3.48	3.48	3.48	3.48	40
3.02	2.26	2.36	4.40	4.40	4.40	3.68	3.38	3.68	3.98	4.46	4.28	41
3.60	2.78	2.63	3.75	3.97	4.11	3.96	3.41	3.41	3.73	3.98	3.98	42
2.93	2.64	3.02	4.13	4.35	4.78	4.62	4.00	4.22	4.32	4.32	4.32	43
4.50	3.90	3.90	7.50	7.50	6.30	6.30	5.70	5.70	6.00	6.60	6.60	44
3.30	2.50	2.50	3.30	3.80	3.80	3.70	3.40	3.30	3.30	3.30	3.40	45
4.67	2.97	3.63	4.46	5.08	4.62	4.62	3.69	3.38	3.38	3.38	3.38	46
5.60	5.40	5.00	5.00	5.50	5.50	5.50	5.50	5.50	5.50	5.50	5.50	47
3.50	2.50	2.55	2.50	2.40	2.40	2.40	2.40	2.40	2.40	2.50	2.50	48
2.88	3.50	3.12	3.37	2.93	2.93	2.93	2.93	2.87	2.87	2.87	2.87	49
4.50	3.20	3.20	3.40	3.40	3.40	3.15	3.15	3.15	3.15	3.15	3.15	50

	1	2	3	4	5	6	7	8	9	10	11	12	13
51	6.43	5.47	4.50	5.54	5.54	5.70	5.70	5.70	5.70	5.00	5.00	4.70	4.95
52	5.24	6.04	5.74	5.74	5.74	5.74	5.74	5.74	5.74	5.74	5.74	6.14	6.14
53	6.30	8.10	3.78	4.95	5.94	6.30	6.30	5.85	5.40	4.50	4.50	4.50	4.50
54	5.43	6.26	4.38	3.62	5.23	5.71	5.80	2.96	2.98	2.90	3.27	3.12	3.27
55	5.45	6.56	3.61	2.95	4.60	4.26	4.26	3.28	3.28	2.95	3.28	2.62	3.28
56	5.50	5.50	4.20	3.10	3.40	3.40	3.50	3.50	3.80	3.00	2.80	2.70	2.80
57	6.44	7.62	6.34	4.05	4.05	4.05	4.31	4.98	4.98	4.98	4.98	4.31	4.31
58	5.89	6.22	4.85	4.39	4.22	4.22	4.22	4.22	4.22	4.22	4.07	3.92	3.92
59	0.0	0.0	0.0	0.0	0.0	0.0	0.0	0.0	0.0	0.0	0.0	0.0	0.0
60	6.86	6.86	5.61	3.78	3.78	3.78	3.78	3.78	3.92	3.92	3.92	3.64	3.08
61	7.00	9.10	5.25	5.04	5.60	5.60	5.60	4.20	4.20	4.20	4.20	4.20	4.20
62	5.18	5.86	4.67	2.96	2.96	2.96	2.96	2.96	2.96	2.96	2.96	2.96	2.96
63	3.30	3.78	3.78	2.64	2.64	2.64	2.64	2.64	2.82	3.12	3.12	3.96	3.84
64	3.73	3.73	3.68	3.04	3.17	3.17	3.17	3.17	3.17	3.22	3.22	3.23	3.23
65	3.17	3.31	3.05	2.41	2.41	2.41	2.41	2.41	2.41	2.41	2.41	3.00	3.35
66	2.90	3.20	2.60	2.00	2.00	2.00	2.00	2.00	2.00	2.10	2.10	2.40	2.50
67	3.30	3.46	3.36	2.96	2.93	2.93	2.93	2.93	2.93	2.98	2.98	3.19	3.25
68	2.80	2.64	2.56	2.16	2.16	2.24	2.40	2.56	2.56	2.56	2.80	2.92	2.92
69	3.76	3.64	3.28	2.84	3.02	3.14	2.02	3.02	3.06	3.16	3.18	3.86	3.96
70	3.24	3.24	3.24	2.20	2.20	2.20	2.20	2.20	2.20	2.20	2.20	2.40	2.40
71	6.30	8.80	7.70	2.90	5.50	5.40	6.00	6.60	6.60	3.90	3.90	3.20	3.00
72	4.44	5.55	4.44	2.89	2.45	2.45	2.22	2.22	2.22	2.22	2.22	2.22	2.18
73	4.97	4.97	3.15	2.32	1.97	1.99	1.93	1.76	1.75	1.70	1.69	1.91	2.29
74	9.45	9.80	5.60	4.80	4.76	4.76	4.20	4.20	4.20	4.20	4.20	3.85	3.85
75	0.0	0.0	0.0	0.0	0.0	0.0	0.0	0.0	0.0	0.0	0.0	0.0	0.0

14	15	16	17	18	19	20	21	22	23	24	25	
4.95	4.21	3.34	4.20	3.20	3.10	3.10	3.10	3.10	3.10	3.10	3.10	51
6.14	5.84	5.84	4.34	4.19	4.19	4.19	4.19	4.19	4.19	4.19	4.19	52
4.50	4.50	4.86	5.04	5.22	5.22	5.22	5.22	5.22	5.22	5.22	5.22	53
3.16	3.15	2.97	3.71	3.13	3.28	3.50	3.51	3.58	3.53	3.50	3.68	54
3.28	2.76	2.63	2.62	2.76	2.82	2.76	2.76	2.76	2.76	2.76	2.82	55
2.90	3.00	3.10	3.10	3.00	3.00	3.00	3.00	3.00	3.00	3.00	3.00	56
4.31	4.31	4.24	4.31	4.22	4.22	4.22	4.22	4.22	4.22	4.31	4.84	57
3.92	4.99	4.10	4.10	4.20	4.20	4.20	4.20	4.10	4.10	4.10	4.30	58
0.0	0.0	0.0	0.0	0.0	0.0	0.0	0.0	0.0	0.0	0.0	0.0	59
3.64	3.64	4.20	4.27	4.20	4.48	4.48	4.20	4.20	4.20	4.20	4.20	60
4.70	4.55	4.90	4.55	4.20	3.85	3.85	3.85	3.85	3.85	3.85	3.85	61
2.96	2.96	2.65	2.81	3.01	3.01	3.01	3.01	3.01	3.01	3.01	3.01	62
3.78	3.12	3.24	3.60	3.48	3.96	3.96	3.96	3.96	3.96	4.08	4.08	63
3.23	3.21	3.13	2.75	2.65	2.65	2.65	2.65	2.65	2.75	2.75	2.75	64
3.35	3.26	2.96	3.26	3.26	3.26	3.26	3.26	3.26	3.26	3.76	3.76	65
2.40	2.40	2.45	2.20	2.27	2.27	2.27	2.25	2.25	2.25	2.25	2.25	66
3.28	3.15	3.20	3.37	3.75	3.87	3.87	3.87	3.87	3.87	3.87	3.87	67
2.60	2.16	2.32	2.32	2.56	2.56	2.56	2.24	2.44	2.44	2.68	2.68	68
3.92	3.64	3.68	3.24	3.24	3.36	3.36	3.28	3.32	3.32	3.36	3.36	69
2.40	2.50	2.50	2.50	3.50	3.50	3.50	3.50	3.50	3.50	3.50	3.50	70
3.70	3.80	3.80	3.92	4.30	4.30	4.30	4.30	4.30	4.20	4.20	3.89	71
2.18	2.36	2.27	2.00	2.00	2.22	2.00	2.00	2.00	2.00	2.00	2.00	72
2.41	2.88	2.96	2.72	3.12	3.21	3.21	3.10	3.15	3.35	3.39	3.41	73
3.85	3.85	4.06	3.85	4.20	4.20	4.20	4.20	4.20	4.20	4.20	4.20	74
0.0	0.0	0.0	0.0	0.0	0.0	0.0	0.0	0.0	0.0	0.0	0.0	75

	1	2	3	4	5	6	7	8	9	10	11	12	13
76	5.70	7.20	3.00	2.16	2.34	2.34	3.60	3.60	3.30	3.30	3.30	2.88	2.70
77	0.0	0.0	0.0	0.0	0.0	0.0	0.0	0.0	0.0	0.0	0.0	0.0	0.0
78	5.21	5.55	4.97	4.35	4.77	5.21	5.92	5.99	5.47	4.54	4.54	3.75	3.62
79	3.58	3.71	3.58	3.20	3.32	3.37	3.50	3.61	3.66	3.77	3.88	3.14	3.03
80	4.80	5.45	4.54	3.78	3.98	4.10	4.22	4.38	4.38	4.40	4.46	4.65	4.78
81	3.61	3.62	3.50	3.50	3.50	3.50	3.50	3.50	3.50	3.50	3.50	3.50	3.50
82	3.60	4.36	3.50	3.20	3.10	3.10	3.10	3.10	3.10	3.30	3.30	3.20	3.20
83	4.00	4.20	5.10	5.20	5.20	4.60	4.40	4.40	4.40	4.40	4.30	4.31	4.25
84	0.0	0.0	0.0	0.0	0.0	0.0	0.0	0.0	0.0	0.0	0.0	0.0	0.0
85	1.93	2.80	4.90	3.40	3.30	3.30	3.30	3.30	3.20	3.10	3.10	3.30	3.30
86	4.00	4.40	7.00	3.50	3.50	3.40	3.60	3.60	3.60	3.50	3.50	3.00	2.50
87	0.0	0.0	0.0	0.0	0.0	0.0	0.0	0.0	0.0	0.0	0.0	0.0	0.0
88	0.0	0.0	0.0	0.0	0.0	0.0	0.0	0.0	0.0	0.0	0.0	0.0	0.0
89	0.0	0.0	0.0	0.0	0.0	0.0	0.0	0.0	0.0	0.0	0.0	0.0	0.0
90	0.0	0.0	0.0	0.0	0.0	0.0	0.0	0.0	0.0	0.0	0.0	0.0	0.0

14	15	16	17	18	19	20	21	22	23	24	25	
2.82	2.58	2.70	2.40	3.12	3.12	3.12	3.12	3.12	3.12	3.12	3.12	76
0.0	0.0	0.0	0.0	0.0	0.0	0.0	0.0	0.0	0.0	0.0	0.0	77
3.91	3.85	4.99	4.29	4.62	5.06	6.31	6.31	6.31	5.12	5.95	6.57	78
3.03	2.63	3.08	3.13	3.79	3.78	3.78	3.52	3.48	3.44	3.49	3.61	79
4.65	4.60	5.00	4.54	5.40	5.54	5.95	6.10	6.15	6.12	6.25	6.40	80
3.50	4.00	3.68	3.78	3.78	3.80	3.80	3.80	3.80	3.80	3.80	3.80	81
3.20	3.20	3.20	3.40	3.30	3.30	3.40	3.30	3.30	3.20	3.20	3.30	82
4.25	4.00	3.80	3.05	3.05	3.00	2.90	2.84	2.75	2.75	2.75	2.75	83
0.0	0.0	0.0	0.0	0.0	0.0	0.0	0.0	0.0	0.0	0.0	0.0	84
3.30	3.31	3.50	3.90	2.90	3.00	3.00	3.00	3.00	3.00	3.00	3.00	85
2.20	2.20	2.20	2.20	2.15	2.15	2.15	2.15	2.15	2.15	2.15	2.30	86
0.0	0.0	0.0	0.0	0.0	0.0	0.0	0.0	0.0	0.0	0.0	0.0	87
0.0	0.0	0.0	0.0	0.0	0.0	0.0	0.0	0.0	0.0	0.0	0.0	88
0.0	0.0	0.0	0.0	0.0	0.0	0.0	0.0	0.0	0.0	0.0	0.0	89
0.0	0.0	0.0	0.0	0.0	0.0	0.0	0.0	0.0	0.0	0.0	0.0	90

ORIGINAL DATA: MILLET PRICE (SILVER), 1900 TO 1910, SHENSI

MONTH / PLACE	1	2	3	4	5	6	7	8	9	10	11	12	13
1	3.00	2.90	3.50	2.40	2.40	2.60	2.90	2.90	2.90	2.90	3.10	2.40	2.60
2	3.40	2.82	2.20	2.17	2.15	2.15	2.30	2.30	2.30	2.48	2.48	2.79	2.54
3	4.24	4.99	0.79	1.56	1.54	1.56	1.88	1.85	1.66	1.34	1.36	1.60	1.81
4	5.68	6.18	1.18	2.09	2.70	1.85	2.05	1.81	1.55	1.70	1.73	1.51	2.13
5	6.22	7.92	1.91	2.28	2.57	2.50	2.57	2.25	1.75	1.75	1.50	1.90	2.75
6	5.17	7.70	1.20	1.20	1.50	1.38	1.32	1.32	1.32	1.38	1.38	1.14	1.89
7	7.80	7.80	2.20	2.16	2.34	2.34	2.34	2.34	1.89	1.89	2.07	2.16	2.24
8	4.90	7.70	1.33	1.33	1.54	1.54	1.54	1.54	1.68	1.68	1.75	1.40	2.31
9	4.00	7.80	1.10	1.10	1.10	1.10	1.17	1.23	1.30	1.23	1.43	1.30	1.75
10	4.83	8.40	1.08	1.35	1.24	1.24	1.24	1.24	1.13	1.23	1.19	1.20	1.35
11	5.80	6.20	5.00	1.90	1.90	1.90	1.80	1.70	1.70	1.70	1.70	1.30	1.20
12	3.64	4.90	1.26	1.12	1.35	1.40	1.12	1.40	1.26	1.40	1.33	1.47	1.75
13	5.88	8.44	1.69	1.71	1.92	2.12	3.12	3.12	2.12	2.12	1.70	2.07	2.10
14	5.18	9.80	2.10	1.61	1.61	1.61	1.61	1.61	1.61	1.61	1.61	1.54	1.89
15	3.30	3.80	1.20	1.45	1.45	1.45	1.45	1.45	1.62	1.50	1.50	1.81	1.71
16	5.53	7.70	1.40	2.66	2.66	2.45	2.66	2.66	2.45	2.31	2.45	2.17	2.45
17	4.76	8.00	1.80	2.80	2.80	2.40	2.20	2.20	2.30	2.30	2.54	2.20	2.40
18	5.94	6.35	2.66	2.07	2.07	2.07	2.07	2.07	2.07	2.07	2.07	2.25	2.03
19	5.68	5.98	4.87	3.10	3.20	3.10	3.00	2.80	2.70	2.45	2.40	1.70	1.65
20	1.81	2.70	0.73	0.71	0.91	1.11	1.19	1.19	1.19	1.19	1.19	1.00	1.00
21	5.70	6.00	4.00	2.50	2.20	1.80	1.50	1.50	1.50	1.50	1.30	1.30	1.30
22	3.96	4.48	5.40	3.16	2.76	2.62	2.33	2.17	1.96	1.68	1.41	1.84	1.74
23	5.51	5.51	3.41	3.41	3.41	2.41	2.41	2.41	2.41	2.41	2.41	2.41	2.41
24	3.50	4.75	1.75	1.75	1.75	1.75	1.75	1.75	1.75	1.75	1.75	1.75	1.75
25	5.25	7.00	2.20	2.40	1.40	1.90	1.90	1.50	1.50	1.50	1.30	2.00	2.00

14	15	16	17	18	19	20	21	22	23	24	25	
2.20	1.70	2.00	2.15	2.00	2.00	2.00	2.00	2.00	2.00	2.00	2.00	1
2.54	2.06	2.35	2.72	2.57	2.84	2.84	2.78	2.78	2.78	2.81	2.81	2
1.63	1.82	1.86	1.79	1.85	1.98	1.99	1.86	1.85	1.85	1.93	1.89	3
2.05	2.03	1.94	1.86	2.02	1.98	1.87	1.67	1.95	1.95	2.21	1.89	4
2.20	2.13	2.25	1.82	2.24	2.71	2.45	1.92	2.06	2.25	2.16	2.25	5
1.77	1.77	2.02	1.83	1.70	1.90	1.90	1.90	1.90	1.90	1.90	1.90	6
2.61	2.70	2.60	2.50	2.98	2.88	3.06	2.79	2.79	2.34	2.70	2.61	7
1.68	1.89	2.10	1.82	2.10	1.89	2.10	1.54	1.54	2.03	2.03	2.03	8
1.69	1.69	1.82	1.56	1.75	1.75	1.75	1.69	1.75	1.75	1.75	1.75	9
1.40	1.51	1.50	1.40	1.40	1.40	1.40	1.40	1.40	1.40	1.40	1.40	10
1.50	1.50	1.50	1.40	1.70	1.70	1.70	1.80	2.00	2.00	2.00	2.00	11
1.96	1.82	1.75	1.68	2.10	2.10	2.10	2.10	2.10	2.10	2.10	2.10	12
2.41	2.37	2.33	2.24	2.64	2.64	2.64	2.18	2.18	2.18	2.18	2.18	13
2.10	1.96	2.31	2.00	2.10	2.10	2.10	2.10	2.10	2.10	2.10	2.10	14
2.01	1.36	1.85	1.80	1.80	1.80	2.10	2.10	2.10	2.10	2.11	2.10	15
2.59	2.66	2.31	2.45	2.94	2.94	2.94	2.94	2.94	2.94	2.94	2.94	16
2.23	2.10	2.38	2.15	2.34	2.32	2.32	2.30	2.30	2.30	2.30	2.30	17
1.85	1.35	1.40	2.25	1.87	1.87	1.87	1.80	1.80	1.80	1.80	1.80	18
1.65	1.50	1.20	1.70	1.60	1.40	1.40	1.40	1.45	1.45	1.50	1.50	19
1.02	1.50	1.22	1.53	1.14	0.98	0.94	0.92	0.92	0.91	0.91	0.91	20
1.20	1.10	1.50	1.40	1.00	1.00	0.90	0.90	0.80	0.80	0.70	0.70	21
1.76	1.48	1.54	1.84	1.26	1.26	1.26	1.26	1.22	1.22	1.22	1.22	22
1.91	1.31	1.31	1.53	1.46	1.46	1.46	1.36	1.36	1.36	1.36	1.36	23
1.75	1.75	1.25	1.75	2.50	1.50	1.50	1.50	1.50	1.50	1.50	1.50	24
1.40	1.10	1.20	2.70	1.60	1.30	1.10	1.10	1.10	1.10	1.10	1.10	25

	1	2	3	4	5	6	7	8	9	10	11	12	13
26	2.85	4.55	2.55	2.55	2.55	2.35	2.35	2.15	1.95	1.95	1.55	2.25	2.25
27	2.95	6.30	2.30	2.60	3.10	3.10	3.10	3.10	3.10	3.10	3.10	3.10	3.10
28	3.57	3.13	1.09	1.18	1.05	1.05	1.05	1.05	1.04	1.04	1.05	1.34	1.31
29	4.81	5.51	0.91	1.16	1.90	1.03	1.09	1.15	1.09	1.12	1.31	1.19	1.39
30	5.52	5.98	1.24	1.42	1.76	1.76	1.76	1.76	1.55	1.55	1.68	1.80	1.92
31	4.50	5.40	1.20	1.20	1.20	1.20	1.26	1.26	1.20	1.20	1.26	1.38	1.50
32	4.53	6.03	1.19	1.57	1.29	1.30	1.32	1.35	1.35	1.35	1.35	1.38	1.81
33	5.59	5.66	1.12	1.37	1.66	1.62	1.82	1.67	1.60	1.56	1.42	1.42	1.72
34	6.50	6.00	1.25	1.50	1.50	1.50	1.50	1.50	1.30	1.30	1.60	1.50	1.50
35	4.12	4.56	2.15	1.16	1.25	1.25	1.25	1.25	1.25	1.25	1.25	1.02	1.13
36	3.72	3.76	2.32	2.04	2.04	2.04	2.04	2.04	1.84	1.76	1.76	2.24	2.36
37	2.30	2.32	1.84	1.92	1.92	1.92	1.92	1.92	1.92	1.92	2.00	2.40	2.40
38	1.92	1.92	2.72	2.32	2.32	2.32	2.42	2.42	2.42	2.42	2.42	2.42	2.42
39	2.49	2.78	2.73	2.45	2.45	2.45	2.45	2.45	2.45	2.45	2.70	2.35	2.30
40	2.05	1.84	2.18	1.76	1.88	2.60	2.60	2.60	2.85	2.79	2.88	2.98	2.82
41	1.48	1.80	2.16	1.98	1.98	2.10	2.22	2.22	2.22	2.22	2.22	3.18	3.30
42	3.16	3.31	3.51	2.97	2.97	2.97	2.97	2.97	2.97	2.97	2.97	2.91	3.13
43	2.63	2.54	3.75	2.59	2.59	2.59	2.59	2.59	2.59	2.59	2.66	3.00	2.40
44	3.00	3.30	3.00	1.80	2.10	2.40	2.40	2.40	2.10	2.10	2.70	3.00	3.60
45	2.30	1.70	2.10	1.80	1.90	2.30	2.30	2.30	2.30	2.30	2.30	2.40	2.50
46	4.44	2.15	1.84	1.85	2.45	2.45	2.45	2.45	2.45	2.45	2.58	2.42	2.67
47	2.00	2.20	2.80	1.60	1.60	1.60	1.60	1.60	1.60	1.60	1.60	1.70	1.70
48	3.36	3.40	2.60	3.00	3.00	3.00	3.00	3.00	3.00	2.10	2.10	1.95	2.00
49	3.81	4.88	4.56	4.44	4.31	4.31	4.19	4.19	4.19	4.19	3.06	2.37	2.37
50	3.95	3.75	1.90	2.70	2.70	2.70	2.70	2.70	2.70	2.70	2.70	3.00	3.00

14	15	16	17	18	19	20	21	22	23	24	25	
2.15	1.75	1.45	1.85	1.10	1.00	1.00	0.85	0.80	0.90	1.00	1.15	26
3.10	2.70	2.20	3.30	2.80	2.80	2.80	2.50	2.50	2.50	2.50	2.50	27
1.31	1.37	1.73	1.44	1.38	1.40	1.40	1.40	1.40	1.40	1.40	1.40	28
1.41	1.39	1.99	1.71	1.92	2.01	1.89	1.84	1.75	1.71	1.75	1.99	29
2.05	1.62	1.56	2.42	2.43	2.73	2.74	2.63	2.69	2.36	2.28	2.52	30
1.44	1.20	1.66	1.74	2.22	2.88	2.10	1.86	1.86	1.86	1.86	1.86	31
1.75	1.63	1.57	2.12	2.00	2.63	2.19	2.30	2.15	2.53	2.20	2.20	32
1.79	1.81	1.62	1.75	2.16	2.29	2.23	2.37	2.40	2.60	1.83	2.09	33
1.70	1.70	1.62	1.70	2.10	2.10	2.10	1.60	1.60	1.16	1.60	1.81	34
1.13	1.43	1.36	1.22	1.57	1.57	1.57	1.32	1.32	1.16	1.16	1.39	35
2.24	1.56	1.24	1.48	1.72	1.72	1.72	1.72	1.72	1.64	1.52	1.52	36
2.28	2.28	1.80	2.48	2.48	2.48	2.48	2.48	2.48	2.48	2.64	2.64	37
2.42	2.22	2.12	2.12	2.12	2.12	2.12	2.12	2.12	2.12	2.12	2.12	38
2.35	1.85	1.85	2.65	2.90	3.00	2.75	2.75	2.75	2.65	2.65	2.65	39
2.13	1.70	1.83	2.10	2.32	2.39	2.02	2.02	2.02	2.02	2.02	2.02	40
2.82	2.28	2.04	3.06	3.12	3.12	3.83	2.46	2.64	2.64	2.82	2.82	41
2.92	2.42	2.35	3.25	3.45	3.53	3.42	3.12	3.12	3.35	3.46	3.46	42
2.12	1.83	2.10	2.61	2.61	2.61	2.31	2.22	2.22	2.27	2.27	2.27	43
2.40	3.00	3.00	3.90	4.80	3.00	3.00	3.30	3.30	3.60	3.60	3.60	44
2.50	2.10	2.10	2.80	3.20	3.20	3.10	2.90	2.80	2.80	2.80	2.90	45
2.67	1.34	1.69	1.69	2.15	2.00	2.00	1.54	1.38	1.38	1.38	1.38	46
1.70	1.70	1.70	1.50	3.60	3.60	3.60	3.60	3.60	3.60	3.60	3.60	47
2.00	1.30	1.55	1.70	1.13	1.13	1.13	1.13	1.13	1.13	1.23	1.33	48
2.06	1.69	1.25	1.75	1.00	1.00	1.00	1.00	1.06	1.06	1.06	1.06	49
2.50	1.50	1.60	1.75	1.70	1.70	1.40	1.40	1.40	1.40	1.40	1.40	50

	1	2	3	4	5	6	7	8	9	10	11	12	13
51	6.22	5.12	3.38	3.23	3.23	3.00	3.00	3.00	3.00	2.50	2.50	2.60	2.32
52	3.87	5.47	3.07	2.87	2.87	2.87	2.87	2.67	2.67	2.67	2.67	2.47	2.37
53	3.33	5.76	1.80	1.89	2.25	2.25	2.70	2.34	2.16	2.16	2.16	2.34	2.34
54	4.33	5.38	1.97	2.17	2.60	3.12	2.52	2.35	2.34	2.26	2.20	2.01	2.45
55	3.94	5.90	1.57	1.57	2.30	2.30	1.97	1.64	1.58	1.64	1.58	1.31	1.51
56	4.30	5.50	1.90	1.70	2.00	2.00	2.00	1.90	1.90	1.40	1.40	1.40	1.50
57	3.97	5.15	1.67	1.49	1.49	1.49	1.49	1.49	1.49	1.49	1.28	1.28	1.28
58	3.09	5.32	1.82	1.67	1.67	1.67	1.47	1.47	1.47	1.47	1.37	1.60	1.60
59	4.00	7.40	1.78	1.83	1.83	1.63	1.63	1.63	1.63	1.50	1.50	1.40	1.40
60	3.71	4.06	1.68	1.40	1.40	1.40	1.40	1.40	1.61	1.61	1.61	1.89	1.82
61	4.90	4.90	3.15	2.80	2.80	2.80	2.80	2.10	2.10	2.10	2.10	2.10	2.66
62	3.86	4.92	2.65	1.15	1.15	1.15	1.15	1.15	1.15	1.15	1.15	1.15	1.15
63	0.0	0.0	0.0	0.0	0.0	0.0	0.0	0.0	0.0	0.0	0.0	0.0	0.0
64	2.41	2.41	2.36	2.14	2.14	2.19	2.19	2.19	2.19	2.19	2.19	2.15	2.15
65	2.25	2.25	2.05	1.86	1.86	1.86	1.86	1.86	1.86	1.86	1.86	2.23	2.23
66	1.40	1.40	1.20	1.20	1.20	1.20	1.20	1.20	1.20	1.20	1.20	1.20	1.20
67	1.35	1.35	1.37	1.08	1.08	1.08	1.08	1.08	1.08	1.08	1.08	1.15	1.17
68	0.0	0.0	0.0	0.0	0.0	0.0	0.0	0.0	0.0	0.0	0.0	0.0	0.0
69	2.12	2.04	1.76	1.48	1.52	1.52	1.52	1.52	1.52	1.56	1.56	1.68	1.68
70	2.19	2.19	2.19	1.80	1.80	1.80	1.80	1.80	1.80	1.80	1.80	2.10	2.10
71	5.60	7.40	1.10	1.30	1.10	1.10	1.10	1.70	1.70	1.70	1.60	1.10	1.10
72	3.25	5.02	0.89	0.76	0.76	0.76	0.76	0.76	0.76	0.76	0.76	0.76	0.76
73	4.71	4.71	1.17	1.24	1.02	1.00	1.00	0.92	0.92	0.90	1.10	1.15	1.22
74	7.00	7.70	2.80	2.24	2.24	2.24	1.89	1.89	1.89	1.89	1.89	1.40	1.40
75	4.52	7.20	2.64	2.28	1.82	1.68	1.50	1.44	1.56	1.68	1.86	1.50	1.74

14	15	16	17	18	19	20	21	22	23	24	25	
2.32	2.00	1.46	1.97	1.30	1.30	1.30	1.03	1.40	1.40	1.40	1.40	51
2.37	2.17	2.32	1.74	1.19	1.19	1.04	1.24	1.24	1.24	1.24	1.24	52
2.52	2.52	1.98	2.25	2.16	2.16	2.16	2.16	2.16	2.16	2.25	2.25	53
1.98	2.17	1.89	2.21	2.16	2.18	2.40	2.28	2.23	2.17	2.27	2.14	54
1.64	1.77	1.31	1.44	1.71	1.77	1.77	1.57	1.57	1.57	1.71	1.90	55
1.40	1.50	1.70	1.60	1.50	1.50	1.50	1.50	1.50	1.50	1.70	1.70	56
1.28	1.41	1.36	1.96	1.45	1.45	1.45	1.45	1.45	1.45	1.45	1.81	57
1.60	1.85	1.40	1.40	1.70	1.70	1.70	1.70	1.50	1.50	1.50	1.80	58
1.30	1.45	1.50	1.50	1.30	1.30	1.30	1.30	1.30	1.30	1.30	1.30	59
1.89	1.96	1.75	1.61	1.61	1.82	1.82	1.68	1.68	1.68	1.82	1.82	60
2.66	2.45	2.45	2.24	2.10	2.24	2.24	2.24	2.24	2.24	2.24	2.24	61
1.15	1.35	1.04	0.98	1.30	1.30	1.30	1.30	1.09	1.09	1.09	1.09	62
0.0	0.0	0.0	0.0	0.0	0.0	0.0	0.0	0.0	0.0	0.0	0.0	63
2.15	2.13	2.15	1.77	1.65	1.65	1.65	1.65	1.65	1.65	1.65	1.75	64
2.23	2.14	2.07	2.09	2.09	2.09	2.09	2.09	2.09	2.09	3.04	3.04	65
1.10	1.10	1.10	0.92	0.90	0.90	0.90	0.90	0.90	0.90	0.90	0.90	66
1.19	1.19	1.16	1.31	1.85	1.85	1.85	1.85	1.85	1.85	1.85	1.85	67
0.0	0.0	0.0	0.0	0.0	0.0	0.0	0.0	0.0	0.0	0.0	0.0	68
1.72	1.74	1.44	1.28	1.28	1.28	1.28	1.24	1.24	1.24	1.24	1.24	69
2.10	2.20	2.20	2.20	2.80	2.80	1.80	2.80	2.80	2.80	2.80	2.80	70
1.30	1.60	1.40	1.45	1.78	1.96	1.94	1.68	1.68	1.54	2.08	1.89	71
0.76	1.07	1.25	1.11	1.11	1.11	1.11	1.11	1.11	1.11	1.20	1.20	72
1.34	1.58	1.72	1.19	1.82	1.92	1.86	1.24	1.36	1.65	1.75	1.74	73
1.40	1.40	1.61	1.75	1.75	2.10	1.89	1.75	1.75	1.75	1.75	1.75	74
1.74	1.80	1.86	1.86	2.04	2.04	2.04	1.98	1.92	1.92	1.92	1.92	75

	1	2	3	4	5	6	7	8	9	10	11	12	13
76	4.80	5.70	1.20	1.20	1.50	1.50	2.10	2.10	1.80	1.80	1.80	1.68	1.68
77	6.16	7.59	2.10	1.78	1.65	1.65	1.65	1.65	1.65	1.65	1.65	1.65	1.65
78	4.16	4.74	2.49	2.90	2.90	3.33	4.07	4.62	4.44	3.96	3.96	3.10	2.94
79	2.02	2.05	2.05	1.76	1.83	1.85	1.93	1.99	2.02	2.07	2.14	1.90	1.82
80	4.30	4.85	3.68	2.47	2.65	2.75	2.86	3.00	3.05	3.10	3.15	3.56	3.66
81	2.82	2.82	2.50	2.45	2.45	2.45	2.45	2.45	2.45	2.45	2.45	2.45	2.45
82	2.70	3.10	2.68	2.53	2.48	2.48	2.48	2.48	2.48	2.58	2.58	2.70	2.70
83	2.50	2.89	3.02	2.52	2.42	2.22	2.20	2.20	2.10	2.10	2.05	1.96	1.90
84	0.96	1.04	1.26	1.26	1.26	1.26	1.26	1.26	1.10	1.10	1.10	1.10	1.10
85	1.18	3.10	3.70	2.80	2.70	2.70	2.60	2.50	2.40	2.40	2.30	2.20	2.20
86	3.60	4.00	3.60	1.70	1.70	1.20	1.20	1.20	1.20	1.20	1.20	1.30	1.00
87	5.55	7.20	2.85	3.60	3.60	3.37	2.85	2.85	2.85	2.10	1.80	2.40	2.55
88	5.74	4.48	3.88	3.57	3.50	3.36	3.22	3.04	2.97	2.90	2.90	3.08	3.08
89	6.10	7.30	2.60	3.00	2.80	2.60	3.00	1.80	1.70	1.40	1.20	1.60	1.50
90	4.90	4.60	2.60	2.30	2.00	1.80	1.60	1.50	1.50	1.60	1.60	2.20	2.10

14	15	16	17	18	19	20	21	22	23	24	25	
1.80	1.80	2.10	1.86	1.92	1.92	1.92	1.92	1.92	1.92	1.92	1.92	76
1.65	1.89	1.93	1.93	1.93	1.93	1.93	1.85	1.85	2.10	2.01	2.01	77
3.54	3.00	4.07	3.89	4.05	4.38	5.28	5.28	5.28	4.05	4.73	4.73	78
1.82	1.61	1.86	1.89	2.25	2.25	2.25	2.11	2.08	2.06	2.01	2.15	79
3.56	3.57	3.80	3.35	3.70	3.75	3.98	4.10	4.14	4.12	4.20	4.25	80
2.45	2.44	2.32	2.37	2.39	2.39	2.39	2.39	2.39	2.39	2.39	2.39	81
2.70	3.10	3.10	3.10	3.10	3.10	3.10	3.10	3.10	3.10	3.10	3.10	82
1.65	1.38	1.31	1.12	1.02	1.05	1.00	0.81	0.80	0.80	0.91	1.02	83
1.10	1.20	1.00	1.05	1.10	1.05	1.05	1.05	1.05	1.05	1.05	1.05	84
2.18	2.20	2.20	2.20	1.10	1.20	1.10	1.10	1.10	1.10	1.10	1.20	85
1.00	1.15	1.15	1.15	1.05	1.05	1.05	0.95	0.95	0.95	0.95	1.20	86
2.25	1.65	1.20	1.80	1.40	1.40	1.40	1.40	1.40	1.40	1.40	1.40	87
3.08	2.17	2.45	3.15	2.59	2.17	2.17	2.17	2.17	2.17	2.17	2.17	88
1.50	1.40	1.40	1.70	1.50	1.50	1.50	1.50	1.50	1.50	1.50	1.50	89
1.70	1.80	2.50	2.10	1.80	1.60	1.50	1.50	1.40	1.40	1.60	1.60	90

ORIGINAL DATA: PEAS PRICES (SILVER), 1900 TO 1910, SHENSI

PLACE \ MONTH	1	2	3	4	5	6	7	8	9	10	11	12	13
1	3.23	2.80	3.58	2.32	2.32	2.82	3.02	3.02	3.02	3.02	3.53	3.05	3.10
2	0.0	0.0	0.0	0.0	0.0	0.0	0.0	0.0	0.0	0.0	0.0	0.0	0.0
3	3.35	3.65	1.14	1.45	1.37	1.38	1.29	1.28	1.33	1.34	1.36	1.28	1.49
4	3.83	4.59	1.97	2.15	1.60	1.31	1.34	1.34	1.27	1.50	1.50	1.16	1.42
5	4.62	5.94	3.13	2.28	2.25	1.91	1.93	1.80	1.75	1.75	1.50	1.25	2.10
6	3.44	4.96	1.44	1.20	1.38	1.32	1.20	1.20	1.20	1.20	1.20	1.05	1.39
7	7.00	6.50	5.10	2.70	2.70	2.52	2.16	2.25	1.98	1.98	2.16	1.62	1.89
8	4.20	5.74	2.45	1.96	1.68	1.89	1.54	1.26	1.61	1.82	1.96	1.40	2.03
9	3.70	5.20	1.82	1.69	1.69	1.75	1.62	1.56	1.49	1.47	1.49	1.23	1.75
10	3.41	6.60	2.16	1.94	1.40	1.40	1.40	1.40	1.40	1.70	1.19	1.20	1.20
11	4.50	4.70	8.50	5.00	5.00	4.70	4.60	4.60	4.50	4.50	4.40	3.30	3.10
12	2.59	4.06	2.80	1.82	1.26	1.33	1.33	1.19	1.19	1.40	1.54	1.26	1.40
13	4.78	7.25	3.64	2.03	1.97	1.97	1.97	1.97	1.97	1.97	1.52	1.54	1.91
14	3.99	8.19	3.85	2.31	1.75	1.75	1.74	1.54	1.54	1.54	1.54	1.40	1.54
15	2.39	3.04	1.50	1.45	1.45	1.45	1.45	1.45	1.45	1.25	1.25	1.20	1.35
16	3.85	5.60	2.45	2.10	2.10	1.40	1.75	1.54	1.54	1.68	1.96	1.75	1.75
17	3.82	5.95	2.10	2.35	2.75	1.60	1.60	1.60	1.60	1.60	1.60	1.47	1.43
18	4.14	4.72	2.93	2.93	2.93	2.70	2.55	2.55	2.55	2.55	2.55	2.52	2.30
19	0.0	0.0	0.0	0.0	0.0	0.0	0.0	0.0	0.0	0.0	0.0	0.0	0.0
20	1.07	2.20	0.75	0.73	0.93	1.05	1.13	1.13	1.13	1.13	1.13	0.95	0.95
21	4.40	5.10	2.40	3.10	2.80	2.50	2.00	1.60	1.60	1.50	1.30	1.30	1.20
22	2.40	2.82	3.80	3.28	3.16	3.00	2.68	2.36	2.00	1.72	1.56	1.20	1.20
23	4.26	4.26	4.06	3.66	3.66	2.86	2.86	2.86	2.86	2.86	2.86	2.86	2.86
24	2.50	3.00	1.75	1.75	1.75	1.75	1.75	1.75	1.75	1.75	1.75	1.75	1.75
25	3.85	4.70	3.00	3.50	3.50	2.30	2.10	2.10	2.10	2.10	1.90	2.20	2.20

14	15	16	17	18	19	20	21	22	23	24	25	
2.70	1.90	2.16	2.60	2.40	2.40	2.40	2.40	2.40	2.40	2.40	2.40	1
0.0	0.0	0.0	0.0	0.0	0.0	0.0	0.0	0.0	0.0	0.0	0.0	2
1.24	1.39	1.35	1.64	1.63	1.94	1.96	1.80	1.79	1.79	1.19	2.06	3
1.24	1.49	1.76	1.60	1.96	2.40	1.81	1.62	1.89	1.95	2.21	2.16	4
1.55	1.50	2.00	1.93	2.10	2.31	2.16	2.02	2.05	2.34	1.60	2.34	5
1.26	1.39	1.58	1.58	1.64	1.58	1.51	1.51	1.51	1.64	1.66	1.64	6
2.07	2.26	2.30	2.10	2.71	2.43	2.34	2.34	2.25	2.34	2.88	2.79	7
1.61	1.68	1.96	1.82	2.10	2.03	1.82	1.82	1.96	2.24	2.38	2.52	8
1.30	1.43	1.69	1.56	1.66	1.69	1.69	1.69	1.69	1.69	1.89	1.82	9
1.30	1.40	1.40	1.30	1.35	1.46	1.46	1.46	1.46	1.46	1.46	1.46	10
3.20	2.80	2.70	2.30	2.90	2.80	2.70	2.70	2.70	2.70	2.70	2.70	11
1.61	1.40	1.40	1.54	2.10	1.82	1.47	2.03	1.89	1.89	1.96	1.89	12
1.97	2.12	1.82	2.04	2.18	2.18	2.18	2.18	2.18	2.18	2.29	2.29	13
1.54	1.54	1.54	1.54	2.10	2.10	1.89	1.89	1.89	1.89	2.10	2.38	14
1.35	1.35	1.25	1.05	1.20	1.20	1.96	2.11	2.11	2.11	2.11	2.11	15
1.75	1.82	1.54	1.96	2.31	2.31	2.31	2.31	2.31	2.31	2.31	2.31	16
1.41	1.40	1.56	1.35	1.67	1.66	1.66	1.65	1.65	1.62	1.80	1.80	17
2.03	1.80	1.80	2.43	1.98	1.98	1.98	1.98	1.98	1.98	1.98	1.98	18
0.0	0.0	0.0	0.0	0.0	0.0	0.0	0.0	0.0	0.0	0.0	0.0	19
0.97	1.60	1.25	1.88	1.42	1.25	1.23	1.23	1.23	1.23	1.23	1.03	20
1.20	1.00	1.20	1.60	1.20	1.20	1.20	1.20	1.10	1.10	1.10	1.10	21
1.10	1.04	1.07	1.40	1.12	1.12	1.12	1.12	1.80	1.80	1.80	1.70	22
2.26	1.86	1.56	1.96	1.71	1.71	1.71	1.61	1.61	1.61	1.61	1.61	23
1.75	1.75	1.25	1.50	1.25	1.25	1.25	1.25	1.25	1.25	1.25	1.25	24
2.00	1.80	1.60	2.80	2.10	2.10	2.00	2.00	2.00	2.00	2.00	2.00	25

	1	2	3	4	5	6	7	8	9	10	11	12	13
26	3.75	5.15	4.75	4.55	3.55	2.95	2.55	2.55	2.35	2.35	2.25	1.85	1.85
27	2.80	4.90	3.20	3.50	3.81	3.81	3.10	3.81	3.81	3.81	3.81	3.80	3.80
28	3.33	3.13	1.99	1.69	1.44	1.18	1.18	1.18	1.22	1.22	1.24	1.79	1.79
29	4.37	4.55	2.03	1.78	1.20	1.13	1.04	1.15	1.00	1.01	1.26	1.11	1.29
30	5.52	4.39	2.16	1.42	1.17	1.17	1.17	1.17	1.04	1.04	1.12	1.47	1.46
31	3.96	4.80	3.00	1.86	1.20	1.08	1.20	1.20	1.08	1.08	1.14	1.20	1.26
32	3.39	4.15	2.33	1.87	1.18	1.15	1.21	1.14	1.14	1.14	1.14	1.09	1.49
33	5.32	5.39	2.81	1.69	1.11	1.00	1.15	1.12	1.17	1.14	1.15	1.39	1.23
34	6.00	5.50	2.50	1.75	1.75	1.75	1.75	1.75	1.50	1.50	1.50	1.60	1.70
35	3.94	4.35	2.38	1.71	1.47	1.48	1.48	1.31	1.31	1.31	1.31	1.13	1.31
36	3.68	3.72	3.16	2.80	2.80	2.80	2.80	2.80	2.56	2.36	2.32	2.62	2.76
37	1.72	1.72	1.60	1.60	1.60	1.60	1.60	1.60	1.60	1.60	1.64	2.00	2.00
38	0.0	0.0	0.0	0.0	0.0	0.0	0.0	0.0	0.0	0.0	0.0	0.0	0.0
39	2.91	2.75	2.55	2.24	2.24	2.24	2.24	2.49	1.58	1.58	2.84	3.59	3.59
40	2.73	2.35	2.83	2.09	2.23	3.63	2.63	2.60	2.50	2.45	2.63	2.68	2.53
41	2.27	1.91	2.90	1.77	1.53	1.65	1.77	1.83	1.83	2.01	2.30	3.03	2.73
42	2.63	2.81	2.97	2.19	2.19	2.19	2.19	2.19	2.19	2.19	2.19	2.21	2.21
43	2.63	2.03	3.21	2.64	2.64	2.64	2.64	2.64	2.64	2.42	2.29	3.24	1.94
44	3.60	3.60	2.10	2.10	2.10	2.70	2.70	2.70	2.70	2.70	3.00	3.30	3.30
45	2.40	1.90	2.10	1.80	1.90	2.40	2.40	2.40	2.40	2.40	2.40	2.40	2.50
46	3.64	2.00	2.30	2.00	2.10	1.94	1.94	1.94	1.94	2.10	2.26	2.46	2.67
47	2.50	2.50	3.30	2.10	2.00	2.00	2.00	2.00	2.00	2.00	2.20	2.20	2.30
48	0.0	0.0	0.0	0.0	0.0	0.0	0.0	0.0	0.0	0.0	0.0	0.0	0.0
49	0.0	0.0	0.0	0.0	0.0	0.0	0.0	0.0	0.0	0.0	0.0	0.0	0.0
50	2.95	2.70	2.05	2.65	2.40	2.25	2.25	2.25	2.25	2.25	2.25	2.50	2.50

14	15	16	17	18	19	20	21	22	23	24	25	
1.85	1.55	1.75	2.95	2.35	2.30	2.20	1.70	1.50	1.50	1.50	1.60	26
3.80	3.40	3.00	3.70	3.40	3.40	3.40	3.20	3.20	3.20	3.20	3.20	27
1.19	1.24	1.23	1.42	2.14	2.17	2.17	2.17	2.17	2.17	2.17	2.17	28
1.15	1.20	0.98	1.60	1.87	1.88	1.78	1.68	1.60	1.66	1.71	1.99	29
1.30	1.02	1.26	1.29	2.08	1.67	1.60	1.61	1.61	1.83	1.64	2.15	30
1.20	1.30	1.44	1.44	1.71	1.74	1.67	1.68	1.68	1.68	1.68	1.68	31
1.31	1.29	1.43	1.40	1.55	2.30	2.20	2.20	2.19	2.40	2.19	2.10	32
1.10	1.37	1.75	1.78	2.16	2.15	1.87	1.23	2.26	2.20	2.22	2.35	33
1.80	1.80	1.75	1.90	2.30	2.30	2.30	1.80	1.80	1.80	1.80	2.10	34
1.07	1.25	1.35	1.16	1.68	1.68	1.68	1.60	1.60	1.60	1.60	1.68	35
2.40	1.92	1.56	2.08	2.04	2.40	2.00	1.76	1.76	1.76	1.76	1.76	36
1.92	1.92	1.60	1.84	1.84	1.84	1.84	1.84	1.84	1.84	1.84	1.84	37
0.0	0.0	0.0	0.0	0.0	0.0	0.0	0.0	0.0	0.0	0.0	0.0	38
2.53	2.54	1.59	3.44	3.44	3.54	3.04	3.04	3.04	2.94	2.94	2.94	39
1.78	1.35	1.46	2.10	2.46	2.55	2.02	2.02	2.02	2.02	2.02	2.02	40
2.01	1.59	1.41	2.25	2.31	2.13	2.13	2.13	2.13	2.13	2.31	2.31	41
1.91	1.57	1.42	2.25	2.39	2.39	2.28	2.11	2.11	2.29	2.51	2.51	42
2.03	1.83	2.33	3.04	3.04	3.04	2.77	2.64	2.86	2.95	2.73	2.73	43
2.10	1.80	2.40	3.30	4.20	3.00	3.00	3.30	3.30	3.30	3.30	3.30	44
2.50	2.20	2.20	2.90	3.20	3.00	2.90	2.50	2.40	2.40	2.40	2.50	45
2.33	1.72	1.23	1.17	3.54	1.69	1.54	1.54	1.45	1.45	1.45	1.45	46
2.00	1.60	1.50	1.50	2.50	2.30	2.30	2.00	2.00	2.00	2.00	2.00	47
0.0	0.0	0.0	0.0	0.0	0.0	0.0	0.0	0.0	0.0	0.0	0.0	48
0.0	0.0	0.0	0.0	0.0	0.0	0.0	0.0	0.0	0.0	0.0	0.0	49
2.00	1.20	1.30	1.50	1.80	1.80	1.40	1.40	1.40	1.40	1.40	1.40	50

	1	2	3	4	5	6	7	8	9	10	11	12	13
51	0.0	0.0	0.0	0.0	0.0	0.0	0.0	0.0	0.0	0.0	0.0	0.0	0.0
52	0.0	0.0	0.0	0.0	0.0	0.0	0.0	0.0	0.0	0.0	0.0	0.0	0.0
53	2.79	4.50	2.25	2.16	2.16	2.25	2.70	1.98	2.07	1.89	1.80	1.89	1.98
54	4.15	4.24	2.30	2.00	2.00	1.91	1.89	1.86	1.85	1.86	1.82	1.17	1.30
55	3.48	4.27	2.10	1.84	1.25	1.11	1.12	1.12	0.99	1.05	0.99	0.98	1.12
56	3.50	4.25	2.40	1.90	1.60	1.60	1.40	1.20	1.40	1.30	1.20	1.00	1.20
57	3.19	4.53	3.43	1.85	1.17	1.17	1.17	1.17	1.17	1.17	1.17	1.01	1.01
58	0.0	0.0	0.0	0.0	0.0	0.0	0.0	0.0	0.0	0.0	0.0	0.0	0.0
59	3.40	4.50	2.80	2.40	1.90	1.70	1.70	1.70	1.70	1.70	1.60	1.15	1.10
60	3.15	3.64	2.94	2.31	1.61	1.61	1.61	1.61	1.61	1.61	1.61	1.26	1.54
61	4.20	4.55	3.50	2.80	2.10	2.10	2.10	1.75	1.75	1.75	1.75	1.54	2.10
62	2.99	3.65	3.29	1.53	1.58	1.53	1.53	1.53	1.53	1.53	1.53	1.53	1.53
63	3.00	3.12	3.12	2.28	2.28	2.28	2.28	2.28	2.28	2.28	2.28	3.30	3.12
64	2.56	2.21	2.01	1.29	1.29	1.29	1.29	1.29	1.29	1.41	1.41	1.54	1.49
65	1.53	1.61	1.61	1.35	1.35	1.35	1.35	1.35	1.35	1.35	1.35	2.23	2.23
66	1.50	1.50	1.00	0.80	0.80	0.85	0.90	0.90	1.00	1.10	1.20	1.40	1.30
67	1.54	1.67	1.54	1.25	1.25	1.25	1.25	1.25	1.25	1.27	1.27	1.35	1.41
68	1.92	1.60	1.60	1.28	1.12	1.20	1.36	1.42	1.44	1.44	1.68	2.48	2.48
69	2.24	2.10	1.76	1.28	1.36	1.40	1.36	1.36	1.44	1.52	1.56	2.36	2.36
70	1.65	1.65	1.65	1.22	1.22	1.22	1.22	1.22	1.22	1.22	1.22	2.00	2.00
71	4.40	6.90	5.30	2.80	1.90	1.90	1.40	1.40	1.40	1.40	1.40	1.60	1.50
72	2.71	4.44	3.56	2.00	1.56	1.56	1.25	1.25	1.25	1.25	1.25	0.95	0.94
73	3.76	3.76	4.50	2.32	1.50	1.29	1.23	1.20	1.20	1.20	1.36	1.24	1.22
74	5.81	8.05	4.20	2.45	2.45	2.45	2.10	2.10	2.10	2.10	2.10	1.75	1.75
75	4.22	6.00	3.93	2.44	1.82	1.68	1.50	1.56	1.62	1.62	1.80	1.50	1.74

14	15	16	17	18	19	20	21	22	23	24	25	
0.0	0.0	0.0	0.0	0.0	0.0	0.0	0.0	0.0	0.0	0.0	0.0	51
0.0	0.0	0.0	0.0	0.0	0.0	0.0	0.0	0.0	0.0	0.0	0.0	52
2.07	2.07	1.80	2.16	2.16	2.34	2.34	2.25	2.34	2.34	2.34	2.34	53
1.24	1.43	1.49	1.80	1.51	1.86	1.75	1.63	1.79	1.74	1.78	1.74	54
1.08	1.01	1.25	1.31	1.31	1.44	1.38	1.38	1.38	1.31	1.38	1.44	55
1.10	1.30	1.40	1.30	1.20	1.30	1.50	1.50	1.50	1.50	1.40	1.40	56
1.00	1.13	1.32	1.33	1.40	1.40	1.45	1.45	1.45	1.45	1.45	1.49	57
0.0	0.0	0.0	0.0	0.0	0.0	0.0	0.0	0.0	0.0	0.0	0.0	58
1.00	1.20	1.20	1.00	1.30	1.30	1.30	1.30	1.30	1.30	1.30	1.30	59
1.40	1.40	1.75	1.54	1.61	1.96	1.96	1.68	1.68	1.68	1.89	1.89	60
2.10	1.75	2.10	1.89	1.82	2.10	2.10	2.10	2.10	2.10	2.10	2.10	61
1.53	1.53	1.20	1.27	1.35	1.35	1.35	1.35	1.35	1.35	1.35	1.35	62
3.00	2.64	2.70	2.76	2.46	2.46	2.46	2.46	2.46	2.46	2.64	2.64	63
1.46	1.46	1.41	1.41	1.37	1.35	1.35	1.35	1.35	1.35	1.37	1.35	64
2.23	2.16	2.05	2.05	2.05	2.05	2.05	2.05	2.05	2.05	2.51	2.51	65
1.30	1.30	1.30	1.28	1.30	1.30	1.30	1.30	1.30	1.30	1.30	1.30	66
1.50	1.50	1.45	1.48	0.99	1.11	1.11	1.99	1.99	1.99	1.99	1.99	67
1.60	1.36	1.28	1.68	1.68	1.68	1.68	1.60	1.60	1.68	1.76	1.76	68
2.24	2.08	1.72	1.68	1.56	3.52	1.52	1.48	1.48	1.48	1.48	1.48	69
1.40	1.40	1.40	1.40	1.90	1.90	1.90	1.90	1.90	1.90	1.90	1.90	70
1.40	1.60	1.40	1.90	2.16	2.42	2.26	1.89	1.89	1.96	2.60	2.74	71
0.94	1.07	1.29	1.70	1.07	1.38	1.07	1.07	1.07	1.07	1.07	1.07	72
1.34	1.44	1.77	1.30	1.96	1.85	1.75	1.37	1.40	1.67	1.84	1.85	73
1.40	1.75	1.75	1.96	2.45	2.80	2.80	2.80	2.80	2.80	2.80	2.80	74
1.74	1.80	1.92	1.80	1.80	1.92	1.86	1.80	1.80	1.80	1.80	2.40	75

	1	2	3	4	5	6	7	8	9	10	11	12	13
76	3.60	4.50	2.40	1.80	1.80	1.80	1.80	1.80	1.80	1.80	1.80	1.62	1.62
77	4.48	6.86	5.40	3.15	2.94	2.94	2.80	2.80	2.80	2.80	2.80	2.52	2.31
78	2.94	3.39	2.67	1.97	1.97	2.07	2.59	2.67	2.12	2.12	2.12	2.39	2.61
79	1.55	1.60	1.76	1.39	1.33	1.40	1.45	1.52	1.57	1.60	1.64	1.44	1.47
80	3.00	3.55	2.55	1.50	1.67	1.76	1.84	1.95	1.95	1.98	1.98	2.20	2.32
81	2.69	2.69	2.50	2.45	2.45	2.45	2.45	2.45	2.45	2.45	2.45	2.45	2.45
82	1.81	2.31	2.50	1.80	1.60	1.60	1.60	1.60	1.60	1.60	1.60	1.60	1.60
83	2.20	2.37	3.40	3.25	3.05	1.70	1.07	1.70	1.60	1.60	1.50	1.71	1.55
84	0.77	0.83	2.55	2.55	2.55	1.01	1.01	1.01	0.90	0.90	0.90	0.90	0.90
85	0.75	0.0	0.0	2.90	2.60	2.40	2.00	2.00	1.90	1.70	1.60	1.40	1.40
86	3.00	3.70	5.20	3.30	3.30	2.30	2.20	2.20	1.90	1.90	1.90	1.50	1.20
87	3.07	4.61	3.30	3.75	2.85	2.62	2.25	2.25	2.25	1.95	1.65	1.80	1.95
88	3.78	3.71	3.41	1.71	3.50	2.94	2.80	2.59	2.52	2.38	2.38	2.45	2.45
89	4.50	5.50	3.00	3.00	2.60	2.10	3.00	1.30	1.20	1.20	1.20	1.60	1.50
90	3.40	3.70	3.30	1.60	1.40	1.30	1.20	1.10	1.10	1.20	1.20	1.80	1.80

14	15	16	17	18	19	20	21	22	23	24	25	
1.74	1.74	1.80	1.44	1.50	1.50	1.50	1.50	1.50	1.50	1.50	1.50	76
2.31	2.31	2.00	2.00	2.00	2.00	2.00	1.90	1.90	2.06	2.46	2.46	77
2.21	2.21	2.22	3.17	3.14	2.69	3.15	3.15	3.15	2.69	2.98	2.98	78
1.27	1.23	1.41	1.60	1.76	1.63	1.56	1.52	1.55	1.57	1.59	1.59	79
2.25	2.23	2.40	2.25	3.62	2.50	2.55	2.60	2.62	2.60	2.70	2.80	80
2.45	2.03	1.84	1.89	1.90	1.90	1.90	1.90	1.90	1.90	1.91	1.91	81
1.40	1.55	1.45	1.80	1.90	1.80	1.90	1.90	1.90	1.80	1.80	1.90	82
1.30	1.10	1.10	1.15	1.05	1.01	1.05	0.99	0.99	0.99	1.05	1.07	83
0.90	0.90	0.90	1.00	1.05	1.00	1.00	1.00	1.00	1.00	1.00	1.00	84
1.38	1.31	2.00	2.00	1.15	1.20	1.10	1.10	1.10	1.10	1.10	1.25	85
1.10	1.10	1.10	1.10	1.10	1.10	1.10	1.10	1.10	1.10	1.10	1.10	86
1.80	1.80	1.72	2.40	2.40	2.40	2.40	2.40	2.40	2.40	2.40	2.40	87
2.45	1.96	2.45	2.94	2.52	2.10	2.10	2.10	2.10	2.10	2.10	2.10	88
1.50	1.40	1.40	1.70	1.50	1.50	1.50	1.50	1.50	1.50	1.50	1.50	89
1.60	2.00	2.50	2.20	1.80	1.60	1.50	1.50	1.50	1.50	1.70	1.70	90

APPENDIX 2

Elementary Analysis of Prices

ELEMENTARY ANALYSIS OF WHEAT PRICES (SILVER), 1900 TO 1910, SHENSI

PLACE \ MONTH	1	2	3	4	5	6	7	8	9	10	11	12	13
1	-1.082	-2.213	-0.319	-0.520	-0.201	0.030	0.518	0.543	0.567	0.568	0.855	0.295	0.364
2	-0.792	-2.044	-1.040	-0.670	-0.342	-0.310	0.127	0.152	0.176	0.227	0.214	-0.236	-0.167
3	0.706	0.864	0.068	-0.232	0.077	0.118	0.085	0.080	-0.085	-0.064	-0.058	-0.438	0.071
4	1.069	1.588	-0.578	0.472	0.160	-0.299	-0.111	-0.146	-0.202	-0.031	-0.104	-0.454	-0.205
5	0.818	2.796	0.630	0.990	0.319	-0.030	-0.043	-0.178	-0.253	-0.252	-0.266	-0.326	0.343
6	1.439	2.987	0.161	-0.139	-0.000	-0.089	-0.281	-0.257	-0.112	-0.231	-0.245	-0.385	0.104
7	3.479	2.648	3.722	1.062	0.120	-0.119	-0.141	-0.016	-0.262	-0.171	0.086	-0.414	-0.095
8	1.185	2.753	0.577	0.397	0.086	-0.093	-0.246	-0.291	-0.126	0.015	0.071	-0.379	0.610
9	0.773	2.242	0.786	0.055	0.174	0.075	0.063	-0.173	-0.148	-0.147	-0.091	-0.180	0.339
10	1.285	4.314	0.628	1.108	0.026	-0.112	-0.125	-0.100	-0.076	0.025	-0.088	0.022	0.041
11	1.368	1.237	4.611	2.431	0.949	1.081	0.868	0.893	0.817	0.818	0.905	-0.155	-0.386
12	0.732	1.461	0.985	0.015	-0.157	-0.335	-0.208	-0.323	-0.299	-0.298	-0.171	-0.241	0.088
13	1.850	3.819	0.643	0.103	0.051	-0.218	-0.230	-0.205	-0.181	-0.180	-0.343	-0.303	-0.054
14	1.357	4.815	1.089	0.149	-0.022	0.009	-0.354	-0.329	-0.654	-0.663	-0.317	-0.347	-0.268
15	-0.197	-0.228	-0.285	-0.665	-0.246	-0.115	-0.127	-0.103	-0.078	-0.277	-0.291	-0.131	-0.161
16	1.193	3.252	0.926	-0.154	-0.326	-0.504	-0.097	-0.072	-0.258	-0.467	-0.340	-0.580	0.129
17	0.660	3.168	0.412	0.862	1.181	0.412	0.399	0.424	0.499	0.510	0.496	-0.274	-0.805
18	1.738	0.667	1.391	1.290	1.149	0.740	0.498	0.522	0.547	0.548	0.534	0.125	-0.096
19	1.396	1.074	1.738	1.788	2.207	2.038	1.625	1.550	1.475	1.276	1.162	0.002	-0.429
20	-1.103	-0.614	-1.550	-0.571	-0.052	0.079	0.147	0.171	0.196	0.197	0.183	0.144	0.013
21	3.266	3.434	-0.292	0.828	1.046	0.878	0.365	0.290	0.314	0.215	-0.098	0.042	-0.189
22	0.386	0.615	1.308	2.208	2.327	2.038	1.506	1.090	0.555	0.346	0.102	0.302	0.012
23	1.864	1.332	1.306	1.326	1.645	0.876	0.863	0.888	0.913	0.914	0.900	0.940	0.809
24	-1.145	-0.427	-0.753	0.267	0.586	0.617	0.605	0.629	0.654	0.655	0.641	0.681	0.550
25	1.130	1.349	1.022	0.442	1.761	0.592	0.380	0.404	0.429	0.430	0.216	0.456	0.326

14	15	16	17	18	19	20	21	22	23	24	25	ROW EFFECT	
0.027	-0.690	-0.399	-0.127	-0.277	-0.293	-0.202	-0.122	-0.091	-0.120	-0.134	-0.171	0.630	1
0.116	-0.521	-0.530	0.242	-0.028	0.126	0.217	-0.063	-0.032	-0.061	0.455	0.418	0.381	2
-0.096	0.137	0.318	-0.050	-0.020	-0.016	-0.004	0.015	0.036	0.007	0.073	0.036	-0.257	3
0.308	0.341	0.502	0.064	0.164	-0.112	-0.191	-0.131	0.060	0.151	0.337	0.040	-0.301	4
0.306	0.369	0.300	-0.128	0.002	0.516	0.048	-0.013	-0.042	0.039	-0.025	-0.012	-0.249	5
0.047	0.100	0.302	0.173	0.174	0.038	0.059	0.078	0.109	0.210	0.197	0.099	-0.571	6
0.358	0.621	0.532	0.134	0.184	-0.102	-0.011	-0.111	-0.080	0.071	0.097	0.020	-0.031	7
0.113	0.186	0.477	0.199	0.129	0.113	-0.075	-0.206	-0.175	0.006	0.062	0.095	-0.336	8
0.071	0.205	0.406	0.148	-0.012	0.012	-0.097	-0.087	-0.117	-0.086	0.041	-0.067	-0.625	9
0.104	0.307	0.198	-0.050	0.050	-0.126	-0.035	0.045	0.076	0.047	0.033	-0.004	-0.797	10
-0.223	-0.290	-0.279	-0.377	-0.177	-0.493	-0.402	-0.422	-0.391	-0.420	-0.334	-0.271	0.480	11
0.361	0.224	0.445	0.167	0.377	0.221	-0.038	0.112	0.073	0.044	0.100	-0.007	-0.444	12
0.319	0.272	0.273	0.015	0.055	0.039	0.130	0.040	0.071	0.042	0.228	0.191	-0.202	13
0.215	0.078	0.509	-0.119	0.301	0.285	0.167	0.246	0.277	0.248	0.234	0.197	-0.298	14
-0.099	-0.065	-0.154	-0.173	0.028	0.012	0.403	0.482	0.513	0.484	0.471	0.433	-0.125	15
-0.018	0.125	-0.074	-0.212	0.278	0.262	0.353	0.433	0.324	0.295	0.281	0.244	0.565	16
-0.112	-1.009	0.222	0.224	-0.226	-0.362	-0.270	-0.191	-0.160	-0.189	-0.203	-0.240	0.249	17
-0.163	-0.330	0.001	0.093	-0.447	-0.463	-0.372	-0.382	-0.351	-0.380	-0.394	-0.432	0.150	18
-0.466	-0.633	-0.722	-0.420	-0.670	-0.936	-0.894	-0.815	-0.734	-0.763	-0.777	-0.814	0.323	19
0.085	0.359	0.130	0.462	-0.108	-0.274	-0.233	-0.163	-0.133	-0.152	-0.165	-0.203	-0.969	20
-0.126	-0.293	0.018	0.520	-0.080	-0.096	-0.105	-0.025	-0.094	-0.123	-0.337	-0.474	-0.817	21
0.154	-0.233	-0.141	0.060	-0.509	-0.525	-0.434	-0.355	-0.394	-0.423	-0.436	-0.474	-0.398	22
-0.128	-0.695	-0.684	-0.332	-0.932	-0.948	-0.856	-0.987	-0.956	-0.985	-0.999	-1.036	0.395	23
0.613	0.546	-0.693	-0.191	-0.690	-0.706	-0.615	-0.536	-0.505	-0.534	-0.547	-0.585	0.593	24
0.188	-0.078	-0.187	0.434	-0.265	-0.581	-0.590	-0.511	-0.480	-0.509	-0.522	-0.560	-0.432	25

	1	2	3	4	5	6	7	8	9	10	11	12	13
26	-0.117	0.652	1.625	2.245	1.564	0.995	0.583	0.607	0.432	0.433	0.319	-0.041	0.129
27	-3.103	-1.684	-1.811	-0.091	0.228	0.259	0.247	0.271	0.296	0.297	0.283	0.323	0.193
28	0.269	-1.092	-0.538	-0.199	0.050	0.021	0.009	0.033	0.038	0.039	0.255	-0.144	-0.275
29	1.229	0.888	-0.549	-0.239	-0.040	-0.129	-0.181	-0.047	-0.182	-0.151	-0.075	-0.225	-0.125
30	1.421	1.129	0.123	-0.527	-0.258	-0.227	-0.240	-0.215	-0.260	-0.259	-0.153	0.047	-0.164
31	0.626	1.114	0.188	-0.292	-0.273	-0.302	-0.255	-0.230	-0.265	-0.324	-0.278	-0.118	-0.069
32	1.363	1.212	0.526	-0.215	-0.376	-0.375	-0.327	-0.373	-0.348	-0.347	-0.361	-0.270	-0.101
33	1.914	1.453	-0.503	-0.434	-0.425	-0.424	-0.186	-0.091	-0.167	-0.196	-0.189	-0.179	-0.090
34	2.179	1.148	-0.428	-0.409	-0.190	-0.159	-0.171	-0.146	-0.322	-0.321	-0.234	-0.094	-0.125
35	0.812	0.721	-0.515	-0.486	-0.077	-0.046	-0.058	-0.034	-0.009	-0.008	-0.022	-0.211	-0.232
36	-0.188	-0.800	-0.746	-0.206	0.113	0.144	0.131	0.156	-0.019	-0.138	-0.072	0.648	0.677
37	-1.370	-1.902	-1.408	-0.348	-0.029	0.002	-0.011	0.014	0.039	0.040	0.146	0.346	0.215
38	-2.476	-3.108	-0.534	0.086	0.305	0.336	0.324	0.348	0.373	0.374	0.360	0.500	0.469
39	-1.744	-2.375	-1.061	-0.592	-0.273	-0.242	-0.254	0.020	0.125	0.126	0.602	0.773	0.642
40	-1.845	-2.647	-0.773	-0.653	-0.174	0.387	0.375	0.399	0.374	0.315	0.681	1.121	0.790
41	-2.259	-3.091	-1.647	-1.107	-0.789	-0.567	-0.350	-0.205	-0.001	0.360	0.647	1.087	1.256
42	-1.684	-2.106	-0.692	-0.402	-0.083	-0.052	-0.065	-0.040	-0.015	-0.014	-0.028	0.392	0.301
43	-1.593	-2.914	-0.610	-0.781	-0.462	-0.431	-0.443	-0.219	-0.194	0.007	0.313	1.264	-0.117
44	-1.475	-2.006	-0.632	-1.613	-1.294	-0.363	-0.075	-0.051	0.574	0.575	1.161	1.202	1.071
45	-1.646	-3.078	-2.204	-1.584	-0.265	0.166	0.153	0.178	0.203	0.204	0.190	0.130	0.099
46	0.196	-2.695	-1.221	-0.812	-0.403	-0.372	-0.224	-0.030	0.465	0.466	0.782	0.812	0.942
47	-0.771	-0.502	-0.428	-0.809	-0.590	-0.559	-0.571	-0.147	-0.122	-0.121	-0.135	0.806	0.775
48	-0.608	-0.810	-1.536	1.404	1.723	1.754	1.741	1.766	1.791	-0.228	-0.242	-0.152	-0.053
49	-0.546	0.053	0.907	-1.073	2.125	2.156	2.014	2.039	2.063	2.064	0.931	0.341	0.210
50	-0.450	-1.382	-0.558	1.462	1.481	1.012	0.849	0.874	0.899	0.900	0.886	0.176	0.045

-0.009	-0.275	-0.164	0.737	-0.412	-0.478	-0.437	-0.658	-0.327	-0.356	-0.369	-0.257	-0.085	26
0.255	-0.211	-0.700	0.301	-0.098	-0.114	-0.023	-0.244	-0.213	-0.242	-0.255	-0.293	1.901	27
-0.223	-0.239	0.102	-0.336	0.014	0.018	0.109	0.189	0.219	0.190	0.177	0.139	-0.751	28
-0.063	-0.089	-0.108	0.023	0.234	0.388	0.329	0.158	0.109	0.150	0.057	0.209	-0.731	29
-0.111	-0.218	-0.117	0.275	0.385	0.119	0.221	0.220	0.211	0.212	0.318	0.491	-0.442	30
-0.066	0.107	0.158	0.060	0.210	0.284	0.376	0.215	0.246	0.217	0.203	0.166	-0.597	31
-0.169	-0.065	0.186	0.038	0.018	0.502	0.493	0.923	0.853	0.524	0.261	0.323	-0.515	32
-0.137	0.076	-0.103	-0.111	0.169	0.553	0.164	0.244	0.305	0.226	0.252	0.285	-0.376	33
0.138	0.071	0.002	-0.316	0.484	0.468	0.559	0.139	0.170	0.141	0.127	0.290	-0.481	34
-0.170	0.064	0.005	-0.133	0.217	0.201	0.292	0.122	0.152	-0.037	-0.050	0.142	-0.744	35
0.220	-0.087	-0.316	-0.154	0.167	0.110	0.122	-0.119	-0.088	-0.117	-0.131	-0.168	-0.103	36
0.078	0.011	-0.738	0.064	0.064	0.048	0.140	-0.021	0.010	-0.019	0.087	0.050	0.439	37
0.432	0.065	-0.324	-0.222	-0.221	-0.237	-0.146	-0.267	-0.236	-0.265	-0.278	-0.316	0.754	38
-0.396	-0.962	-0.901	1.151	1.351	0.805	0.046	0.126	0.156	0.127	0.114	0.076	1.082	39
-0.157	-0.874	-0.722	0.209	1.060	0.094	-0.305	-0.226	-0.195	-0.224	-0.237	-0.275	0.603	40
-0.241	-0.788	-0.857	0.465	0.585	0.269	-0.120	-0.040	0.171	0.322	0.608	0.391	0.568	41
-0.026	-0.643	-0.852	0.040	0.271	0.294	0.226	0.845	-0.124	0.107	0.253	0.216	0.742	42
-0.204	-0.541	-0.180	0.512	0.512	0.496	0.337	0.297	-0.452	0.599	0.585	0.778	0.871	43
-0.966	-1.333	-1.022	2.280	1.380	-0.736	-0.645	0.335	0.366	0.637	0.623	0.586	2.223	44
0.162	-0.705	-0.694	0.108	0.508	0.292	0.284	0.063	-0.606	-0.135	-0.149	0.014	1.095	45
0.414	-0.502	-0.521	0.220	1.481	0.235	-0.134	-0.054	-0.024	-0.053	-0.616	-0.264	0.112	46
0.538	-0.029	-0.318	-0.516	0.584	0.368	0.459	0.239	0.270	0.241	0.227	0.190	0.019	47
0.010	-0.637	0.244	-0.124	-0.273	-0.290	-0.198	-0.119	-0.088	-0.117	-0.181	-0.218	0.226	48
-0.097	-0.544	-0.913	-0.471	-0.841	-0.857	-0.766	-0.686	-0.595	-0.624	-0.638	-0.675	0.244	49
-0.092	-0.559	-0.148	0.104	-0.396	-0.412	-0.670	-0.591	-0.560	-0.589	-0.603	-0.640	0.049	50

	1	2	3	4	5	6	7	8	9	10	11	12	13
51	0.425	-1.367	-0.323	1.567	1.886	1.297	1.285	1.309	1.334	0.735	0.721	0.361	-0.150
52	-0.761	-0.093	0.181	1.001	1.320	0.951	0.939	0.663	0.688	0.689	0.675	0.515	0.134
53	-0.366	0.722	0.366	-0.144	0.175	0.116	0.553	-0.052	-0.027	-0.296	-0.400	-0.180	-0.131
54	0.644	0.943	0.557	0.506	0.195	0.186	0.274	0.208	0.223	0.224	0.250	-0.529	-0.570
55	0.316	0.765	0.169	0.668	0.067	-0.162	-0.114	-0.219	-0.255	-0.254	-0.267	-0.237	0.362
56	0.383	0.652	1.026	0.446	0.064	0.095	0.083	-0.192	-0.168	-0.267	-0.280	-0.240	-0.071
57	0.702	1.120	1.074	0.424	0.023	0.004	-0.009	0.016	0.041	0.042	0.028	-0.262	-0.393
58	-0.360	0.458	1.472	0.812	0.260	0.092	-0.121	-0.096	-0.072	-0.071	-0.184	-0.114	-0.245
59	0.436	0.705	0.969	0.198	C.167	0.098	0.086	0.110	0.135	0.036	0.022	-0.137	-0.118
60	0.085	0.184	1.428	0.697	0.176	0.207	0.195	0.219	-0.106	-0.105	-0.119	-0.289	0.071
61	0.576	0.745	0.519	0.488	0.457	0.488	0.476	-0.339	-0.315	-0.314	-0.327	-0.357	0.072
62	0.279	0.277	1.931	0.491	0.370	0.131	0.118	0.143	0.168	0.169	0.155	0.065	-0.066
63	-1.856	-2.388	-1.334	-1.214	-0.896	-0.864	-0.877	-0.852	-0.527	-0.526	-0.420	1.420	1.409
64	-1.054	-1.935	-0.961	-0.341	-0.023	0.058	0.046	0.071	0.095	0.196	0.183	0.443	0.212
65	-2.218	-2.629	-1.676	-0.986	-0.667	-0.636	-0.648	-0.624	-0.599	-0.598	-0.612	0.608	0.478
66	-1.193	-1.425	-1.651	-0.831	-0.513	-0.481	-0.494	-0.469	-0.345	-0.194	-0.157	0.283	0.252
67	-1.914	-2.275	-1.241	-0.552	-0.233	-0.202	-0.214	-0.190	-0.165	-0.124	-0.138	-0.327	-0.818
68	-1.515	-2.607	-1.433	-0.893	-0.575	-0.463	-0.396	-0.131	-0.107	-0.106	0.121	1.041	0.910
69	-1.252	-1.964	-1.370	-0.790	-0.291	-0.240	-0.332	-0.308	-0.223	-0.082	-0.076	0.924	0.883
70	-1.809	-2.341	-1.167	-0.667	-0.348	-0.317	-0.330	-0.305	-0.280	-0.279	-0.293	-0.553	-0.684
71	1.969	3.338	3.411	0.231	-0.050	-0.019	0.269	0.193	0.218	0.219	0.105	-0.355	-0.585
72	0.024	1.132	0.976	0.436	0.315	0.346	0.114	0.138	0.163	0.164	0.150	0.010	-0.391
73	1.192	0.661	0.895	0.474	-0.047	-0.146	-0.198	-0.223	-0.179	-0.178	-0.051	-0.221	-0.072
74	2.822	4.110	0.944	0.214	0.532	0.564	0.201	0.226	0.251	0.252	0.238	-0.072	-0.203
75	0.761	2.310	1.503	0.343	0.042	-0.067	-0.259	-0.175	-0.090	-0.089	0.137	-0.183	0.047

14	15	16	17	18	19	20	21	22	23	24	25	ROW EFFECT	
-0.387	-0.454	-0.673	0.239	-0.560	-0.776	-0.685	-0.606	-0.475	-0.504	-0.517	-0.555	0.663	51
0.147	-0.070	0.142	0.043	-0.656	-0.672	-0.981	-0.802	-0.771	-0.800	-0.813	-0.851	0.439	52
0.022	-0.045	-0.124	0.058	-0.031	0.042	0.134	0.123	0.154	0.125	0.111	0.074	0.094	53
-0.078	0.056	0.017	0.039	-0.261	0.073	-0.056	0.014	-0.066	-0.145	-0.118	-0.146	-0.166	54
0.155	0.418	0.239	0.101	0.101	0.155	0.046	0.066	0.097	-0.002	0.054	0.147	-0.758	55
-0.058	0.275	0.236	-0.062	-0.162	0.022	0.213	0.293	0.324	0.295	-0.019	-0.056	-0.635	56
-0.210	0.133	0.144	-0.054	-0.033	-0.050	0.042	0.121	0.062	0.033	0.019	0.112	-0.834	57
-0.182	0.181	0.152	0.154	0.084	0.068	0.059	0.139	-0.030	-0.059	-0.073	0.290	-0.581	58
-0.235	-0.002	0.189	-0.009	-0.109	-0.125	-0.034	0.046	0.077	0.048	0.034	-0.003	-0.788	59
-0.007	0.417	0.288	-0.061	-0.270	-0.146	-0.055	-0.045	-0.015	-0.044	-0.057	-0.095	-0.497	60
0.135	0.138	0.079	-0.269	-0.269	-0.005	0.086	0.166	0.197	0.168	0.154	0.117	0.272	61
0.107	0.460	0.051	-0.047	-0.007	-0.023	-0.091	-0.012	-0.291	-0.320	-0.334	-0.371	-0.690	62
1.172	0.085	-0.264	0.218	0.098	0.322	0.413	0.493	0.764	0.735	0.961	0.924	1.405	63
0.255	0.188	0.159	-0.269	-0.319	-0.335	-0.244	-0.164	-0.133	0.138	0.124	0.087	0.222	64
0.540	0.354	0.005	0.266	0.267	0.251	0.342	0.421	0.452	0.423	0.760	0.722	0.416	65
0.415	0.348	0.359	-0.109	0.161	0.145	0.236	0.316	0.347	0.318	0.304	0.267	-0.258	66
-0.725	-0.062	0.099	-0.749	0.491	0.585	0.676	0.846	0.877	0.848	0.834	0.797	-0.138	67
0.013	-0.374	-0.283	0.359	0.199	0.183	0.274	0.034	0.145	0.196	0.382	0.345	0.024	68
0.836	0.329	-0.179	0.022	0.023	0.127	0.178	0.097	0.128	0.099	0.166	0.128	0.840	69
0.079	0.012	0.023	0.025	0.626	0.610	0.701	0.780	0.811	0.782	0.768	0.731	-0.123	70
-0.223	0.011	0.022	-0.067	0.044	0.028	0.009	-0.132	-0.101	-0.160	0.107	0.189	-0.521	71
-0.328	-0.175	0.016	0.428	-0.201	0.093	-0.126	-0.047	-0.016	-0.045	-0.098	-0.136	-0.826	72
0.051	0.234	0.425	-0.123	0.157	0.311	0.232	-0.258	-0.227	0.194	0.230	0.223	-0.704	73
-0.490	-0.207	-0.196	0.016	-0.334	0.140	-0.119	-0.039	-0.008	-0.037	-0.051	-0.088	-0.153	74
-0.711	0.163	0.234	-0.005	0.056	0.160	0.071	0.090	0.121	0.032	0.019	0.101	-0.293	75

	1	2	3	4	5	6	7	8	9	10	11	12	13
76	1.887	2.256	0.730	-0.531	-0.212	-0.181	-0.193	-0.169	-0.144	-0.143	-0.157	-0.296	-0.127
77	2.000	2.638	2.342	-0.718	-0.540	0.492	0.199	0.224	0.249	0.250	0.236	-0.004	-0.345
78	-1.399	-1.930	-1.546	-1.527	-1.208	-0.817	0.161	0.305	0.530	0.071	0.057	-0.502	-0.683
79	-1.313	-1.845	-0.391	-0.871	-0.653	-0.501	-0.364	0.501	0.605	0.666	0.763	-0.167	-0.048
80	-1.343	-1.324	-1.340	-1.501	-1.082	-0.971	-0.883	-0.699	-0.494	-0.443	-0.307	0.054	0.063
81	-1.368	-1.890	-0.956	0.014	0.332	0.364	0.351	0.376	0.400	0.401	0.388	0.428	0.297
82	-1.763	-1.874	-0.620	-0.531	-0.412	-0.381	-0.393	-0.369	-0.144	-0.043	-0.057	-0.017	-0.147
83	-1.076	-1.208	2.016	2.436	2.555	0.986	0.974	0.848	0.873	0.874	0.760	0.500	0.319
84	-2.179	-2.650	-0.056	0.964	1.282	0.414	0.401	0.426	0.220	0.121	0.108	0.148	0.017
85	-2.731	-1.002	1.472	1.091	1.110	0.941	0.729	0.754	0.778	0.479	0.466	0.456	0.325
86	0.083	0.051	5.225	1.445	1.764	0.995	0.782	0.807	0.832	0.733	0.719	0.059	-0.272
87	1.010	2.429	1.132	2.072	1.271	1.702	0.840	0.864	0.889	0.290	-0.024	0.316	0.336
88	0.656	-0.646	0.488	1.198	1.377	0.918	0.556	0.370	0.325	0.256	0.242	0.422	0.291
89	1.901	1.670	1.144	1.363	1.282	0.813	1.701	0.025	-0.050	-0.049	-0.063	0.278	0.047
90	0.220	0.489	1.063	1.082	1.101	0.432	0.020	-0.056	-0.031	0.070	0.056	0.397	0.266
COL EFFS	1.77	2.30	1.13	0.11	-0.21	-0.24	-0.23	-0.25	-0.28	-0.28	-0.27	-0.31	-0.18

14	15	16	17	18	19	20	21	22	23	24	25	ROW EFFECT	
0.175	0.169	0.390	-0.058	0.002	-0.014	0.077	0.157	0.187	0.158	0.145	0.107	-0.239	76
-0.282	0.001	-0.058	-0.196	-0.116	-0.132	-0.041	-0.061	-0.030	0.081	0.067	0.030	-0.151	77
-0.621	-0.687	-0.146	0.086	0.266	0.080	0.491	0.571	0.601	0.532	0.869	0.831	1.517	78
-0.485	-0.662	-0.351	0.191	0.511	0.255	0.206	0.076	0.217	0.228	-0.296	0.357	0.402	79
-0.045	-0.111	0.240	0.142	0.662	0.646	0.737	0.867	0.947	0.888	0.975	0.967	1.591	80
0.360	-0.077	-0.346	-0.354	-0.334	-0.350	-0.259	-0.179	-0.148	-0.177	-0.171	-0.158	0.047	81
-0.085	0.249	0.060	0.261	0.262	0.246	0.237	0.317	0.347	0.318	0.305	0.367	0.041	82
0.112	-0.195	-0.244	-0.452	-0.601	-0.587	-0.546	-0.647	-0.606	-0.635	-0.578	-0.476	-0.526	83
0.080	0.113	-0.196	-0.194	-0.154	-0.210	-0.119	-0.039	-0.008	-0.037	-0.051	-0.088	-0.903	84
0.308	0.181	0.082	-0.016	-0.916	-0.832	-0.841	-0.761	-0.730	-0.759	-0.773	-0.710	-0.081	85
-0.409	-0.326	-0.315	-0.263	-0.413	-0.429	-0.337	-0.358	-0.327	-0.356	-0.370	-0.257	-0.634	86
0.098	-0.349	-0.257	-0.106	-0.655	-0.671	-0.580	-0.501	-0.470	-0.499	-0.512	-0.550	-0.042	87
0.354	-0.623	-0.261	0.230	-0.189	-0.625	-0.534	-0.455	-0.424	-0.453	-0.466	-0.504	0.682	88
0.109	-0.057	-0.046	0.256	-0.294	-0.310	-0.219	-0.139	-0.109	-0.138	-0.151	-0.189	-0.753	89
0.129	0.262	0.673	0.075	-0.125	-0.341	-0.350	-0.270	-0.239	-0.268	-0.082	-0.120	-0.372	90
-0.24	-0.17	-0.18	-0.18	-0.18	-0.17	-0.26	-0.34	-0.37	-0.34	-0.33	-0.29	2.28	

ELEMENTARY ANALYSIS OF RICE PRICES (SILVER), 1900 TO 1910, SHENSI

PLACE \ MONTH	1	2	3	4	5	6	7	8	9	10	11	12	13
1	-0.882	-1.556	0.605	0.298	0.026	0.300	0.431	0.484	0.544	0.598	0.898	0.407	0.699
2	-0.526	-1.021	-0.299	0.074	-0.188	-0.215	0.137	0.190	0.250	0.643	0.644	0.093	-0.256
3	0.616	2.202	-0.857	-0.184	0.214	1.058	0.929	0.542	-0.198	-0.125	-0.034	-0.575	-0.134
4	0.0	0.0	0.0	0.0	0.0	0.0	0.0	0.0	0.0	0.0	0.0	0.0	0.0
5	2.237	4.603	0.044	0.057	0.525	-0.051	-0.109	-0.057	0.003	-0.443	-0.942	-0.883	-0.442
6	1.678	3.924	-0.275	-0.102	-0.374	-0.400	-0.459	-0.406	-0.346	-0.292	-0.292	-0.113	-0.081
7	1.523	0.899	1.960	0.343	0.521	0.495	2.236	2.289	1.449	-0.388	0.153	-1.138	-0.926
8	2.125	2.600	-0.688	-0.656	1.172	-2.054	0.038	0.790	0.150	0.204	-0.495	-0.996	0.205
9	1.383	6.009	-0.360	-0.017	1.271	1.375	1.446	0.849	0.259	-0.207	-0.657	-0.608	-0.336
10	0.878	4.494	0.735	1.108	0.836	0.810	0.751	0.804	-0.056	-0.003	-0.002	0.357	0.298
11	1.849	2.074	3.336	1.969	1.497	1.470	1.312	1.265	1.025	1.078	1.079	0.138	-0.121
12	0.160	1.986	-0.053	-0.920	0.558	1.582	0.123	0.176	0.396	-0.271	0.290	-0.841	-0.410
13	2.816	3.962	0.483	0.046	-0.226	-0.172	-0.231	0.712	1.022	1.075	-0.174	0.225	-0.274
14	1.100	6.075	1.587	-0.330	-1.302	-1.329	-1.387	-1.334	-1.274	-1.221	-1.220	-0.111	-0.170
15	-0.066	0.360	-0.469	-0.486	-0.758	-0.485	-0.243	-0.190	0.120	-0.227	-0.226	0.083	0.024
16	0.302	3.528	0.089	-0.358	0.210	0.674	1.116	0.948	0.308	-0.618	-0.407	-1.118	-1.247
17	0.274	2.849	0.361	1.244	0.972	0.185	0.127	0.180	0.400	0.483	0.504	-0.787	-0.376
18	0.0	0.0	0.0	0.0	0.0	0.0	0.0	0.0	0.0	0.0	0.0	0.0	0.0
19	0.0	0.0	0.0	0.0	0.0	0.0	0.0	0.0	0.0	0.0	0.0	0.0	0.0
20	0.0	0.0	0.0	0.0	0.0	0.0	0.0	0.0	0.0	0.0	0.0	0.0	0.0
21	0.0	0.0	0.0	0.0	0.0	0.0	0.0	0.0	0.0	0.0	0.0	0.0	0.0
22	0.413	-0.021	2.320	1.573	0.941	0.755	0.016	-0.011	-0.551	-0.497	-0.497	-0.117	-0.176
23	0.0	0.0	0.0	0.0	0.0	0.0	0.0	0.0	0.0	0.0	0.0	0.0	0.0
24	0.0	0.0	0.0	0.0	0.0	0.0	0.0	0.0	0.0	0.0	0.0	0.0	0.0
25	-2.105	-1.280	-0.818	0.715	0.443	0.416	0.358	0.411	0.471	0.524	0.525	0.584	0.525

14	15	16	17	18	19	20	21	22	23	24	25	ROW EFFECT	
0.243	-0.580	-0.239	-0.199	-0.399	-0.449	-0.447	-0.399	-0.396	-0.362	-0.419	-0.447	-0.706	1
-0.212	-0.555	-0.284	0.277	-0.203	0.017	0.018	0.027	0.030	0.064	0.007	-0.021	-0.021	2
0.011	0.058	-0.061	-0.091	-0.291	-0.001	0.041	0.209	0.182	-0.144	0.139	0.101	-0.184	3
0.0	0.0	0.0	0.0	0.0	0.0	0.0	0.0	0.0	0.0	0.0	0.0	0.0	4
-0.398	0.249	0.670	-0.239	-0.190	0.170	-0.058	0.230	0.234	0.167	0.690	0.082	0.385	5
-0.037	0.140	0.221	0.191	0.021	0.171	0.173	0.221	0.224	0.258	0.201	0.173	-1.586	6
0.288	0.175	-0.084	-0.544	0.006	-0.494	-0.492	0.006	0.009	0.043	-0.464	0.048	2.139	7
-0.451	-0.274	-0.383	-0.192	0.758	0.007	0.009	0.057	0.061	0.444	0.387	0.359	0.438	8
0.228	-0.175	-0.224	-0.384	-0.164	-0.214	0.118	0.496	0.569	-0.247	-0.054	-0.012	0.029	9
0.363	0.540	0.661	-0.639	-0.689	-0.739	-0.737	-0.689	-0.686	-0.652	-0.709	-0.737	-0.856	10
0.023	-0.100	-0.509	-0.868	-0.968	-1.118	-1.117	-1.069	-1.065	-1.031	-1.088	-1.116	0.664	11
-0.506	-0.189	-0.297	0.243	0.423	0.373	0.095	0.143	0.146	-0.170	-0.227	-0.255	-0.348	12
0.351	0.248	0.589	0.049	-0.241	-0.291	-0.289	-0.381	-0.378	-0.344	-0.301	-0.329	-0.464	13
0.154	0.051	0.502	0.483	0.593	0.543	0.544	0.592	0.596	0.630	0.573	0.545	-0.587	14
0.218	0.045	-0.113	-0.123	-0.023	-0.073	0.278	0.327	0.330	0.364	0.307	0.279	-1.032	15
-0.783	-0.606	-0.155	-0.104	0.285	-0.465	0.237	0.285	0.289	0.322	0.265	0.237	0.910	16
-0.952	-0.165	-0.134	-0.393	-0.043	-0.073	-0.072	-0.074	-0.070	-0.036	-0.093	-0.121	-0.211	17
0.0	0.0	0.0	0.0	0.0	0.0	0.0	0.0	0.0	0.0	0.0	0.0	0.0	18
0.0	0.0	0.0	0.0	0.0	0.0	0.0	0.0	0.0	0.0	0.0	0.0	0.0	19
0.0	0.0	0.0	0.0	0.0	0.0	0.0	0.0	0.0	0.0	0.0	0.0	0.0	20
0.0	0.0	0.0	0.0	0.0	0.0	0.0	0.0	0.0	0.0	0.0	0.0	0.0	21
-0.012	-0.305	0.296	0.696	-0.004	-0.054	-0.052	-0.004	-0.000	0.033	-0.024	-0.052	0.299	22
0.0	0.0	0.0	0.0	0.0	0.0	0.0	0.0	0.0	0.0	0.0	0.0	0.0	23
0.0	0.0	0.0	0.0	0.0	0.0	0.0	0.0	0.0	0.0	0.0	0.0	0.0	24
0.569	-0.154	-0.262	0.178	-0.222	-0.472	-0.471	-0.422	-0.419	-0.385	-0.442	-0.470	2.917	25

	1	2	3	4	5	6	7	8	9	10	11	12	13
26	0.0	0.0	0.0	0.0	0.0	0.0	0.0	0.0	0.0	0.0	0.0	0.0	0.0
27	-4.545	-2.119	-1.958	-0.525	0.683	0.657	0.598	0.571	0.631	0.684	0.685	0.744	0.685
28	0.485	-1.099	-0.637	-0.155	-0.407	-0.403	-0.461	-0.409	-0.419	-0.365	-0.324	0.655	0.136
29	1.484	1.860	-0.649	-0.046	-0.138	-0.184	0.277	0.260	0.290	0.193	-0.184	-0.507	-0.346
30	1.840	1.536	0.108	-0.500	-0.172	-0.198	-0.256	-0.204	-0.174	-0.120	-0.399	-0.310	-0.379
31	1.117	2.343	0.204	-0.403	-0.375	-0.402	0.200	0.253	0.073	-0.054	-0.053	-0.234	-0.293
32	1.050	2.286	-0.102	0.180	-0.422	-0.518	-0.486	-0.534	-0.464	-0.100	-0.099	-0.460	-0.089
33	2.169	2.385	-0.654	-0.241	-0.283	-0.239	0.003	-0.305	-0.345	-0.351	-0.370	-0.561	-0.100
34	1.948	1.424	-0.114	-0.132	-0.404	-0.430	-0.488	-0.436	-0.576	-0.522	-0.521	0.188	0.129
35	0.0	0.0	0.0	0.0	0.0	0.0	0.0	0.0	0.0	0.0	0.0	0.0	0.0
36	0.460	0.066	-0.233	0.060	-0.212	-0.238	-0.297	-0.044	0.016	0.069	0.070	0.729	0.831
37	-0.540	-0.774	-0.833	-0.180	-0.452	-0.478	-0.536	-0.484	-0.424	-0.370	-0.249	0.530	0.471
38	-1.436	-1.711	-0.899	-0.567	-0.899	-0.765	-0.723	-0.671	-0.511	-0.357	-0.356	0.603	0.644
39	-0.569	-0.883	-0.512	-0.349	-0.521	-0.447	-0.506	-0.453	-0.393	0.161	0.661	-0.230	-0.038
40	-1.542	-2.326	-0.325	-0.242	-0.084	0.629	0.571	0.624	0.204	0.177	0.428	0.647	0.368
41	-1.899	-2.773	-0.352	-0.659	-0.331	-0.117	0.124	-0.423	-0.303	0.230	0.531	0.300	0.541
42	-1.393	-1.488	0.204	0.057	-0.215	-0.242	-0.300	-0.357	-0.297	-0.144	-0.193	0.336	0.497
43	-1.132	-2.126	1.335	-0.292	-0.564	-0.580	-0.639	-0.676	-0.556	-0.293	0.038	0.547	-0.021
44	-1.321	-1.095	-1.134	-0.401	-0.173	0.701	0.042	0.095	-0.145	-0.092	0.509	-0.032	0.510
45	0.174	-1.200	-0.039	-1.206	-0.278	0.195	0.137	0.190	0.250	0.303	0.304	-0.037	0.004
46	1.429	-2.065	-1.224	0.039	0.327	0.301	0.242	0.295	0.355	0.408	-1.271	0.308	0.650
47	-2.701	-1.876	-1.314	-0.881	-1.353	-1.380	-1.438	-1.085	-1.025	-0.972	-0.971	0.988	0.929
48	-0.573	-1.248	-0.286	1.496	1.224	1.198	1.140	1.192	1.252	0.656	0.657	0.166	0.557
49	-0.967	0.139	1.160	1.633	1.231	1.205	1.026	1.079	1.139	1.192	1.193	0.562	0.503
50	-1.056	-1.180	-0.569	1.314	1.042	1.016	1.007	1.060	1.120	1.174	1.174	1.183	1.125

14	15	16	17	18	19	20	21	22	23	24	25	ROW EFFECT	
0.0	0.0	0.0	0.0	0.0	0.0	0.0	0.0	0.0	0.0	0.0	0.0	0.0	26
0.730	0.507	-0.002	-0.062	-0.462	-0.512	-0.510	-0.662	-0.659	-0.625	-0.682	-0.710	3.657	27
0.160	0.487	-0.802	0.409	0.168	0.158	0.160	0.208	0.212	0.245	0.188	0.160	-0.343	28
-0.071	0.036	0.307	0.017	0.077	0.097	-0.051	-0.063	-0.110	-0.136	-0.223	0.089	-1.222	29
0.015	-0.388	-0.127	0.224	0.153	0.313	0.295	0.213	0.207	0.100	0.043	0.565	-0.918	30
-0.369	-0.012	0.650	-0.100	0.100	0.230	0.112	0.040	0.043	0.077	0.020	-0.008	-1.105	31
-0.075	0.012	-0.367	0.374	-0.146	0.203	0.035	0.353	0.157	0.940	0.533	0.505	-0.858	32
-0.336	0.261	0.792	-0.327	-0.008	0.392	0.314	0.362	0.266	0.219	0.152	0.384	-1.137	33
0.173	0.350	0.191	0.232	0.431	0.381	0.383	0.031	0.035	0.068	0.011	0.083	-0.536	34
0.0	0.0	0.0	0.0	0.0	0.0	0.0	0.0	0.0	0.0	0.0	0.0	0.0	35
0.755	-0.068	-0.217	-0.257	0.003	-0.047	-0.045	0.003	0.006	-0.040	-0.217	-0.245	-0.828	36
0.355	0.532	-0.497	0.384	0.283	0.233	0.235	0.083	0.087	0.120	0.303	0.275	-0.148	37
0.688	0.365	0.456	0.497	0.297	0.246	0.248	0.296	0.300	0.333	0.276	0.248	0.669	38
0.006	-0.567	-0.676	0.714	1.594	1.544	0.296	0.344	0.347	0.381	0.324	0.296	0.181	39
-0.398	-1.231	-1.169	0.841	0.121	0.201	-0.177	-0.129	-0.126	-0.092	-0.149	-0.177	-0.096	40
-0.495	-1.078	-1.086	0.794	0.694	0.644	-0.074	-0.326	-0.023	0.311	0.734	0.526	0.001	41
0.201	-0.442	-0.700	0.260	0.380	0.470	0.321	-0.180	-0.177	0.177	0.370	0.342	-0.115	42
-0.647	-0.760	-0.489	0.461	0.581	0.961	0.803	0.231	0.454	0.588	0.531	0.503	0.064	43
-1.246	-1.669	-1.778	1.662	1.562	0.312	0.314	-0.238	-0.235	0.099	0.642	0.614	2.233	44
0.048	-0.575	-0.683	-0.043	0.357	0.307	0.208	-0.043	-0.140	-0.106	-0.163	-0.091	-0.262	45
0.764	-0.759	-0.208	0.462	0.982	0.472	0.474	-0.408	-0.715	-0.681	-0.738	-0.766	0.393	46
0.873	0.850	0.341	0.182	0.582	0.532	0.533	0.582	0.585	0.619	0.562	0.534	1.213	47
0.601	-0.222	-0.281	-0.490	-0.690	-0.741	-0.739	-0.691	-0.687	-0.654	-0.611	-0.639	-0.614	48
-0.762	0.035	-0.454	-0.364	-0.904	-0.954	-0.952	-0.904	-0.961	-0.927	-0.984	-1.012	0.129	49
0.669	-0.454	-0.563	-0.523	-0.623	-0.673	-0.921	-0.873	-0.870	-0.836	-0.893	-0.921	0.318	50

	1	2	3	4	5	6	7	8	9	10	11	12	13
51	0.659	-0.575	-0.084	1.489	1.217	1.351	1.292	1.345	1.405	0.758	0.759	0.518	0.709
52	-1.406	-0.880	0.282	0.814	0.542	0.516	0.458	0.510	0.570	0.624	0.625	1.084	1.025
53	-0.232	1.294	-1.565	0.138	0.856	1.190	1.131	0.734	0.344	-0.503	-0.502	-0.443	-0.501
54	0.554	1.110	0.691	0.464	1.802	2.256	2.287	-0.500	-0.420	-0.447	-0.076	-0.167	-0.076
55	0.988	1.824	0.335	0.208	1.586	1.220	1.162	0.234	0.294	0.018	0.349	-0.252	0.349
56	0.915	0.641	0.802	0.235	0.263	0.236	0.278	0.331	0.691	-0.056	-0.255	-0.296	-0.255
57	0.587	1.493	1.674	-0.083	-0.355	-0.382	-0.180	0.543	0.603	0.656	0.657	0.046	-0.013
58	0.252	0.308	0.399	0.472	0.030	0.004	-0.055	-0.002	0.058	0.111	-0.038	-0.129	-0.167
59	0.0	0.0	0.0	0.0	0.0	0.0	0.0	0.0	0.0	0.0	0.0	0.0	0.0
60	1.351	1.077	1.488	-0.009	-0.281	-0.307	-0.366	-0.313	-0.113	-0.060	-0.059	-0.280	-0.898
61	1.178	3.004	0.615	0.938	1.226	1.200	1.141	-0.206	-0.146	-0.092	-0.092	-0.033	-0.091
62	0.741	1.146	1.418	0.241	-0.031	-0.058	-0.116	-0.063	-0.004	0.050	0.051	0.110	0.051
63	-1.607	-1.401	0.060	-0.547	-0.819	-0.845	-0.904	-0.851	-0.611	-0.258	-0.257	0.642	0.464
64	-0.726	-1.000	0.411	0.304	0.162	0.136	0.077	0.130	0.190	0.293	0.294	0.363	0.305
65	-1.268	-1.402	-0.201	-0.308	-0.580	-0.606	-0.665	-0.612	-0.552	-0.498	-0.498	0.152	0.443
66	-0.782	-0.756	0.105	0.038	-0.234	-0.260	-0.319	-0.266	-0.206	-0.053	-0.052	0.307	0.348
67	-1.536	-1.651	-0.289	-0.156	-0.458	-0.485	-0.543	-0.490	-0.430	-0.327	-0.326	-0.057	-0.056
68	-1.139	-1.574	-0.192	-0.059	-0.331	-0.278	-0.176	0.037	0.097	0.150	0.391	0.570	0.511
69	-0.987	-1.382	-0.280	-0.187	-0.279	-0.186	-1.364	-0.311	-0.212	-0.058	-0.037	0.702	0.743
70	-0.982	-1.256	0.205	-0.302	-0.574	-0.600	-0.659	-0.606	-0.546	-0.493	-0.492	-0.233	-0.292
71	0.533	2.759	3.121	-1.147	1.181	1.055	1.597	2.249	2.309	-0.337	-0.336	-0.977	-1.236
72	0.803	1.638	1.990	0.972	0.260	0.234	-0.054	-0.002	0.058	0.112	0.113	0.172	0.073
73	0.849	0.574	0.216	-0.081	-0.703	-0.710	-0.828	-0.945	-0.895	-0.892	-0.901	-0.622	-0.301
74	3.830	3.906	1.167	0.900	0.588	0.562	-0.057	-0.004	0.056	0.109	0.110	-0.181	-0.240
75	0.0	0.0	0.0	0.0	0.0	0.0	0.0	0.0	0.0	0.0	0.0	0.0	0.0

14	15	16	17	18	19	20	21	22	23	24	25	ROW EFFECT	
0.754	0.191	-0.788	-0.088	-1.188	-1.338	-1.336	-1.288	-1.285	-1.251	-1.308	-1.336	0.683	51
1.069	0.946	0.837	-0.822	-1.073	-1.123	-1.121	-1.073	-1.069	-1.036	-1.093	-1.121	1.558	52
-0.457	-0.280	-0.029	-0.009	0.071	0.021	0.023	0.071	0.074	0.108	0.051	0.023	1.444	53
-0.141	0.026	-0.263	-0.317	-0.363	-0.263	-0.041	0.017	0.090	0.074	-0.013	0.139	-0.212	54
0.393	0.050	-0.189	-0.358	-0.319	-0.309	-0.367	-0.319	-0.315	-0.282	-0.339	-0.307	-0.626	55
-0.111	0.166	0.158	-0.002	-0.202	-0.252	-0.251	-0.202	-0.199	-0.165	-0.222	-0.250	-0.503	56
0.031	0.208	0.030	-0.060	-0.250	-0.300	-0.299	-0.250	-0.247	-0.213	-0.180	0.322	0.765	57
-0.143	1.104	0.105	-0.055	-0.055	-0.105	-0.103	-0.055	-0.152	-0.118	-0.175	-0.003	0.550	58
0.0	0.0	0.0	0.0	0.0	0.0	0.0	0.0	0.0	0.0	0.0	0.0	0.0	59
-0.294	-0.117	0.334	0.244	0.074	0.304	0.306	0.074	0.077	0.111	0.054	0.026	0.421	60
0.453	0.480	0.721	0.211	-0.239	-0.639	-0.637	-0.589	-0.586	-0.552	-0.609	-0.637	0.734	61
0.095	0.272	-0.147	-0.146	-0.046	-0.097	-0.095	-0.047	-0.043	-0.009	-0.067	-0.094	-0.648	62
0.448	-0.035	-0.024	0.176	-0.044	0.386	0.388	0.436	0.439	0.473	0.536	0.508	-0.181	63
0.349	0.506	0.317	-0.223	-0.423	-0.473	-0.471	-0.423	-0.420	-0.286	-0.343	-0.371	-0.632	64
0.487	0.574	0.165	0.305	0.205	0.155	0.157	0.205	0.209	0.242	0.685	0.657	-0.650	65
0.293	0.470	0.411	0.001	-0.029	-0.079	-0.077	-0.049	-0.046	-0.012	-0.069	-0.097	-1.406	66
0.018	0.065	0.006	0.017	0.297	0.367	0.368	0.417	0.420	0.454	0.397	0.369	-0.252	67
0.235	-0.028	0.023	-0.136	0.004	-0.046	-0.045	-0.316	-0.113	-0.079	0.104	0.076	-1.148	68
0.747	0.644	0.575	-0.024	-0.124	-0.055	-0.053	-0.085	-0.041	-0.007	-0.025	-0.052	-0.340	69
-0.247	0.030	-0.079	-0.239	0.661	0.611	0.613	0.661	0.664	0.698	0.641	0.613	-0.866	70
-0.492	-0.215	-0.324	-0.363	-0.083	-0.134	-0.132	-0.084	-0.080	-0.147	-0.204	-0.542	0.679	71
0.117	0.474	0.275	-0.154	-0.254	-0.085	-0.303	-0.255	-0.251	-0.218	-0.275	-0.303	-1.450	72
-0.137	0.510	0.481	0.082	0.382	0.422	0.423	0.362	0.415	0.649	0.632	0.624	-0.966	73
-0.195	-0.018	0.083	-0.287	-0.037	-0.087	-0.085	-0.037	-0.034	0.000	-0.057	-0.085	0.532	74
0.0	0.0	0.0	0.0	0.0	0.0	0.0	0.0	0.0	0.0	0.0	0.0	0.0	75

	1	2	3	4	5	6	7	8	9	10	11	12	13
76	1.277	2.502	-0.236	-0.543	-0.635	-0.662	0.540	0.593	0.352	0.406	0.407	0.046	-0.193
77	0.0	0.0	0.0	0.0	0.0	0.0	0.0	0.0	0.0	0.0	0.0	0.0	0.0
78	-1.230	-1.165	-0.283	-0.371	-0.222	0.191	0.843	0.966	0.505	-0.371	-0.370	-1.101	-1.290
79	-1.299	-1.443	-0.112	0.041	-0.111	-0.087	-0.016	0.147	0.257	0.420	0.531	-0.150	-0.318
80	-1.556	-1.181	-0.629	-0.856	-0.928	-0.835	-0.773	-0.560	-0.501	-0.427	-0.366	-0.117	-0.046
81	-1.483	-1.747	-0.406	0.127	-0.145	-0.172	-0.230	-0.177	-0.117	-0.064	-0.063	-0.004	-0.063
82	-1.105	-0.620	-0.018	0.214	-0.157	-0.184	-0.242	-0.189	-0.130	0.124	0.125	0.084	0.025
83	-1.231	-1.306	1.056	1.689	1.417	0.790	0.532	0.585	0.644	0.698	0.599	0.668	0.549
84	0.0	0.0	0.0	0.0	0.0	0.0	0.0	0.0	0.0	0.0	0.0	0.0	0.0
85	-2.692	-2.097	1.465	0.498	0.126	0.099	0.041	0.094	0.054	0.007	0.008	0.267	0.208
86	-0.090	0.036	4.097	1.130	0.858	0.731	0.873	0.926	0.986	0.939	0.940	0.499	-0.060
87	0.0	0.0	0.0	0.0	0.0	0.0	0.0	0.0	0.0	0.0	0.0	0.0	0.0
88	0.0	0.0	0.0	0.0	0.0	0.0	0.0	0.0	0.0	0.0	0.0	0.0	0.0
89	0.0	0.0	0.0	0.0	0.0	0.0	0.0	0.0	0.0	0.0	0.0	0.0	0.0
90	0.0	0.0	0.0	0.0	0.0	0.0	0.0	0.0	0.0	0.0	0.0	0.0	0.0
COL EFFS	1.33	1.61	0.15	-0.39	-0.11	-0.09	-0.03	-0.08	-0.14	-0.20	-0.20	-0.26	-0.20

14	15	16	17	18	19	20	21	22	23	24	25	ROW EFFECT	
-0.029	-0.092	-0.081	-0.540	0.080	0.029	0.031	0.079	0.083	0.117	0.059	0.032	-0.664	76
0.0	0.0	0.0	0.0	0.0	0.0	0.0	0.0	0.0	0.0	0.0	0.0	0.0	77
-0.956	-0.839	0.192	-0.667	-0.437	-0.048	1.204	1.252	1.256	0.100	0.872	1.465	1.353	78
-0.274	-0.497	-0.156	-0.266	0.284	0.234	0.236	0.024	-0.013	-0.019	-0.026	0.066	-0.209	79
-0.132	-0.005	0.286	-0.333	0.427	0.516	0.928	1.126	1.180	1.184	1.256	1.379	1.269	80
-0.019	0.658	0.230	0.170	0.070	0.040	0.042	0.090	0.093	0.127	0.070	0.042	0.005	81
0.069	0.246	0.137	0.178	-0.022	-0.073	0.029	-0.023	-0.019	-0.085	-0.143	-0.070	-0.382	82
0.593	0.520	0.211	-0.698	-0.798	-0.899	-0.997	-1.009	-1.095	-1.061	-1.119	-1.146	0.144	83
0.0	0.0	0.0	0.0	0.0	0.0	0.0	0.0	0.0	0.0	0.0	0.0	0.0	84
0.252	0.439	0.520	0.761	-0.339	-0.289	-0.288	-0.239	-0.236	-0.202	-0.259	-0.287	-0.465	85
-0.316	-0.139	-0.247	-0.407	-0.557	-0.607	-0.606	-0.557	-0.554	-0.520	-0.577	-0.455	-0.998	86
0.0	0.0	0.0	0.0	0.0	0.0	0.0	0.0	0.0	0.0	0.0	0.0	0.0	87
0.0	0.0	0.0	0.0	0.0	0.0	0.0	0.0	0.0	0.0	0.0	0.0	0.0	88
0.0	0.0	0.0	0.0	0.0	0.0	0.0	0.0	0.0	0.0	0.0	0.0	0.0	89
0.0	0.0	0.0	0.0	0.0	0.0	0.0	0.0	0.0	0.0	0.0	0.0	0.0	90
-0.24	-0.42	-0.31	-0.15	-0.05	0.00	-0.00	-0.05	-0.05	-0.09	-0.03	-0.00	3.75	

ELEMENTARY ANALYSIS OF MILLET PRICES (SILVER), 1900 TO 1910, SHENSI

PLACE \ MONTH	1	2	3	4	5	6	7	8	9	10	11	12	13
1	-1.391	-2.182	1.173	0.170	0.124	0.335	0.618	0.638	0.670	0.680	0.884	0.136	0.269
2	-1.207	-2.478	-0.343	-0.276	-0.343	-0.332	-0.199	-0.179	-0.147	0.044	0.048	0.309	-0.007
3	0.415	0.474	-0.972	-0.104	-0.171	-0.140	0.163	0.153	-0.005	-0.314	-0.290	-0.099	0.044
4	1.701	1.510	-0.735	0.272	0.836	-0.004	0.179	-0.041	-0.268	-0.108	-0.074	-0.342	0.211
5	1.948	2.957	-0.298	0.169	0.413	0.353	0.406	0.106	-0.361	-0.351	-0.597	-0.245	0.538
6	1.429	3.268	-0.477	-0.380	-0.126	-0.236	-0.313	-0.293	-0.260	-0.190	-0.186	-0.474	0.209
7	3.249	2.558	-0.287	-0.230	-0.096	-0.085	-0.103	-0.082	-0.500	-0.490	-0.306	-0.264	-0.251
8	1.037	3.146	-0.469	-0.372	-0.208	-0.198	-0.215	-0.195	-0.022	-0.012	0.062	-0.336	0.507
9	0.387	3.496	-0.449	-0.352	-0.398	-0.387	-0.335	-0.254	-0.152	-0.212	-0.008	-0.186	0.197
10	1.407	4.286	-0.279	0.088	-0.068	-0.058	-0.075	-0.055	-0.132	-0.022	-0.058	-0.096	-0.013
11	2.000	1.709	3.264	0.261	0.215	0.225	0.108	0.028	0.061	0.071	0.075	-0.373	-0.540
12	-0.142	0.427	-0.458	-0.501	-0.317	-0.256	-0.553	-0.253	-0.361	-0.211	-0.277	-0.185	0.028
13	1.548	3.417	-0.578	-0.461	-0.298	-0.087	0.896	0.916	-0.052	-0.041	-0.457	-0.136	-0.173
14	1.205	5.134	0.189	-0.204	-0.251	-0.240	-0.257	-0.237	-0.205	-0.194	-0.190	-0.309	-0.026
15	-0.520	-0.711	-0.556	-0.209	-0.256	-0.245	-0.262	-0.242	-0.040	-0.149	-0.145	0.116	-0.051
16	0.804	2.283	-1.262	0.095	0.049	-0.150	0.043	0.063	-0.115	-0.245	-0.101	-0.429	-0.216
17	0.385	2.934	-0.512	0.586	0.539	0.150	-0.067	-0.047	0.085	0.096	0.340	-0.049	0.084
18	1.916	1.635	0.700	0.207	0.161	0.171	0.154	0.174	0.207	0.217	0.221	0.353	0.066
19	1.686	1.295	2.940	1.267	1.320	1.231	1.114	0.934	0.866	0.627	0.581	-0.168	-0.284
20	-1.333	-1.134	-0.349	-0.272	-0.119	0.092	0.155	0.175	0.207	0.218	0.222	-0.016	-0.083
21	2.392	2.001	2.756	1.353	1.006	0.617	0.300	0.320	0.352	0.363	0.167	0.118	0.052
22	0.268	0.097	3.772	1.629	1.183	1.053	0.746	0.606	0.429	0.159	-0.107	0.275	0.108
23	1.506	0.815	1.470	1.567	1.521	0.531	0.514	0.534	0.567	0.577	0.581	0.533	0.466
24	-0.253	0.306	0.061	0.158	0.112	0.122	0.105	0.125	0.158	0.168	0.172	0.124	0.057
25	1.708	2.767	0.722	1.019	-0.027	0.483	0.466	0.086	0.119	0.129	-0.067	0.585	0.518

14	15	16	17	18	19	20	21	22	23	24	25	ROW EFFECT	*
-0.089	-0.582	-0.261	-0.172	-0.396	-0.396	-0.379	-0.337	-0.341	-0.336	-0.350	-0.377	0.378	1
0.035	-0.438	-0.128	0.181	-0.042	0.227	0.245	0.226	0.223	0.228	0.243	0.217	0.595	2
-0.094	-0.103	0.164	0.033	0.019	0.149	0.177	0.088	0.074	0.080	0.145	0.078	-0.187	3
0.173	0.160	0.090	-0.050	0.036	-0.005	-0.097	-0.255	0.021	0.026	0.272	-0.075	-0.034	4
0.030	-0.033	0.107	-0.384	-0.037	0.432	0.190	-0.298	-0.162	0.033	-0.071	-0.008	0.259	5
0.131	0.138	0.408	0.157	-0.046	0.153	0.171	0.213	0.209	0.214	0.200	0.173	-0.272	6
0.161	0.258	0.179	0.018	0.424	0.323	0.521	0.293	0.289	-0.156	0.190	0.073	0.538	7
-0.081	0.136	0.366	0.025	0.232	0.021	0.249	-0.269	-0.273	0.222	0.208	0.181	-0.150	8
0.179	0.186	0.337	0.016	0.132	0.131	0.149	0.131	0.187	0.192	0.178	0.151	-0.400	9
0.079	0.196	0.206	0.046	-0.028	-0.029	-0.011	0.031	0.027	0.032	0.018	-0.009	-0.590	10
-0.198	-0.191	-0.171	-0.331	-0.105	-0.106	-0.088	0.054	0.250	0.255	0.241	0.214	-0.213	11
0.260	0.147	0.098	-0.033	0.313	0.313	0.330	0.372	0.368	0.373	0.359	0.332	-0.231	12
0.179	0.147	0.127	-0.024	0.302	0.302	0.320	-0.099	-0.103	-0.097	-0.112	-0.138	0.320	13
0.226	0.094	0.464	0.093	0.119	0.119	0.137	0.178	0.174	0.180	0.165	0.139	-0.037	14
0.291	-0.351	0.159	0.048	-0.026	-0.026	0.292	0.333	0.329	0.335	0.330	0.294	-0.192	15
-0.034	0.043	-0.286	-0.207	0.209	0.209	0.226	0.268	0.264	0.269	0.255	0.228	0.713	16
-0.044	-0.167	0.134	-0.157	-0.041	-0.061	-0.043	-0.022	-0.026	-0.020	-0.035	-0.062	0.363	17
-0.072	-0.565	-0.495	0.294	-0.159	-0.160	-0.142	-0.170	-0.174	-0.169	-0.183	-0.210	0.011	18
-0.242	-0.385	-0.665	-0.226	-0.399	-0.600	-0.582	-0.540	-0.494	-0.489	-0.454	-0.480	-0.018	19
-0.021	0.466	0.206	0.455	-0.008	-0.169	-0.191	-0.169	-0.173	-0.178	-0.193	-0.219	-0.870	20
-0.006	-0.099	0.321	0.160	-0.313	-0.314	-0.396	-0.354	-0.458	-0.453	-0.568	-0.594	-0.704	21
0.170	-0.103	-0.023	0.217	-0.437	-0.438	-0.420	-0.378	-0.422	-0.417	-0.431	-0.458	-0.321	22
0.008	-0.585	-0.565	-0.405	-0.549	-0.550	-0.532	-0.590	-0.594	-0.589	-0.603	-0.630	-0.009	23
0.099	0.106	-0.374	0.065	0.742	-0.259	-0.241	-0.199	-0.203	-0.198	-0.212	-0.239	-0.260	24
-0.040	-0.333	-0.213	1.227	0.053	-0.248	-0.430	-0.388	-0.392	-0.387	-0.401	-0.428	-0.471	25

	1	2	3	4	5	6	7	8	9	10	11	12	13
26	-0.936	0.073	0.828	0.925	0.878	0.689	0.672	0.492	0.324	0.335	-0.061	0.590	0.523
27	-1.976	0.683	-0.563	-0.165	0.288	0.299	0.282	0.302	0.334	0.345	0.349	0.300	0.233
28	0.227	-0.904	-0.189	-0.002	-0.178	-0.168	-0.185	-0.165	-0.142	-0.132	-0.118	0.124	0.027
29	1.227	1.236	-0.609	-0.262	0.432	-0.428	-0.385	-0.305	-0.332	-0.292	-0.098	-0.266	-0.133
30	1.435	1.204	-0.781	-0.504	-0.210	-0.200	-0.217	-0.197	-0.374	-0.364	-0.230	-0.158	-0.105
31	0.891	1.100	-0.345	-0.248	-0.295	-0.284	-0.241	-0.221	-0.249	-0.238	-0.174	-0.103	-0.049
32	0.703	1.512	-0.573	-0.096	-0.422	-0.402	-0.399	-0.349	-0.316	-0.306	-0.302	-0.320	0.043
33	1.690	1.069	-0.716	-0.369	-0.125	-0.155	0.028	-0.102	-0.139	-0.169	-0.305	-0.353	-0.120
34	2.807	1.616	-0.379	-0.032	-0.078	-0.068	-0.085	-0.065	-0.232	-0.222	0.082	-0.066	-0.133
35	0.746	0.495	0.839	-0.053	-0.010	0.001	-0.016	0.004	0.036	0.047	0.051	-0.228	-0.185
36	-0.194	-0.845	0.470	0.287	0.241	0.251	0.234	0.254	0.087	0.017	0.021	0.453	0.506
37	-2.005	-2.676	-0.401	-0.224	-0.270	-0.259	-0.276	-0.256	-0.224	-0.214	-0.130	0.222	0.155
38	-2.422	-3.113	0.442	0.139	0.093	0.103	0.186	0.206	0.239	0.249	0.253	0.205	0.138
39	-2.107	-2.508	0.197	0.014	-0.032	-0.021	-0.038	-0.018	0.014	0.024	0.278	-0.120	-0.237
40	-2.283	-3.184	-0.089	-0.412	-0.338	0.392	0.375	0.395	0.678	0.628	0.722	0.774	0.547
41	-3.098	-3.469	-0.354	-0.437	-0.484	-0.353	-0.250	-0.230	-0.198	-0.187	-0.183	0.728	0.781
42	-2.010	-2.551	0.404	-0.039	-0.085	-0.075	-0.092	-0.072	-0.039	-0.029	-0.025	-0.133	0.020
43	-1.879	-2.660	1.304	0.242	0.195	0.206	0.189	0.209	0.241	0.252	0.326	0.617	-0.050
44	-1.951	-2.342	0.113	-0.990	-0.736	-0.426	-0.443	-0.423	-0.690	-0.680	-0.076	0.176	0.709
45	-2.291	-3.582	-0.427	-0.630	-0.577	-0.166	-0.183	-0.163	-0.131	-0.120	-0.116	-0.064	-0.031
46	0.334	-2.647	-0.202	-0.095	0.459	0.469	0.452	0.472	0.505	0.515	0.649	0.441	0.624
47	-2.250	-2.741	0.614	-0.489	-0.535	-0.525	-0.542	-0.522	-0.489	-0.479	-0.475	-0.423	-0.490
48	-0.597	-1.248	0.707	1.204	1.158	1.168	1.151	1.171	1.204	0.314	0.318	0.120	0.103
49	-0.557	-0.178	2.256	2.234	2.057	2.068	1.931	1.951	1.983	1.994	0.868	0.129	0.062
50	-0.207	-1.098	-0.193	0.704	0.658	0.669	0.652	0.672	0.704	0.714	0.718	0.970	0.903

14	15	16	17	18	19	20	21	22	23	24	25	ROW EFFECT	
0.465	0.073	-0.207	0.132	-0.692	-0.792	-0.774	-0.883	-0.937	-0.831	-0.746	-0.622	-0.226	26
0.275	-0.117	-0.597	0.442	-0.132	-0.132	-0.114	-0.373	-0.377	-0.371	-0.386	-0.412	0.914	27
0.069	0.136	0.516	0.165	0.032	0.051	0.069	0.111	0.107	0.112	0.098	0.071	-0.670	28
-0.071	-0.084	0.536	0.196	0.332	0.421	0.319	0.311	0.217	0.182	0.208	0.421	-0.430	29
0.067	-0.356	-0.396	0.404	0.340	0.639	0.667	0.599	0.655	0.330	0.236	0.449	0.072	30
-0.067	-0.300	0.180	0.199	0.606	1.265	0.503	0.304	0.301	0.306	0.291	0.265	-0.403	31
0.025	-0.088	-0.128	0.362	0.168	0.797	0.375	0.527	0.373	0.758	0.414	0.387	-0.186	32
-0.008	0.019	-0.151	-0.081	0.255	0.384	0.342	0.524	0.550	0.755	-0.029	0.204	-0.113	33
0.109	0.116	0.056	0.075	0.402	0.401	0.419	-0.039	-0.043	-0.478	-0.052	0.131	-0.320	34
-0.143	0.164	0.115	-0.086	0.190	0.190	0.208	-0.001	-0.005	-0.159	-0.174	0.029	-0.638	35
0.428	-0.245	-0.545	-0.365	-0.199	-0.200	-0.182	-0.140	-0.144	-0.219	-0.353	-0.380	-0.099	36
0.077	0.084	-0.375	0.244	0.170	0.170	0.187	0.229	0.225	0.230	0.376	0.349	0.292	37
0.180	-0.013	-0.093	-0.154	-0.227	-0.228	-0.210	-0.168	-0.172	-0.167	-0.181	-0.208	0.329	38
-0.145	-0.638	-0.617	0.122	0.298	0.398	0.166	0.207	0.203	0.109	0.094	0.067	0.584	39
-0.101	-0.524	-0.374	-0.164	-0.018	0.051	-0.301	-0.259	-0.263	-0.258	-0.272	-0.299	0.320	40
0.343	-0.189	-0.409	0.550	0.536	0.536	1.264	-0.065	0.111	0.117	0.282	0.256	0.566	41
-0.148	-0.641	-0.691	0.149	0.275	0.354	0.262	0.004	-0.000	0.235	0.331	0.304	1.157	42
-0.288	-0.571	-0.280	0.169	0.095	0.095	-0.187	-0.236	-0.240	-0.184	-0.199	-0.226	0.497	43
-0.449	0.158	0.178	1.018	1.844	0.043	0.061	0.403	0.399	0.704	0.690	0.663	0.938	44
0.011	-0.382	-0.362	0.277	0.604	0.603	0.521	0.363	0.259	0.264	0.249	0.323	0.578	45
0.666	-0.657	-0.287	-0.347	0.039	-0.112	-0.094	-0.512	-0.676	-0.671	-0.685	-0.712	0.093	46
-0.448	-0.441	-0.421	-0.681	1.345	1.344	1.362	1.404	1.400	1.405	1.391	1.364	0.237	47
0.145	-0.548	-0.278	-0.188	-0.832	-0.833	-0.815	-0.773	-0.777	-0.772	-0.686	-0.613	-0.056	48
-0.206	-0.569	-0.988	-0.549	-1.373	-1.373	-1.355	-1.314	-1.258	-1.252	-1.267	-1.294	0.355	49
0.445	-0.548	-0.427	-0.338	-0.462	-0.462	-0.745	-0.703	-0.707	-0.702	-0.716	-0.743	0.144	50

	1	2	3	4	5	6	7	8	9	10	11	12	13
51	1.960	0.169	1.184	1.131	1.084	0.865	0.848	0.868	0.900	0.411	0.415	0.467	0.120
52	-0.318	0.591	0.946	0.843	0.797	0.807	0.790	0.610	0.643	0.653	0.657	0.409	0.242
53	-0.989	0.750	-0.455	-0.268	0.046	0.056	0.489	0.149	0.002	0.012	0.016	0.148	0.081
54	0.012	0.371	-0.284	0.013	0.397	0.927	0.310	0.160	0.183	0.113	0.057	-0.181	0.192
55	0.218	1.487	-0.088	0.009	0.693	0.703	0.356	0.046	0.019	0.089	0.033	-0.285	-0.152
56	0.614	1.123	0.278	0.175	0.429	0.439	0.422	0.342	0.375	-0.115	-0.111	-0.159	-0.126
57	0.433	0.922	0.197	0.114	0.068	0.079	0.062	0.092	0.114	0.124	-0.082	-0.130	-0.197
58	-0.564	0.975	0.230	0.177	0.131	0.141	-0.076	-0.056	-0.023	-0.013	-0.109	0.073	0.006
59	0.474	3.183	0.318	0.465	0.418	0.229	0.212	0.232	0.264	0.145	0.149	0.000	-0.066
60	-0.037	-0.378	-0.003	-0.186	-0.232	-0.222	-0.239	-0.219	0.024	0.034	0.038	0.270	0.133
61	0.489	-0.202	0.803	0.550	0.503	0.514	0.497	-0.183	-0.150	-0.140	-0.136	-0.184	0.309
62	0.610	0.979	1.464	0.061	0.015	0.025	0.008	0.028	0.061	0.071	0.075	0.027	-0.040
63	0.0	0.0	0.0	0.0	0.0	0.0	0.0	0.0	0.0	0.0	0.0	0.0	0.0
64	-1.657	-2.348	0.357	0.234	0.188	0.249	0.232	0.252	0.284	0.294	0.298	0.210	0.143
65	-1.870	-2.561	-0.006	-0.099	-0.146	-0.135	-0.152	-0.132	-0.100	-0.089	-0.085	0.236	0.169
66	-1.749	-2.440	0.115	0.212	0.166	0.176	0.159	0.179	0.212	0.222	0.226	0.178	0.111
67	-2.077	-2.768	0.007	-0.186	-0.232	-0.222	-0.239	-0.219	-0.186	-0.176	-0.172	-0.150	-0.197
68	0.0	0.0	0.0	0.0	0.0	0.0	0.0	0.0	0.0	0.0	0.0	0.0	0.0
69	-1.420	-2.191	0.284	0.101	0.094	0.105	0.088	0.108	0.140	0.191	0.195	0.266	0.200
70	-2.068	-2.759	-0.005	-0.297	-0.344	-0.333	-0.350	-0.330	-0.298	-0.287	-0.283	-0.032	-0.099
71	1.979	3.088	-0.457	-0.160	-0.407	-0.396	-0.413	0.207	0.239	0.250	0.154	-0.395	-0.462
72	0.236	1.315	-0.061	-0.093	-0.140	-0.129	-0.146	-0.126	-0.094	-0.083	-0.079	-0.128	-0.195
73	1.303	0.612	-0.173	-0.006	-0.273	-0.282	-0.299	-0.359	-0.327	-0.336	-0.132	-0.131	-0.127
74	3.137	3.146	1.000	0.538	0.491	0.502	0.135	0.155	0.187	0.198	0.202	-0.337	-0.404
75	0.621	2.610	0.805	0.542	0.036	-0.093	-0.290	-0.330	-0.178	-0.048	0.136	-0.272	-0.099

14	15	16	17	18	19	20	21	22	23	24	25	ROW EFFECT	
0.162	-0.151	-0.671	-0.222	-0.965	-0.966	-0.948	-1.176	-0.810	-0.805	-0.820	-0.846	0.247	51
0.284	0.091	0.261	-0.380	-1.003	-1.004	-1.136	-0.894	-0.898	-0.893	-0.907	-0.934	0.175	52
0.303	0.310	-0.210	-0.000	-0.164	-0.165	-0.147	-0.105	-0.109	-0.104	-0.028	-0.055	0.306	53
-0.236	-0.039	-0.299	-0.039	-0.163	-0.144	0.094	0.016	-0.038	-0.093	-0.007	-0.164	0.305	54
0.020	0.157	-0.283	-0.214	-0.017	0.042	0.060	-0.098	-0.102	-0.097	0.029	0.192	-0.291	55
-0.184	-0.077	0.143	-0.017	-0.191	-0.192	-0.174	-0.132	-0.136	-0.131	0.055	0.028	-0.327	56
-0.155	-0.018	-0.047	0.492	-0.092	-0.092	-0.075	-0.033	-0.037	-0.032	-0.046	0.287	-0.476	57
0.048	0.305	-0.125	-0.185	0.041	0.040	0.058	0.100	-0.104	-0.099	-0.113	0.160	-0.359	58
-0.124	0.033	0.103	0.042	-0.231	-0.232	-0.214	-0.173	-0.176	-0.171	-0.186	-0.212	-0.486	59
0.245	0.322	0.132	-0.069	-0.142	0.067	0.085	-0.013	-0.017	-0.012	0.114	0.087	-0.266	60
0.351	0.148	0.168	-0.103	-0.316	-0.177	-0.159	-0.117	-0.121	-0.116	-0.130	-0.157	0.398	61
0.002	0.209	-0.081	-0.202	0.045	0.044	0.062	0.104	-0.110	-0.105	-0.119	-0.146	-0.763	62
0.0	0.0	0.0	0.0	0.0	0.0	0.0	0.0	0.0	0.0	0.0	0.0	0.0	63
0.185	0.172	0.213	-0.228	-0.422	-0.422	-0.405	-0.363	-0.367	-0.362	-0.376	-0.303	0.054	64
0.211	0.129	0.079	0.038	-0.036	-0.036	-0.018	0.023	0.019	0.025	0.960	0.934	0.108	65
0.053	0.060	0.080	-0.160	-0.254	-0.255	-0.237	-0.195	-0.199	-0.194	-0.208	-0.235	-0.864	66
-0.135	-0.128	-0.138	-0.048	0.418	0.417	0.435	0.477	0.473	0.478	0.464	0.437	-0.586	67
0.0	0.0	0.0	0.0	0.0	0.0	0.0	0.0	0.0	0.0	0.0	0.0	0.0	68
0.282	0.309	0.029	-0.192	-0.265	-0.266	-0.248	-0.246	-0.250	-0.245	-0.260	-0.286	-0.472	69
-0.057	0.050	0.071	0.010	0.536	0.536	-0.446	0.595	0.591	0.597	0.582	0.555	0.246	70
-0.220	0.088	-0.092	-0.103	0.153	0.333	0.331	0.112	0.108	-0.026	0.499	0.283	-0.391	71
-0.153	0.164	0.365	0.164	0.090	0.090	0.108	0.149	0.145	0.151	0.226	0.199	-0.998	72
0.035	0.282	0.442	-0.149	0.408	0.507	0.465	-0.114	0.003	0.298	0.383	0.347	-0.605	73
-0.362	-0.355	-0.124	-0.045	-0.119	0.231	0.039	-0.060	-0.064	-0.058	-0.073	-0.100	-0.149	74
-0.057	0.010	0.091	0.030	0.136	0.136	0.154	0.135	0.071	0.077	0.062	0.035	-0.114	75

	1	2	3	4	5	6	7	8	9	10	11	12	13
76	0.889	1.038	-0.647	-0.550	-0.296	-0.285	0.297	0.318	0.050	0.060	0.064	-0.104	-0.171
77	2.269	3.008	0.273	0.050	-0.127	-0.116	-0.133	-0.113	-0.081	-0.070	-0.066	-0.115	-0.182
78	-1.839	-1.950	-1.445	-0.938	-0.984	-0.544	0.179	0.749	0.602	0.132	0.136	-0.772	-0.999
79	-2.037	-2.698	0.056	-0.136	-0.113	-0.082	-0.019	0.061	0.123	0.184	0.258	-0.031	-0.178
80	-1.295	-1.436	0.149	-0.964	-0.830	-0.719	-0.626	-0.466	-0.384	-0.324	-0.270	0.092	0.125
81	-1.681	-2.372	0.063	0.110	0.064	0.075	0.057	0.078	0.110	0.120	0.124	0.076	0.009
82	-2.176	-2.467	-0.133	-0.185	-0.282	-0.271	-0.288	-0.268	-0.236	-0.125	-0.121	-0.050	-0.117
83	-1.151	-1.452	1.433	1.030	0.884	0.695	0.658	0.678	0.610	0.620	0.574	0.436	0.309
84	-2.228	-2.839	0.135	0.233	0.186	0.197	0.180	0.200	0.072	0.083	0.087	0.038	-0.029
85	-2.866	-1.637	1.718	0.915	0.769	0.780	0.663	0.583	0.515	0.525	0.429	0.281	0.214
86	0.411	0.120	2.474	0.672	0.625	0.136	0.119	0.139	0.171	0.182	0.186	0.237	-0.130
87	1.424	2.383	0.787	1.635	1.588	1.369	0.832	0.852	0.884	0.145	-0.151	0.400	0.483
88	0.895	-1.056	1.099	0.886	0.769	0.640	0.483	0.323	0.285	0.226	-0.230	0.361	0.295
89	2.428	2.937	0.992	1.489	1.243	1.053	1.436	0.256	0.189	-0.101	-0.297	0.055	-0.112
90	1.096	0.105	0.860	0.657	0.310	0.121	-0.096	-0.176	-0.144	-0.033	-0.029	0.523	0.356
COL EFFS	1.89	2.58	-0.17	-0.27	-0.22	-0.23	-0.22	-0.24	-0.27	-0.28	-0.28	-0.23	-0.17

14	15	16	17	18	19	20	21	22	23	24	25	ROW EFFECT	
-0.009	-0.002	0.319	0.018	0.004	0.003	0.021	0.063	0.059	0.064	0.050	0.023	-0.102	76
-0.140	0.108	0.168	0.107	0.033	0.033	0.051	0.012	0.008	0.264	0.159	0.133	-0.121	77
-0.357	-0.890	0.200	-0.040	0.046	0.375	1.293	1.335	1.331	0.106	0.772	0.745	1.986	78
-0.136	-0.339	-0.068	-0.099	0.187	0.187	0.205	0.106	0.072	0.058	-0.007	0.106	0.045	79
0.067	0.084	0.335	-0.176	0.100	0.150	0.398	0.559	0.595	0.581	0.646	0.669	1.582	80
0.051	0.048	-0.051	-0.062	-0.116	-0.117	-0.099	-0.057	-0.061	-0.056	-0.070	-0.097	0.488	81
-0.075	0.333	0.353	0.232	0.218	0.218	0.236	0.277	0.273	0.279	0.264	0.238	0.864	82
0.101	-0.162	-0.211	-0.462	-0.636	-0.606	-0.638	-0.787	-0.801	-0.795	-0.700	-0.617	-0.362	83
0.013	0.120	-0.059	-0.070	-0.094	-0.144	-0.126	-0.085	-0.089	-0.083	-0.098	-0.125	-0.024	84
0.236	0.263	0.284	0.223	-0.951	-0.851	-0.934	-0.892	-0.896	-0.891	-0.905	-0.832	0.033	85
-0.088	0.069	0.090	0.029	-0.145	-0.145	-0.127	-0.186	-0.190	-0.184	-0.199	0.024	-0.823	86
0.225	-0.368	-0.797	-0.258	-0.732	-0.732	-0.714	-0.673	-0.677	-0.671	-0.686	-0.713	0.114	87
0.337	-0.566	-0.266	0.373	-0.260	-0.681	-0.663	-0.621	-0.625	-0.620	-0.635	-0.661	0.833	88
-0.070	-0.163	-0.143	0.097	-0.177	-0.178	-0.160	-0.118	-0.122	-0.117	-0.131	-0.158	-0.341	89
-0.002	0.105	0.825	0.364	-0.009	-0.210	-0.292	-0.250	-0.354	-0.349	-0.164	-0.190	-0.209	90
-0.21	-0.22	-0.24	-0.18	-0.10	-0.10	-0.12	-0.16	-0.16	-0.16	-0.15	-0.12	2.12	

ELEMENTARY ANALYSIS OF PEAS PRICES (SILVER), 1900 TO 1910, SHENSI

PLACE \ MONTH	1	2	3	4	5	6	7	8	9	10	11	12	13
1	-0.730	-1.726	0.290	-0.421	-0.213	0.300	0.534	0.562	0.562	0.554	1.063	0.579	0.564
2	0.0	0.0	0.0	0.0	0.0	0.0	0.0	0.0	0.0	0.0	0.0	0.0	0.0
3	0.445	0.179	-1.095	-0.237	-0.108	-0.085	-0.141	-0.123	-0.073	-0.071	-0.052	-0.136	0.009
4	0.818	1.012	-0.372	0.356	0.014	-0.262	-0.198	-0.171	-0.240	-0.018	-0.020	-0.364	-0.168
5	1.292	2.047	0.473	0.171	0.349	0.023	0.076	-0.026	-0.076	-0.084	-0.335	-0.589	0.196
6	0.652	1.606	-0.678	-0.370	0.018	-0.028	-0.114	-0.087	-0.086	-0.094	-0.096	-0.250	0.025
7	3.335	2.269	2.105	0.253	0.462	0.295	-0.031	0.087	-0.183	-0.191	-0.012	-0.556	-0.351
8	0.945	1.919	-0.135	-0.077	-0.148	0.075	-0.241	-0.493	-0.143	0.059	0.198	-0.366	0.199
9	0.703	1.637	-0.507	-0.088	C.120	0.193	0.097	0.065	-0.005	-0.033	-0.014	-0.278	0.177
10	0.618	3.242	0.038	0.366	0.034	0.048	0.082	0.109	0.110	0.402	-0.110	-0.104	-0.168
11	-0.199	-0.564	4.472	1.520	1.728	1.442	1.375	1.403	1.303	1.295	1.194	0.090	-0.175
12	-0.363	0.541	0.517	0.085	-0.266	-0.183	-0.149	-0.261	-0.261	-0.059	0.080	-0.205	-0.129
13	1.349	3.254	0.880	-0.182	-0.034	-0.020	0.014	0.041	0.042	0.033	-0.418	-0.402	-0.097
14	0.859	4.494	1.390	0.398	0.046	0.060	0.084	-0.089	-0.088	-0.097	-0.098	-0.242	-0.167
15	-0.510	-0.426	-0.730	-0.232	-0.023	-0.010	0.024	0.052	0.052	-0.156	-0.157	-0.211	-0.126
16	0.506	1.691	-0.223	-0.025	0.183	-0.503	-0.119	-0.302	-0.301	-0.169	0.109	-0.105	-0.170
17	0.824	2.389	-0.225	0.573	1.181	0.045	0.079	0.106	0.107	0.098	0.097	-0.037	-0.142
18	0.532	0.547	-0.007	0.541	0.749	0.533	0.416	0.444	0.444	0.436	0.435	0.401	0.116
19	0.0	0.0	0.0	0.0	0.0	0.0	0.0	0.0	0.0	0.0	0.0	0.0	0.0
20	-1.454	-0.889	-1.104	-0.575	-0.167	-0.034	0.080	0.108	0.108	0.100	0.099	-0.085	-0.150
21	1.690	1.824	0.360	1.608	1.517	1.230	0.764	0.392	0.392	0.284	0.083	0.079	-0.086
22	-0.543	-0.689	1.527	1.555	1.643	1.497	1.211	0.918	0.559	0.271	0.109	-0.255	-0.320
23	0.616	0.050	1.086	1.235	1.443	0.656	0.690	0.718	0.718	0.710	0.709	0.705	0.640
24	-0.409	-0.475	-0.489	0.059	0.268	0.281	0.315	0.343	0.343	0.335	0.334	0.330	0.265
25	0.420	0.705	0.241	1.289	1.497	0.311	0.145	0.172	0.173	0.165	-0.037	0.259	0.194

14	15	16	17	18	19	20	21	22	23	24	25	ROW EFFECT	
0.263	-0.505	-0.265	0.033	-0.258	-0.288	-0.261	-0.223	-0.250	-0.261	-0.272	-0.313	0.762	1
0.0	0.0	0.0	0.0	0.0	0.0	0.0	0.0	0.0	0.0	0.0	0.0	0.0	2
-0.142	0.040	-0.020	0.128	0.027	0.307	0.354	0.232	0.195	0.184	-0.427	0.402	-0.293	3
-0.249	0.033	0.282	-0.019	0.250	0.659	0.096	-0.056	0.188	0.237	0.486	0.395	-0.186	4
-0.254	-0.273	0.207	-0.005	0.075	0.254	0.131	0.029	0.332	0.311	-0.440	0.260	0.129	5
-0.005	0.157	0.326	0.185	0.154	0.063	0.020	0.058	0.032	0.150	0.160	0.099	-0.410	6
-0.072	0.150	0.170	-0.172	0.347	0.037	-0.026	0.011	-0.105	-0.026	0.503	0.372	0.467	7
-0.122	-0.020	0.240	-0.042	0.147	0.047	-0.136	-0.098	0.015	0.284	0.413	0.512	0.057	8
-0.174	-0.012	0.228	-0.044	-0.035	-0.035	-0.008	0.030	0.003	-0.008	0.181	0.071	-0.202	9
0.031	0.163	0.142	-0.099	-0.140	-0.061	-0.034	0.004	-0.022	-0.033	-0.044	-0.085	-0.406	10
0.025	-0.344	-0.464	-1.006	-0.496	-0.627	-0.700	-0.662	-0.689	-0.700	-0.711	-0.751	1.500	11
0.180	0.002	-0.018	-0.020	0.449	0.139	-0.184	0.413	0.247	0.236	0.295	0.184	-0.245	12
0.063	0.244	-0.076	0.002	0.052	0.021	0.048	0.086	0.059	0.048	0.147	0.107	0.232	13
-0.067	-0.036	-0.056	-0.198	0.272	0.241	0.058	0.096	0.069	0.058	0.257	0.497	-0.068	14
-0.027	0.005	-0.115	-0.457	-0.398	-0.428	0.359	0.547	0.520	0.509	0.498	0.457	-0.298	15
-0.070	0.031	-0.269	0.010	0.269	0.238	0.265	0.303	0.276	0.265	0.254	0.214	0.145	16
-0.062	-0.041	0.099	-0.253	-0.023	-0.064	-0.037	-0.009	-0.036	-0.077	0.092	0.052	-0.203	17
-0.054	-0.253	-0.273	0.215	-0.325	-0.356	-0.329	-0.291	-0.318	-0.329	-0.340	-0.380	0.409	18
0.0	0.0	0.0	0.0	0.0	0.0	0.0	0.0	0.0	0.0	0.0	0.0	0.0	19
-0.030	0.631	0.261	0.749	0.199	-0.002	0.005	0.043	0.016	0.005	-0.006	-0.246	-0.675	20
0.013	-0.155	0.025	0.283	-0.208	-0.238	-0.211	-0.174	-0.300	-0.311	-0.322	-0.363	-0.488	21
-0.320	-0.348	-0.339	-0.150	-0.521	-0.552	-0.525	-0.487	0.167	0.155	0.145	0.004	-0.255	22
0.139	-0.229	-0.549	-0.291	-0.632	-0.662	-0.635	-0.697	-0.724	-0.735	-0.746	-0.787	0.446	23
0.364	0.396	-0.124	-0.016	-0.357	-0.387	-0.360	-0.323	-0.349	-0.360	-0.371	-0.412	-0.289	24
0.094	-0.075	-0.295	0.764	-0.027	-0.058	-0.131	-0.093	-0.120	-0.131	-0.142	-0.182	0.231	25

	1	2	3	4	5	6	7	8	9	10	11	12	13
26	0.282	1.116	1.952	2.300	1.509	0.922	0.556	0.584	0.384	0.376	0.275	-0.130	-0.194
27	-2.054	-0.520	-0.984	-0.135	0.383	0.396	-0.280	0.458	0.458	0.450	0.449	0.435	0.370
28	0.343	-0.423	-0.327	-0.079	-0.120	-0.367	-0.333	-0.305	-0.265	-0.273	-0.254	0.292	0.227
29	1.593	1.208	-0.077	0.222	-0.150	-0.207	-0.263	-0.125	-0.275	-0.273	-0.024	-0.178	-0.063
30	2.749	1.054	0.059	-0.132	-0.174	-0.161	-0.127	-0.099	-0.229	-0.237	-0.158	0.188	0.113
31	1.154	1.429	0.865	0.273	-0.179	-0.285	-0.132	-0.104	-0.224	-0.232	-0.173	-0.117	-0.122
32	0.450	0.644	0.060	0.149	-0.333	-0.350	-0.256	-0.298	-0.298	-0.306	-0.307	-0.361	-0.026
33	2.375	1.879	0.535	-0.037	-0.408	-0.505	-0.321	-0.323	-0.273	-0.311	-0.302	-0.066	-0.291
34	2.807	1.741	-0.023	-0.225	-0.016	-0.003	0.031	0.059	-0.191	-0.199	-0.200	-0.104	-0.069
35	1.105	0.349	0.215	0.093	0.062	0.085	0.119	-0.023	-0.023	-0.031	-0.032	-0.216	-0.101
36	0.074	-0.452	0.224	0.412	0.621	0.634	0.668	0.696	0.456	0.248	0.207	0.502	0.578
37	-1.387	-1.953	-0.837	-0.289	-0.081	-0.067	-0.033	-0.006	-0.005	-0.013	0.025	0.381	0.316
38	0.0	0.0	0.0	0.0	0.0	0.0	0.0	0.0	0.0	0.0	0.0	0.0	0.0
39	-1.115	-1.841	-0.805	-0.567	-0.359	-0.345	-0.311	-0.034	-0.943	-0.951	0.307	1.053	0.988
40	-0.844	-1.790	-0.074	-0.265	0.083	1.496	0.530	0.528	0.428	0.370	0.549	0.595	0.380
41	-1.116	-2.041	0.185	-0.397	-0.429	-0.295	-0.141	-0.054	-0.053	0.118	0.407	1.133	0.768
42	-0.931	-1.316	0.080	-0.152	0.056	0.070	0.104	0.131	0.132	0.123	0.122	0.138	0.073
43	-1.342	-2.508	-0.092	-0.114	0.095	0.108	0.142	0.170	0.170	-0.058	-0.189	0.757	-0.608
44	-0.673	-1.239	-1.503	-0.954	-0.746	-0.133	-0.099	-0.071	-0.071	-0.079	0.220	0.516	0.451
45	-1.424	-2.489	-1.053	-0.805	-0.497	0.017	0.051	0.078	0.079	0.071	0.069	0.065	0.100
46	0.466	-1.739	-0.203	0.045	0.353	0.207	0.241	0.268	0.269	0.420	0.579	0.775	0.920
47	-0.892	-1.457	0.578	-0.073	0.035	0.048	0.082	0.110	0.110	0.102	0.301	0.297	0.332
48	0.0	0.0	0.0	0.0	0.0	0.0	0.0	0.0	0.0	0.0	0.0	0.0	0.0
49	0.0	0.0	0.0	0.0	0.0	0.0	0.0	0.0	0.0	0.0	0.0	0.0	0.0
50	-0.248	-1.064	-0.478	0.670	0.628	0.492	0.526	0.554	0.554	0.546	0.545	0.790	0.726

14	15	16	17	18	19	20	21	22	23	24	25	ROW EFFECT	
-0.095	-0.363	-0.183	0.875	0.184	0.104	0.030	-0.432	-0.658	-0.669	-0.680	-0.621	0.270	26
0.469	0.101	-0.319	0.239	-0.152	-0.182	-0.155	-0.317	-0.344	-0.355	-0.366	-0.406	1.656	27
-0.274	-0.192	-0.222	-0.174	0.455	0.455	0.482	0.519	0.493	0.482	0.471	0.430	-0.211	28
-0.103	-0.022	-0.262	0.216	0.396	0.375	0.302	0.240	0.133	0.182	0.221	0.461	-0.422	29
0.053	-0.196	0.024	-0.088	0.612	0.171	0.128	0.176	0.149	0.358	0.157	0.627	-0.428	30
-0.082	0.049	0.169	0.027	0.207	0.206	0.163	0.211	0.184	0.173	0.162	0.122	-0.393	31
-0.107	-0.095	0.025	-0.147	-0.088	0.632	0.559	0.597	0.560	0.759	0.538	0.407	-0.258	32
-0.322	-0.020	0.340	0.228	0.517	0.477	0.224	-0.378	0.625	0.554	0.563	0.652	-0.253	33
0.130	0.162	0.092	0.100	0.409	0.379	0.406	-0.057	-0.083	-0.094	-0.105	0.154	-0.005	34
-0.242	-0.030	0.050	-0.282	0.147	0.117	0.144	0.102	0.075	0.064	0.053	0.092	-0.363	35
0.317	-0.131	-0.511	-0.133	-0.264	0.066	-0.308	-0.510	-0.536	-0.547	-0.558	-0.599	0.408	36
0.336	0.368	0.027	0.126	0.035	0.004	0.031	0.069	0.043	0.031	0.021	-0.020	-0.091	37
0.0	0.0	0.0	0.0	0.0	0.0	0.0	0.0	0.0	0.0	0.0	0.0	0.0	38
0.028	0.070	-0.901	0.808	0.717	0.786	0.313	0.351	0.325	0.213	0.203	0.162	0.827	39
-0.271	-0.669	-0.579	-0.081	0.188	0.248	-0.255	-0.217	-0.244	-0.255	-0.266	-0.306	0.375	40
0.148	-0.241	-0.441	0.257	0.227	0.016	0.043	0.081	0.054	0.043	0.212	0.172	0.187	41
-0.127	-0.436	-0.606	0.083	0.132	0.101	0.018	-0.114	-0.141	0.028	0.237	0.197	0.362	42
-0.419	-0.587	-0.107	0.461	0.370	0.340	0.097	0.004	0.198	0.277	0.046	0.005	0.774	43
-0.650	-0.918	-0.338	0.420	1.229	-0.001	0.026	0.364	0.337	0.326	0.315	0.274	1.075	44
0.200	-0.069	-0.089	0.470	0.679	0.448	0.375	0.013	-0.114	-0.125	-0.136	-0.076	0.625	45
0.680	0.101	-0.409	-0.611	1.669	-0.212	-0.335	-0.297	-0.414	-0.425	-0.436	-0.476	-0.025	46
0.132	-0.237	-0.357	-0.499	0.411	0.180	0.207	-0.055	-0.082	-0.093	-0.104	-0.144	0.193	47
0.0	0.0	0.0	0.0	0.0	0.0	0.0	0.0	0.0	0.0	0.0	0.0	0.0	48
0.0	0.0	0.0	0.0	0.0	0.0	0.0	0.0	0.0	0.0	0.0	0.0	0.0	49
0.325	-0.443	-0.364	-0.305	-0.096	-0.127	-0.500	-0.462	-0.488	-0.499	-0.510	-0.551	-0.000	50

	1	2	3	4	5	6	7	8	9	10	11	12	13
51	0.0	0.0	0.0	0.0	0.0	0.0	0.0	0.0	0.0	0.0	0.0	0.0	0.0
52	0.0	0.0	0.0	0.0	0.0	0.0	0.0	0.0	0.0	0.0	0.0	0.0	0.0
53	-0.738	0.407	-0.607	-0.149	0.059	0.163	0.647	-0.046	0.045	-0.144	-0.235	-0.149	-0.124
54	1.051	0.576	-0.128	0.120	0.328	0.252	0.265	0.263	0.253	0.255	0.214	-0.440	-0.375
55	0.867	1.091	0.157	0.445	0.063	-0.063	-0.019	0.008	-0.121	-0.069	-0.131	-0.145	-0.070
56	0.745	0.930	0.315	0.364	0.272	0.285	0.119	-0.053	0.147	0.039	-0.062	-0.266	-0.131
57	0.520	1.294	1.430	0.399	-0.073	-0.060	-0.026	0.002	0.002	-0.006	-0.007	-0.171	-0.236
58	0.0	0.0	0.0	0.0	0.0	0.0	0.0	0.0	0.0	0.0	0.0	0.0	0.0
59	0.616	1.150	0.686	0.834	0.542	0.356	0.390	0.418	0.418	0.410	0.309	-0.146	-0.260
60	0.102	0.026	0.562	0.480	-0.011	0.002	0.036	0.064	0.064	0.056	0.055	-0.299	-0.084
61	0.829	0.613	0.799	0.647	0.156	0.169	0.203	-0.119	-0.119	-0.127	-0.128	-0.342	0.153
62	0.173	0.267	1.143	-0.069	0.190	0.153	0.187	0.215	0.215	0.207	0.206	0.202	0.137
63	-0.825	-1.270	-0.034	-0.326	-0.118	-0.104	-0.070	-0.043	-0.042	-0.051	-0.052	0.964	0.719
64	-0.180	-1.096	-0.060	-0.232	-0.024	-0.010	0.024	0.052	0.052	0.164	0.163	0.288	0.174
65	-1.665	-2.151	-0.915	-0.626	-0.418	-0.405	-0.371	-0.343	-0.343	-0.351	-0.352	0.524	0.459
66	-1.043	-1.609	-0.873	-0.525	-0.316	-0.253	-0.169	-0.141	-0.041	0.051	0.150	0.346	0.181
67	-1.272	-1.708	-0.602	-0.344	-0.135	-0.122	-0.088	-0.060	-0.060	-0.048	-0.049	0.027	0.022
68	-1.001	-1.887	-0.651	-0.423	-0.375	-0.281	-0.087	0.000	0.021	0.013	0.251	1.047	0.982
69	-0.677	-1.383	-0.487	-0.419	-0.131	-0.077	-0.083	-0.056	0.025	0.097	0.135	0.931	0.866
70	-1.272	-1.838	-0.602	-0.484	-0.276	-0.262	-0.228	-0.201	-0.200	-0.208	-0.210	0.566	0.501
71	1.234	3.168	2.804	0.852	0.160	0.174	-0.292	-0.265	-0.264	-0.272	-0.274	-0.078	-0.243
72	0.130	1.294	1.650	0.639	0.407	0.420	0.144	0.172	0.172	0.164	0.163	-0.141	-0.216
73	0.896	0.331	2.306	0.675	0.063	-0.134	-0.160	-0.162	-0.162	-0.170	-0.011	-0.135	-0.220
74	2.108	3.783	1.169	-0.033	0.175	0.189	-0.127	-0.100	-0.099	-0.107	-0.109	-0.463	-0.528
75	1.051	2.266	1.432	0.490	0.078	-0.048	-0.194	-0.107	-0.046	-0.055	0.124	-0.180	-0.005

14	15	16	17	18	19	20	21	22	23	24	25	ROW EFFECT	
0.0	0.0	0.0	0.0	0.0	0.0	0.0	0.0	0.0	0.0	0.0	0.0	0.0	51
0.0	0.0	0.0	0.0	0.0	0.0	0.0	0.0	0.0	0.0	0.0	0.0	0.0	52
0.066	0.097	-0.193	0.026	-0.065	0.084	0.111	0.059	0.122	0.111	0.100	0.060	0.329	53
-0.335	-0.114	-0.074	0.094	-0.286	0.033	-0.050	-0.132	0.001	-0.060	-0.031	-0.111	-0.100	54
-0.010	-0.048	0.171	0.090	-0.001	0.098	0.065	0.103	0.077	-0.005	0.055	0.074	-0.585	55
-0.131	0.100	0.180	-0.062	-0.252	-0.183	0.044	0.082	0.055	0.044	-0.067	-0.107	-0.444	56
-0.147	0.015	0.185	0.053	0.032	0.002	0.079	0.117	0.090	0.079	0.068	0.067	-0.528	57
0.0	0.0	0.0	0.0	0.0	0.0	0.0	0.0	0.0	0.0	0.0	0.0	0.0	58
-0.261	-0.029	-0.050	-0.391	-0.182	-0.213	-0.186	-0.148	-0.174	-0.185	-0.196	-0.237	-0.414	59
-0.125	-0.093	0.237	-0.115	-0.136	0.184	0.211	-0.032	-0.058	-0.069	0.130	0.089	-0.150	60
0.252	-0.066	0.264	-0.088	-0.249	0.001	0.028	0.066	0.039	0.028	0.017	-0.024	0.173	61
0.236	0.268	-0.082	-0.154	-0.165	-0.195	-0.168	-0.131	-0.157	-0.168	-0.179	-0.220	-0.381	62
0.699	0.370	0.410	0.329	-0.062	-0.093	-0.066	-0.028	-0.055	-0.066	0.103	0.063	0.626	63
0.243	0.275	0.204	0.063	-0.068	-0.119	-0.092	-0.054	-0.080	-0.091	-0.082	-0.143	-0.458	64
0.558	0.520	0.390	0.248	0.157	0.127	0.154	0.192	0.165	0.154	0.603	0.562	-0.003	65
0.280	0.312	0.292	0.130	0.059	0.029	0.056	0.094	0.067	0.056	0.045	0.004	-0.655	66
0.211	0.243	0.173	0.061	-0.520	-0.430	-0.403	0.514	0.488	0.477	0.466	0.425	-0.386	67
0.202	-0.006	-0.107	0.152	0.061	0.030	0.057	0.015	-0.011	0.057	0.127	0.086	-0.277	68
0.846	0.718	0.337	0.156	-0.055	1.874	-0.099	-0.101	-0.127	-0.139	-0.149	-0.190	-0.281	69
0.001	0.033	0.012	-0.129	0.280	0.249	0.276	0.314	0.288	0.276	0.266	0.225	-0.276	70
-0.243	-0.011	-0.232	0.127	0.296	0.525	0.392	0.060	0.034	0.092	0.722	0.821	-0.032	71
-0.117	0.045	0.245	0.513	-0.208	0.072	-0.211	-0.173	-0.200	-0.211	-0.222	-0.263	-0.618	72
-0.000	0.131	0.441	-0.171	0.399	0.258	0.185	-0.157	-0.154	0.105	0.264	0.234	-0.335	73
-0.778	-0.397	-0.417	-0.348	0.051	0.370	0.397	0.435	0.408	0.397	0.386	0.346	0.503	74
0.095	0.186	0.286	0.024	-0.066	0.023	-0.010	-0.032	-0.059	-0.070	-0.081	0.479	-0.030	75

	1	2	3	4	5	6	7	8	9	10	11	12	13
76	0.559	0.893	0.029	-0.022	0.186	0.199	0.233	0.261	0.261	0.253	0.252	0.068	0.003
77	0.690	2.504	2.280	0.579	0.577	0.590	0.484	0.512	0.512	0.504	0.503	0.219	-0.056
78	-0.985	-1.101	-0.585	-0.737	-0.528	-0.415	0.133	0.247	-0.303	-0.311	-0.312	-0.046	0.109
79	-1.323	-1.839	-0.443	-0.265	-0.117	-0.033	0.051	0.148	0.199	0.221	0.259	0.055	0.020
80	-0.655	-0.671	-0.435	-0.937	-0.559	-0.455	-0.341	-0.204	-0.203	-0.181	-0.183	0.033	0.089
81	-0.848	-1.414	-0.368	0.131	0.339	0.352	0.386	0.414	0.414	0.406	0.405	0.401	0.336
82	-1.257	-1.322	0.104	-0.048	-0.040	-0.026	0.008	0.035	0.036	0.028	0.026	0.022	-0.043
83	-0.454	-0.849	1.417	1.615	1.823	0.487	-0.109	0.548	0.449	0.440	0.339	0.545	0.320
84	-1.573	-2.079	0.877	1.425	1.634	0.107	0.141	0.169	0.059	0.051	0.050	0.046	-0.019
85	-2.133	0.0	0.0	1.235	1.144	0.957	0.591	0.619	0.519	0.311	0.210	0.006	-0.059
86	0.212	0.346	3.082	1.730	1.939	0.952	0.886	0.914	0.614	0.606	0.605	0.201	-0.164
87	-0.523	0.451	0.377	1.375	0.684	0.467	0.131	0.159	0.159	-0.149	-0.450	-0.304	-0.219
88	0.041	-0.595	0.741	-0.811	1.188	0.641	0.535	0.353	0.283	0.135	0.134	0.200	0.135
89	1.624	2.059	0.795	1.343	1.151	0.665	1.599	-0.074	-0.173	-0.182	-0.183	0.213	0.048
90	0.527	0.261	1.097	-0.055	-0.047	-0.133	-0.199	-0.272	-0.271	-0.179	-0.181	0.415	0.350
COL EFFS	1.24	1.80	0.57	0.02	-0.19	-0.20	-0.24	-0.26	-0.27	-0.26	-0.26	-0.25	-0.19

14	15	16	17	18	19	20	21	22	23	24	25	ROW EFFECT	
0.222	0.254	0.294	-0.208	-0.239	-0.269	-0.242	-0.204	-0.231	-0.242	-0.253	-0.293	-0.158	76
0.043	0.075	-0.255	-0.397	-0.438	-0.518	-0.491	-0.553	-0.580	-0.431	-0.042	-0.082	0.592	77
-0.192	-0.160	-0.170	0.638	0.517	0.037	0.524	0.561	0.535	0.064	0.343	0.302	0.727	78
-0.080	-0.088	0.071	0.120	0.189	0.028	-0.015	-0.017	-0.013	-0.005	0.005	-0.036	-0.325	79
0.118	0.130	0.279	-0.012	1.257	0.116	0.193	0.281	0.275	0.244	0.333	0.392	0.457	80
0.435	0.047	-0.163	-0.255	-0.336	-0.366	-0.339	-0.301	-0.328	-0.339	-0.340	-0.381	0.340	81
-0.143	0.038	-0.082	0.127	0.136	0.005	0.132	0.170	0.143	0.032	0.021	0.081	-0.132	82
0.170	0.001	-0.019	-0.111	-0.301	-0.372	-0.305	-0.327	-0.354	-0.365	-0.316	-0.336	-0.545	83
0.080	0.112	0.092	0.050	0.009	-0.071	-0.044	-0.006	-0.033	-0.044	-0.055	-0.096	-0.855	84
0.020	-0.018	0.652	0.510	-0.431	-0.411	-0.484	-0.446	-0.473	-0.484	-0.495	-0.386	-0.315	85
-0.165	-0.133	-0.153	-0.295	-0.386	-0.416	-0.389	-0.352	-0.378	-0.389	-0.400	-0.441	-0.410	86
-0.270	-0.233	-0.338	0.200	0.109	0.079	0.106	0.144	0.117	0.106	0.095	0.054	0.395	87
0.234	-0.224	0.246	0.594	0.083	-0.367	-0.340	-0.302	-0.329	-0.340	-0.351	-0.392	0.541	88
0.148	0.079	0.059	0.218	-0.073	-0.104	-0.077	-0.039	-0.066	-0.077	-0.088	-0.128	-0.323	89
0.250	0.682	1.161	0.720	0.229	-0.002	-0.075	-0.037	-0.063	-0.075	0.115	0.074	-0.325	90
-0.29	-0.32	-0.30	-0.16	-0.07	-0.03	-0.06	-0.10	-0.07	-0.06	-0.05	-0.01	1.96	

References cited

1. Chinese manuscript sources

2. Chinese printed sources, to 1911

3. Books and articles in Chinese, post 1911

4. Books and articles in Japanese

5. Books and articles in English, French and German

Manuscript Sources

The Shensi Reports

1. Shan-sheng Kuang-hsü erh-shih-liu nien wu yüeh-fen yin liang chia-chih 陝省光緒貳拾陸年伍月分銀糧價值 (Reports on prices of grains and silver from ninety district towns in Shensi with prefectural and departmental summaries for the fifth month of the twenty-sixth year of Kuang-hsü, May 28 to June 26, 1900). MSS in the Ōki Bunko, Tōyōbunka Kenkyūjo, Tokyo University

Same for:

2.	Kuang-hsü 26/8	August 25 to Sept 23 1900
3.	Kuang-hsü 28/4	May 8 to June 5 1902
4.	Kuang-hsü 29/4	April 27 to May 26 1903
5.	Kuang-hsü 29/5 (inter-callary)	June 25 to July 23 1903
6.	Kuang-hsü 29/6	July 24 to August 22 1903
7.	Kuang-hsü 29/7	August 23 to Sept 20 1903
8.	Kuang-hsü 29/8	Sept 21 to Oct 19 1903
9.	Kuang-hsü 29/9	Oct 20 to Nov 18 1903
10.	Kuang-hsü 29/10	Nov 19 to Dec 18 1903
11.	Kuang-hsü 29/11	Dec 19 to Jan 16 1903-4
12.	Kuang-hsü 31/1	Feb 4 to March 5 1905
13.	Kuang-hsü 31/5	June 3 to July 2 1905
14.	Kuang-hsü 31/8	August 30 to Sept 28 1905

15.	Kuang-hsü 32/2	Feb 23 to March 24 1906
16.	Kuang-hsü 32/10	Nov 16 to Dec 15 1906
17.	Kuang-hsü 34/5	May 30 to June 28 1908
18.	Hsüan-t'ung 1/3	April 20 to May 18 1909
19.	Hsüan-t'ung 1/5	June 18 to July 16 1909
20.	Hsüan-t'ung 1/6	July 17 to August 15 1909
21.	Hsüan-t'ung 1/8	Sept 14 to Oct 13 1909
22.	Hsüan-t'ung 1/9	Oct 14 to Nov 12 1909
23.	Hsüan-t'ung 1/10	Nov 13 to Dec 12 1909
24.	Hsüan-t'ung 1/11	Dec 13 to Jan 10 1909-10
25.	Hsüan-t'ung 1/12	Jan 11 to Feb 9 1910

The Szechwan Reports

1. Szu-ch'uan t'ung-sheng ko fu, t'ing, chou, hsien Kuang-hsü san-shih-szu nien chiu yüeh-fen mi-liang chia-chih 四川通省各府廳州縣光緒叁拾肆年玖月分米糧價值 (Rice and grain price reports from every prefecture, sub-prefecture, department and district in the province of Szechwan for the ninth month of the thirty-fourth year of Kuang-hsü, Sept 25 to Oct 24 1908). MSS in the Ōki Bunko, Tōyōbunka Kenkyūjo, Tokyo University.

Same for:

2. Kuang-hsü 34/10 Oct 25 to Nov 23 1908

3.	Kuang-hsü 34/11	Nov 24 to Dec 22 1908
4.	Kuang-hsü 34/12	Dec 23 to Jan 21 1908-9
5.	Hsüan-t'ung 1/1	Jan 22 to Feb 19 1909
6.	Hsüan-t'ung 1/2 (intercallary)	Feb 20 to March 21 1909
7.	Hsüan-t'ung 1/2	March 22 to April 19 1909
8.	Hsüan-t'ung 1/3	April 20 to May 18 1909
9.	Hsüan-t'ung 1/4	May 19 to June 17 1909
10.	Hsüan-t'ung 1/5	June 18 to July 16 1909
11.	Hsüan-t'ung 1/6	July 17 to August 15 1909
12.	Hsüan-t'ung 1/7	August 16 to Sept 13 1909
13.	Hsüan-t'ung 1/8	Sept 14 to Oct 13 1909

Account Books

1. Shih-fei chang 使費賬 (Household expenditures of a Christian for 64 days, Nov 19 1739 to Jan 1 1740). MS in Bibliotheque nationale, Paris, Chinois 4992.

2. Ch'u-ju yin-liang liu-shui chang (Te-sheng tien) 出入銀兩流水賬(德盛店) (Daily receipts and expenditures of a general store in Hopei (Fang-shan ?), June 11 to December 4, 1782. MS

3. No title: charge accounts of cotton dealer in Hopei, 1806, MS

4. Same as 3, 1813. MS

5. No title: accounts of grain dealer's purchases, Peking area, 1850-1852. MS

6. Lai-wang lao-chang 來往老賬 (miscellaneous charge accounts of store in Peking area, 1857-1863. MS

7. Shou-liang lao-chang 收糧老賬 (grain purchase accounts of store in Hopei (Ch'ang-p'ing ?), 1858. MS

Account books 2 through 7 were formerly in the possession of Sydney Gamble. They were given by his widow to the Library of the Far Eastern Institute, Columbia University.

Handbooks for secretarial assistants in charge of financial matters (ch'ien-ku 錢穀)*

1. Ch'ien-ku chai-yao 錢穀摘要 2 ch'üan, anon. 1823 ? Handwritten copy in the Toyo Bunko, Tokyo. Contains Shantung regulations, c. 1723-1823.

2. Ch'ien-ku ch'ieh-yao 錢穀挈要 10 ch'üan, anon. c. 1850. Handwritten copy in Taiwan Provincial Library. Contains Fukien regulations, 1750-1850.

3. Ch'ien-ku pei-yao 錢谷備要 20 ts'e, anon. c. 1850. Handwritten copy in the Toyo Bunko, Tokyo. With the exception of the title this work is identical with No. 2. It should not be confused with No. 7 which although it has the same title is a completely different work.

4. Ch'ien-ku pi-tu 錢穀必讀 1 ts'e, compiled by Liu Yu-jung 劉有容, preface dated 1811. Handwritten copy in the Chinese-Japanese Library, Harvard University. Contains Kiangnan regulations, late 18th and early 19th centuries.

5. Ch'ien-ku shih-ch'eng 錢穀視成 2 ch'üan, compiled by Hsieh Ming-huang 謝鳴篁. Original preface dated 1788. Copied with additions by Chan Yün-hsiu 湛允修 in 1907. Contains Kiangnan regulations. Handwritten copy in the Chinese-Japanese Library, Harvard University.

6. Ch'ien-ku yao-lüeh 錢谷要略 1 ts'e, anon. c. 1820. Handwritten copy in the Toyo Bunko, Tokyo. Contains Shantung regulations, c. 1723-1820.

7. Ch'ien-ku pei-yao 錢穀備要 8 ch'üan, originally compiled by Wang Yu-huai 王又槐 in 1793. This work ran through many wood-block editions each containing much different material. All editions however contain empire wide regulations making them more general than the other handbooks listed above. Apart from the 1793 edition I have used the 1814 edition and the 1893 copper-plate edition.

---

*-For a more detailed description of this type of source see Wilkinson (1970).

Chinese printed sources, to 1911

1. Administrative regulations, statutes, laws etc.

Ch'ing-yüan t'iao-fa shih-lei 慶元條法事類,12[illegible](Sub-statutes to the Code arranged by categories, Ch'ing-yüan period, 1195-1201), 1202. Koten Kenkyūkai reprint, Tokyo, 1965.

Chu-ssu chih-chang 諸司職掌 (Statutes for the organization of the central government), 1393, included in Huang Ming chih-shu 皇明制書, Koten Kenkyūkai reprint, Tokyo, 1966-67.

Ho-nan kung-pu wu-liao chia-chih tse-li 河南工部物料價值則例 (Regulations for the prices of materials used by the Board of Works, Honan), 1768.

Hsien-kang shih-lei 憲綱事類 (Regulations for the activities of the censorial office), 1371, included in Huang Ming chih-shu, Koten Kenkyūkai reprint, Tokyo, 1966-67.

Huang Ming t'iao-fa shih-lei tsuan 皇明條法事類纂 (Sub-statutes to the Code arranged by categories), 1531? Koten Kenkyukai reprint, Tokyo 1966.

Hu-nan sheng-li ch'eng-an 湖南省例成案 (Administrative precedents and leading cases of Hunan), 1820.

Hu-pu tse-li 户部則例 (Regulations of the Board of Revenue), 1776; 1783; 1791; 1831; 1865; 1874.

(Li-tai) Ch'ien-ku t'iao-li 歷代錢穀條例 (Financial statutes arranged chronologically from 1751 to 1817), 1817.

Liu-pu tse-li 六部則例 (Regulations of the Six Boards), 1670.

Nan-ching hu-pu chih 南京户部志 (Handbook of the Nanking Board of Revenue), 1595.

Shan-hsi ch'ing-li ts'ai-cheng shuo-ming shu 陝西清理財政說明書 (Guide to the reform of Shensi finances), published by the Bureau for the Reform of the Shensi Finances, 1909.

Shan-hsi sheng fu-i ch'üan shu 陝西省賦役全書 (Complete book of taxes and labour services of Shensi province), 1844.

Sheng-li (Fu-chien) 省例福建 (Administrative precedents of Fukien, 1752 to 1872), 1873. Handwritten copy in the Toyo Bunko, Tokyo.

Ta Ch'ing hui-tien (shih-li) 大清會典事例 (Collected statutes of the Ch'ing dynasty, and precedents), 1690; 1733; 1763; 1818; 1899. Unless otherwise indicated all references are to the 1899 edition (abbreviated as shih-li) in the Taipei reprint, 1963.

Ta Ch'ing li-ch'ao shih-lu 大清歷朝實錄 (Veritable records of the Ch'ing dynasty), Mukden, 1938.

Ta Ch'ing lü-li hui-t'ung hsin-tsuan 大清律例會通新纂 (Comprehensive new edition of the statutes and sub-statutes of the Ch'ing Code), 1873.

Ta Ming hui-tien 大明會典 (Collected statutes of the Ming dynasty), 2nd edition, 1587. Taipei reprint, 1963.

Ta Ming ling 大明令 (Legal rules of the Ming), 1368, included in Huang Ming chih-shu, Koten Kenkyūkai reprint, Tokyo, 1966-67.

Ta Ming lü 大明律 (The Ming Code), 1397, included in Huang Ming chih-shu, Koten Kenkyūkai reprint, Tokyo, 1966-67.

Tse-li lei-pien (pen-ch'ao hsü-tseng) 則例類編(本朝續增) (Collected administrative regulations, Ch'ing additions), 1703.

Tse-li pien-lan 則例便覽 (Guide to administrative regulations), 1793.

(Yung-cheng) Chu-p'i yü-chih 雍正硃批諭旨 (Vermilion endorsements and edicts, Yung-cheng period, 1723-1735), 1738, Taipei reprint, 1965.

2. Works of individual authors

Chang Hsüeh-ch'eng 章学誠, Hu-pei t'ung-chih wei-ch'eng kao 湖北通志未成稿 (Incomplete draft of general gazetteer of Hupeh province), 1790. Contained in Chang-shih i-shu, Chia Yeh t'ang library edition, 1922.

Cheng Kuang-tsu 鄭光祖, I-pan lu 一斑錄 (Partial records), 1855? Printed separately and also as an appendix to his Chou-chü suo chih, 1855.

Ch'ien Yung 钱泳, Li-yuan ts'ung-hua 履園叢話 (Collected conversations of Li-yüan), 1870.

Lin Tse-hsü 林则徐, Lin Wen-chung cheng-shu 林文忠政書 (Memorials of Duke Lin Wen-chung), 1885.

Tung Wei 董煟, Chiu-huang huo-min shu 救荒活民書 (Book of preventing calamities and saving the people),

Wang Ch'ing-yün 王慶雲, Shih-ch'ü yü-chi 石渠餘紀, 1851.

Wang Hui-tsu 汪輝祖, Ping-t'a meng-hen lu 病榻夢痕錄 (Traces of dreams from a sick-bed), 1796 and Meng-hen yü-lu 夢痕餘錄 (The same, continued), 1806.

Yeh Meng-chu 葉夢珠, Yüeh shih pien 閱世編 (Notes on practical affairs), 1700? printed in Shanghai chang-ku ts'ung-shu, Shanghai, 1935.

Books and articles in Chinese, post 1911

Chang Chia-hsiang 張家驤, Chung-hua pi-chih shih 中華幣制史 (A history of China's monetary system in the early Republic), Peking, 1925.

Chang Lü-lan 張履鸞, "Chiang-su Wu-chin wu-chia chih yen-chiu" 江蘇武進物價之研究 (Farm prices in Wu-chin, Kiangsu), Chin-ling hsüeh-pao, vol 3, 1, 1933, pp. 153-216.

Ch'en Chao-nan 陳昭南, Yung-cheng Ch'ien-lung nien chien ti yin ch'ien pi-chia pien-tung, 1723-1795 雍正乾隆年間的銀錢比價變動 (Fluctuations in the cash/-silver exchange rates during the Yung-cheng and Ch'ien-lung periods), Taipei, 1966.

Ch'en Heng-li 陳恆力, Pu nung shu yen-chiu 補農書研究 (Studies on the Pu nung shu), Peking, 1958.

Chung-kuo chin-tai huo-pi shih tzu-liao 中国貨幣史近代資料 (Materials on the history of currency in modern China), compiled by the group in charge of preparing materials on the history of currency under the advisory office of the head-office of the People's Bank of China (Chung-kuo jen-min yin-hang tsung-hang ts'an shih shih chin-yung shih-liao tsu 中国人民銀行總行參事室金融史料組編), part 1, 1840-1911, 2 vols, Peking, 1964.

Ch'üan Han-sheng 全漢昇, "Mei-chou pai-yin yü shih-pa shih-chi Chung-kuo wu-chia ko-ming ti kuan-hsi" 美洲白銀與十八世紀中國物價革命的關係 (American silver and the price revolution in China in the eighteenth century), Chung-yang yen-chiu yüan li-shih yü-yen yen-chiu suo chi-k'an (hereafter abbreviated as LYYC), vol 28, 1957, pp. 517-528.

---------------- "Ch'ien-lung shih-san nien ti mi kuei wen-t'i" 乾隆十三年的米貴問題 (The problem of high rice prices in 1748), in Ch'ing-chu Li Chi hsien-sheng ch'i-shih sui lun-wen chi, part 1, pp. 332-352, Taipei, 1965.

---------------- and Wang Yeh-chien 王業鍵, "Ch'ing Yung-cheng nien chien ti mi-chia" 清雍正年間的米價 (Rice prices in the Yung-cheng period, 1723-1735), LYYC, vol 30, 1959, pp. 157-185.

---------------- and Wang Yeh-chien 王業鍵, "Ch'ing chung-yeh i-ch'ien Chiang-Che mi-chia ti pien-tung ch'ü-shih" 清中葉以前江浙米價的變動趨勢 (Fluctuation trends of rice prices in southeast China in the early Ch'ing), in *Ch'ing-chu Tung Tso-pin hsien-sheng liu-shih-wu sui lun-wen chi*, pp. 351-357, Taipei, 1960-61.

---------------------------------- "Chin-tai Ssu-ch'uan Ho-chiang hsien wu-chia yü kung-tzu ti pien-tung ch'ü-shih" 近代四川合江縣物價與工資的變動趨勢 (Fluctuation trends of prices and wages in Ho-chiang district, Szechwan, 1875-1925), LYYC, vol 34, 1962, pp. 265-274.

Fu I-ling 傅衣凌, *Ming Ch'ing nung-ts'un she-hui ching-chi* 明清農村社會經濟 (Rural society and economy in Ming and Ch'ing), Peking, 1968.

Li Chien-nung 李劍農, "Ming-tai ti i-ko kuan-ting ti wu-chia piao yü pu-huan chih-pi" 明代的一個官定的物價表與不換紙幣 (A government price list and irredeemable paper money in the Ming dynasty), *Wu-han ta-hsüeh she-hui k'o-hsüeh chi-k'an*, vol 1, 3, 1930, pp. 501-526.

------------- *Hsien Ch'in liang Han ching-chi shih kao* 先秦兩漢經濟史稿 (A draft economic history of the pre-Ch'in and Han periods), Peking, 1962.

Li Wen-chih 李文治, "Ch'ing-tai ya-p'ien chan-cheng ch'ien ti ti-tsu, shang-yeh tzu-pen, kao-li tai yü nung-min sheng-huo" 清代鴉片戰爭前的地租，商業資本，高利貸與農民生活 (Land rent, commercial capital, high interest rates, and the peasants' standard of living in the Ch'ing period prior to the opium war), reprinted in *Chung-kuo tzu-pen chu-i meng-ya wen-t'i t'ao-lun chi*, vol 2, pp. 609-656, Peking, 1957.

----------- and Chang Yu-i 章有義 (compilers), *Chung-kuo chin-tai nung-yeh shih tzu-liao* 中国近代农业史资料 (Materials on the history of agriculture in modern China), 3 vols, Peking, 1957.

Liang Ch'i-ch'ao 梁啟超, *Chung-kuo li-shih yen-chiu fa* 中国歷史研究法 (Research methods in Chinese history), Shanghai, 1925.

Liu I-cheng 柳詒徵, "Chiang-su ko ti ch'ien liu-pai nien chien chih mi-chia" 江蘇各地千六百年間之米價 (Rice prices in Kiangsu during the last sixteen hundred years), *Shih-hsüeh tsa-chih*, vol 2, 3, 1930, pp. 1-8 plus tables.

P'eng Hsin-wei 彭信威, Chung-kuo huo-pi shih 中国货币史 (A history of Chinese money), Shanghai, 1958.

P'eng Tse-i 彭泽益, "Ya-p'ien chan hou shih nien chien yin kuei ch'ien chien p'o-tung hsia ti Chung-kuo ching-chi yü chieh-chi kuan-hsi" 鸦片战后十年間銀贵錢賤波动下的中国經济与阶級关系 (The economy and class relations under the impact of the appreciation of silver and the depreciation of cash in the decade following the opium war in China), Lishi yanjiu, vol 6, 1961, pp. 40-68.

Sheng Chün 盛俊, "Ch'ing Ch'ien-lung ch'ao Chiang-su sheng wu-chia kung-tzu t'ung-chi" 清乾隆朝江苏省物價工資統計 (Price and wage data from Kiangsu during the Ch'ien-lung period), Hsüeh Lin, vol 2, 1940, pp. 105-136.

Ts'ai Shen-chih 蔡申之, Ch'ing-tai chou hsien ku-shih 清代州縣故事 (Informal materials on Chinese local government during the Ch'ing dynasty), Hong Kong 1968.

Wu Ch'eng-lo 吳承洛, Chung-kuo tu liang heng shih 中国度量衡史 (A history of Chinese weights and measures), Shanghai, 1957.

Yang Tuan-liu 楊端六, Ch'ing-tai huo-pi chin-yung shih kao 清代货幣金融史稿 (A draft history of money and currency during the Ch'ing dynasty), Peking, 1962.

Yen Chung-p'ing 嚴中平 (ed.), Chung-kuo chin-tai ching-chi shih t'ung-chi hsüan chi 中国近代經濟史統計資料選輯 (A selection of statistics on modern Chinese economic history), Peking, 1955.

--------------- Ch'ing-tai Yün-nan t'ung-cheng k'ao 清代雲南銅政考 (A study of the government copper monopoly in Yunnan during the Ch'ing dynasty), Shanghai, 1957.

Addenda

Wang Shih-ch'ing 王世慶, "Ch'ing-tai T'ai-wan ti mi-chia" 清代臺灣的米價 (Rice prices in Taiwan during the Ch'ing dynasty), Tai-wan wen-hsien, vol 9, 4, 1958, pp. 11-20.

Books and articles in Japanese

Abe Takeo 安部健夫, "Beikoku jukyū no kenkyū" 米穀需給の研究 (A study of the supply and demand for grain in the Yung-cheng period), Tōyōshi kenkyū, vol 15, 4, 1957, pp. 120-213.

Hoshi Ayao 星斌夫, Mindai sōun no kenkyū 明代漕運の研究 (The Ming tribute grain system), Tokyo 1963.

---------- Chūgoku shakai keizai shi goi 中国社会経済史語彙 (Glossary of socio-economic terms in Chinese history), Tokyo, 1966.

Ikeda On 池田温, "Chūgoku kodai bukka no ichi kōsatsu 中国古代の物価の一考察 (A study on prices in ancient China), Shigaku zasshi, vol 77, 1 and 2, 1968, pp. 1-45 and 45-61.

Imahori Seiji 今堀誠二, Chūgoku hōken shakai no kikō 中国封建社会の機構 (The structure of Chinese feudal society), Tokyo, 1955.

Katō Shigeshi 加藤繁, part author, Shinkoku gyōseihō 清国行政法 (Administrative laws of the Ch'ing dynasty), Tokyo, 1905-1915.

------------- "Shindai ni okeru senhō senshō no hattatsu ni tsuite" 清代に於ける銭舗銭荘の発達に就いて (On the development of money shops and money banking shops in the Ch'ing dynasty), Tōyōgakuhō, vol 31, 3, 1947, (reprinted in Shina keizaishi kōsho, pp. 463-477 (vol 2))

Miyashita Tadao 宮下忠雄, Chūgoku heisei no tokushu kenkyū: Kindai Chūgoku ginryo seido no kenkyū 中国幣制の特殊研究：近代中国銀両制度の研究 (A special study of the Chinese currency system: a study of the silver tael system of modern China), Tokyo, 1952.

Negishi Tadashi 根岸佶, Shanghai no girudo 上海のギルド (The guilds of Shanghai), Tokyo, 1951.

-------------- Chūgoku no girudo 中国のギルド (The guilds of China), Tokyo, 1953.

Niida Noboru 仁井田陞, Tōryō shūi 唐令拾遺 (Collected vestiges of the T'ang Statutes), Tokyo, 1933.

Niida Noboru 仁井田陞, *Chūgoku hōseishi kenkyū* 中国法制史研究 (Studies in the history of Chinese law), vol 2, Tokyo, 1960.

Otake Fumio 小竹文夫, "Shindai ni okeru gin.sen hika no hendō" 清代における銀.銭比価の変動 (Fluctuations in the cash/silver exchange rates during the Ch'ing dynasty), in his *Kinsei Shina keizaishi kenkyū*, pp. 77-139, Tokyo, 1942.

Saeki Tomi 佐伯富, "Shindai Yōseichō ni okeru tsuka mondai" 清代雍正朝における通貨問題 (The currency problem in the Yung-cheng period), *Tōyōshi kenkyū*, vol 18, 3, 1959, pp. 142-211.

Sasaki Masaya 佐々木正哉 "Ahen sensō izen no tsūka mondai" 阿片戦争以前の通貨問題 (Currency problems prior to the opium war), *Tōhōgaku*, vol 8, 1954, pp. 84-117.

Shiba Yoshinobu 斯波義信, *Sōdai shōgyō shi kenkyū* 宋代商業史研究 (Commercial activities during the Sung dynasty), Tokyo, 1968.

Shina shōbetsu zenshi 支那省別全誌 (Comprehensive gazetteer of China by provinces) compiled by members of the Tōa Dōbunkai, Tōa Dōbun Gakuin, Shanghai, 18 vols, Tokyo, 1918.

--------------------- New and revised edition, 8 vols, Tokyo, 1941-1946.

Terada Takanobu 寺田隆信, "Mindai ni okeru hokuhen beika mondai ni tsuite" 明代における北辺米価問題について (On the problem of rice prices at the northern frontier during the Ming dynasty), *Tōyōshi kenkyū*, vol 1967, pp. 48-70.

Wada Sei 和田清 (ed.), *Minshi shokkashi yakuchū* 明史食貨志譯註 (An integral translation of the Treatise on Finance of the Ming History), 2 vols, Tokyo, 1957.

Yamane Yukio 山根幸夫 (ed.), *Kōmin seisho* 皇明制書 (Collection of 18 basic works on early Ming government, first published 1579), 2 vols, Tokyo, for the Koten Kenkyūkai, 1966/67.

Addendum

Kobayashi Kojiro 小林高四郎, "Tō-Sō gajin kō," 唐宋牙人考 (A study of the brokers in the T'ang and Sung periods), *Shigaku*, 8, 1, 1932, pp. 53-101 and supplement in *Shigaku*, 8, 3, 1932, pp. 165-167.

Books and articles in English, French and German

Baehrel, R. "Économie et histoire à propos des prix" in Hommage à Lucien Febvre, pp. 287-310, Paris, 1953.

Block, K. "On the copper currencies in China," Nanking Soc- and Economic Quarterly, vol 8, 3, 1935, pp. 616-632.

Braudel, F. and Spooner, F. "Prices in Europe from 1450 to 1750," chapter 7, Cambridge Economic History of Europe, vol 4, pp. 378-486, Cambridge, 1967.

Brewitt-Taylor, C.H. "A Handful of Cash," China Review, vol 17, 1889, pp. 357-359.

Buck, J.L. "Price Changes in China," Journal of the American Statistical Association, New Series, No. 149, 1925, pp. 238-241.

---------- Land Utilization in China, vol 1, Text; vol 2, Atlas; vol 3, Statistics, Shanghai, 1937.

Canton Register and Price Current, The, Canton, 1827-1839.

Clark, C. and Haswell, M. The Economics of Subsistence Agriculture, New York, 1967.

Ch'ü T'ung-tsu Local Government in China under the Ch'ing, Cambridge, Mass., 1962.

Fisher, I. The Purchasing Power of Money, New York, 1911.

Feuerwerker, A. "The Chinese Economy, ca. 1870-1911," Michigan Papers in Chinese Studies, 5, 1969.

Gamble, S.D. "Prices, Wages and Standard of Living in Peking," Chinese Social and Political Science Review, Special Supplement, July, 1926.

------------ "Daily Wages of Unskilled Chinese Labourers," Far Eastern Quarterly, vol 3, 1944, pp. 41-73.

------------ Ting Hsien: A North China Rural Community, New York, 1954.

------------ North China Villages, Berkeley, 1963.

Hammarström, I. "The 'Price Revolution' of the 16th century, some Swedish Evidence," Scandinavian Economic History Review, vol 2, 1957, pp.

Ho, P'ing-ti Studies on the Population of China, Cambridge, Mass. 1959.

Hsiao, Kung-chuan Rural China, Seattle, 1960.

Jamieson, G. (ed.) "Tenure of Land in China and the Condition of the Rural Population," Journal of the Royal Asiatic Society of Great Britain and Ireland, North China Branch, vol 23, 1888, pp. 59-174.

King, F.H. Money and Monetary Policy in China, 1845-1895, Cambridge, Mass., 1965.

Kingsmill, T.W. (ed.) "Inland Communications in China," Journal of the China Branch of the Royal Asiatic Society, vol 28, 1898, pp. 1-214.

Miyashita, Tadao "The Silver Tael System in Modern China," Kobe University Economic Review, vol 2, 1956, pp. 11-32.

Morse, H.B. (ed.) "Abstract of Information on Currency and Measures in China," Journal of the China Branch of the Royal Asiatic Society, vol 29, 1889, pp. 46-135.

Muramatsu, Yuji "A Documentary Study of Chinese Landlordism in Late Ch'ing and Early Republical Kiangnan," Bulletin of the School of Oriental and African Studies, Vol 29, 33, 1966, pp. 566-599.

Nichols, F.A. Through Hidden Shensi, New York, 1902.

Parkes, H. "Account of the Paper Currency and Banking System of Fuchowfoo," Journal of the Royal Asiatic Society, vol 13, 1852, pp. 179-191.

Perkins, D. Agricultural Development in China, 1368-1968, Chicago, 1969.

Pernitzsch, M.G. and Tittel, H. "Chinesische Buchhaltung," Mitteilungen der Deutschen Gesellschaft für Natur- und Völkerkunde Ostasiens, Supplement 10, 1927, pp. 1-84.

Shepherd, G.S. Agricultural Price Analysis, Iowa, 1963.

Silver Prices in China, Report of the Committee for the Study of Silver Values and Commodity Prices, Ministry of Industries, Shanghai, 1935.

Spence, J. Ts'ao Yin and the K'ang-hsi Emperor, New Haven, 1966.

Tukey, J.W. unpublished preliminary version of Introduction to Exploratory Data Analysis, Fall 1969.

Twitchett, D.C. "The T'ang Market System," Asia Major, New Series, vol 12, part 2, 1966, pp. 202-248.

Wagel, S.R. Chinese Currency and Banking, Shanghai, 1915.

Warntz, W. Toward a Geograophy of Price, A Study in Geo-econometrics, Philadelphia, 1959.

Wilkinson, E.P. "Chinese Grain Price Quotations, 1600-1900," Transactions of the International Conference of Orientalists in Japan, vol 14, 1969, pp. 54-65.

--------------- "New Sources for Local History" to appear in Fall 1970 number of Ch'ing Shih Wen-t'i.

Williams, T. "Silver in China and its Relation to Chinese Copper Coinage," Annals of the American Philosophical Society, vol 9, 1897, pp.

Yang, L.S. Money and Credit in China, A Short History, Cambridge, Mass. 1952.

Addenda

China Year Book, 1914, (by Woodhead, H.G.W. and Bell, H.T.M.), London, 1914.

Ho, P.T. The Ladder of Success in Imperial China, New York, 1963.

Lu, Lien-tching. Les greniers publics de prévoyance sous la dynastie des Ts'ing, Paris, 1932.

MacGowan, D.J. "Chinese guilds or chambers of commerce and trades unions," Journal of the China Branch of the Royal Asiatic Society, vol 21, 1886, pp. 133-192.

Martin, R.M. China; Political, Commercial and Social, 2 vols, London, 1847.

Titles in the Modern Chinese Economy Series

THE LATE IMPERIAL PERIOD

(late nineteenth and early twentieth centuries)

1. Ball, Samuel. **An Account of the Cultivation and Manufacture of Tea in China.** London, 1848.

2. Chen, Jerome. **State Economic Policies of the Ch'ing Government, 1840–1895.** New York, Garland, 1979.

3. Edkins, Joseph. **The Revenue and Taxation of the Chinese Empire.** Shanghai, 1903.

4. Fortune, Robert. **Three Years' Wanderings in the Northern Provinces of China.** London, 1847.

5. King, Paul. **In the Chinese Customs Service: A Personal Record of Forty-Seven Years.** London, 1924.

6. Parker, E.H. **China: The History, Diplomacy, and Commerce from the Earliest Times to the Present Day.** London, 1917.

7. Parsons, William Barclay. **An American Engineer in China.** New York, 1900.

8. Wilkinson, Endymion Porter. **Studies in Chinese Price History.** [Ph.D. Dissertation, Princeton University, 1970.] New York, Garland, 1979.

9. Wright, Stanley. **Kiangsi Native Trade and Its Taxation.** Shanghai, 1920.

THE AGRARIAN ECONOMY

10. Buck, John Lossing. **Three Essays on Chinese Farm Economy.** New York, Garland, 1979.

11. **Economic Facts.** [published by the Department of Agricultural Economics of the University of Nanking, Chengtu.] September 1936–January 1946. Nos. 1–53. Four volumes.

12. Lamb, Jefferson D.H. **The Development of the Agrarian Movement and Agrarian Legislation in China.** Shanghai, 1934.

13. Roll, Charles Robert, Jr. **The Distribution of Rural Incomes in China: A Comparison of the 1930s and 1950s.** [Ph.D. Dissertation, Harvard University, 1974.] New York, Garland, 1979.

14. Tang, Chi-Yu. **An Economic Study of Chinese Agriculture.** Cornell, 1924. [Ph.D. Thesis.]

15. Wagner, Wilhelm. **Die Chinesische Landwirtschaft.** Berlin, 1926.

FOREIGN TRADE AND INVESTMENT

the Rise of the Modern State, and Their Impact upon the Hinterland

16. Arnold, Julean. **Commercial Handbook of China.** Washington, 1919, 1920. Two volumes.

17. Burrill, Harry R. and Raymond F. Crist. **Report on Trade Conditions in China.** Washington, 1906.

18. Chen Han-seng. **Industrial Capital and Chinese Peasants: A Study of the Livelihood of Chinese Tobacco Cultivators.** Shanghai, 1939.

Bound With

The China Institute of Economic and Statistical Research. **A Study of the Rural Economy of Wuhing, Chekiang.** Shanghai, 1939.

Bound With

Chin Chien Yen. **Wool Industry and Trade in China.** Tientsin, 1937.

19. **The Commercial, Industrial and Economic Situation in China.** London, 1926, 1927, 1928, 1930.

Bound With

Moser, Charles K. **Where China Buys and Sells.** Washington, 1935.

20. Wagel, Srinvas R. **Finance in China.** Shanghai, 1914.

TWENTIETH-CENTURY ECONOMIC DEVELOPMENT

21. The American Presbyterian Mission. **The Isle of Palms: Sketches of Hainan.** Shanghai, 1919.

22. China International Famine Relief Commission. **Herr Raiffeisen Among Chinese Farmers.** Peiping, 1930.

23. Duncan, Robert Moore. **Peiping Municipality and the Diplomatic Quarter.** Peiping, 1933.

24. Hosie, Alexander. **Manchuria: Its People, Resources and Recent History.** London, 1904.

25. Institute of Pacific Relations. **Economic Trends and Problems in the Early Republican Period.** 1931.

26. Kann, Edward. **The History of China's Internal Loan Issues.** Shanghai, 1934.
Bound With
B. Lyn Yu Shen: **China's Currency Reform: A Historical Survey.** Shanghai, 1941.

27. King-yi Hsu. **Political Mobilization and Economic Extraction: Chinese Communist Agrarian Policies During the Kiangsi Period.** New York, Garland, 1979.

28. Kraus, Richard A. **Cotton and Cotton Goods in China, 1918–1936.** [Ph.D. Dissertation, Harvard University, 1968.] New York, Garland, 1979.

29. Myers, Ramon H., ed. **Selected Essays in Chinese Economic Development.** New York, Garland, 1979.

30. Remer, C.F. **Readings in Economics for China.** Shanghai, 1933.

31. Sakatani, Baron Y. **Manchuria: A Survey of Its Economic Development.** [Revised by Grover Clark, prepared for the Division of Economics and History of the Carnegie Endowment for International Peace.] 1932.

32. Woodhead, H.G.W. **Extraterritoriality in China: The Case Against Abolition.** Tientsin, 1929.
Bound With
Fong, H.D. **The Growth and Decline of Rural Industrial Enterprise in North China.** Tientsin, 1936.
Bound With
Ho, Franklin L. and Hsien Ding Fong. **Extent and Effects of Industrialization in China.** Tientsin, 1929.

LABOR AND THE ECONOMY

33. Epstein, Israel. **Notes on Labor Problems in Nationalist China.** New York, 1949.

34. Fang Fu-an. **Chinese Labour: An Economic and Statistical Survey of the Labour Conditions and Labour Movements in China.** Shanghai, 1931.

35. Wagner, Augusta. **Labor Legislation in China.** Peking, 1938.

THE WARTIME ECONOMY AND POSTWAR PROBLEMS

36. Ch'ao-ting Chi. **War-time Economic Development in China.** New York, 1939.

37. Dawson, Owen L. "Food." No. 6 in **Studies of Relief and Rehabilitation in China.** August 1943.
Bound With
Dawson, Owen L. "Rehabilitation Problems in Agriculture." No. 14 in **Studies of Relief and Rehabilitation in China.** August 1943.
Bound With
Problems of Economic Reconstruction in China Series. H.D. Fong, K.Y. Lin, and Tso-Fan Koh, **Principles of Postwar Economic Reconstruction in China** (Part I) and **Capitol Stock in China** (Part II). Quebec, China Council, 1942.

38. Phillips, Ralph W., Ray G. Johnson and Raymond T. Moyer. **The Livestock of China.** Washington, 1945.

39. Taylor, George E. **Japanese Sponsored Regime in North China.** New York, 1939.

40. United Nations Relief and Rehabilitation Administration. **UNRRA in China.** Washington, 1948.
Bound With
Ray, J. Franklin, Jr. **UNRRA in China: A Case Study of the Interplay of Interest in a Program of International Aid to an Underdeveloped Country.** New York, 1947.
Bound With
Committee on Foreign Affairs, House of Representatives. **Text of Proposed China Aid Bill and Background Information on Economic Assistance Program for China.** Washington, 1948.